Hermann Bahr

Twayne's World Authors Series
German Literature

Ulrich Weisstein, Editor
Indiana University

TWAS 744

HERMANN BAHR
(1863–1934)

Hermann Bahr

By Donald G. Daviau

University of California, Riverside

Twayne Publishers • Boston

Hermann Bahr

Donald G. Daviau

Copyright © 1985 by G. K. Hall & Company
All Rights Reserved
Published by Twayne Publishers
A Division of G. K. Hall & Co.
A publishing subsidiary of ITT
70 Lincoln Street
Boston, Massachusetts 02111

Book Production by Elizabeth Todesco
Book Design by Barbara Anderson

Printed on permanent/durable acid-free
paper and bound in the United States of
America.

Library of Congress Cataloging in Publication Data

Daviau, Donald G.
   Hermann Bahr.

    (Twayne's world authors series.   German literature)
    Bibliography: p. 157
    Includes index.
  1. Bahr, Hermann, 1863–1934—
Criticism and interpretation.   I. Title. II. Series.
PT2603.A33Z65 1985   838'.91209   84-19232
ISBN 0-8057-6592-1

Contents

About the Author
Preface
Chronology

    Chapter One
    Hermann Bahr: A Mirror of his Time   1

    Chapter Two
    Paris: The Decadent Phase   22

    Chapter Three
    Catalyst of Modernity and Cultural Mediator   35

    Chapter Four
    The Modernization of Art: Secessionism   56

    Chapter Five
    Theater and Burgtheater   70

    Chapter Six
    The Creative Mirror: The Novels   90

    Chapter Seven
    The World as Theater   114

    Chapter Eight
    Conclusion and Assessment   140

Notes and References   145
Selected Bibliography   157
Index   164

About the Author

Donald G. Daviau, literary critic, translator, and editor, is professor of Austrian and German literature at the University of California at Riverside. In 1953–54 he was a Fulbright student at the University of Vienna. Professor Daviau is president of the International Arthur Schnitzler Research Association and editor of the literary journal *Modern Austrian Literature;* he is also president of the American Council for the Study of Austrian Literature and a member of the Austrian P. E. N. Club and other international literary organizations. He has published scholarly books and articles on Hermann Bahr, Hugo von Hofmannsthal, Arthur Schnitzler, Karl Kraus, Stefan Zweig, and Raoul Auernheimer, among others, in American, Austrian, and German publications. In 1977 he was awarded the Austrian Cross of Honor for Science and Art.

Preface

In one of his many attempts at self-characterization Hermann Bahr—the Austrian writer, dramatist, novelist, essayist, diarist, newspaper editor, journalist, political commentator, popular philosopher, theater director, and critic of the theater, art, and culture in general—coined the descriptive motto "Never and always the same." While this concise and convenient formulation fails to give the unsuspecting reader any real notion of the extraordinary range and complexity of this literary Proteus and cultural seismograph, it does convey the essence of his worldview and temperament. By nature Bahr was an extroverted, flamboyant, larger-than-life personality, prone to exaggeration and overstatement. He feared nothing so much as being considered boring, and so he needed to dazzle, to provoke, and to stimulate, in order to ensure a reaction, whether friendly or hostile. He loved life, which he once claimed he was born to affirm, and, like the true impressionist that he was, surrendered freely and willingly to its blandishments in order to experience to the utmost everything that the world had to offer. He threw himself into the mainstream of his age, participating actively and often to extremes in every trend of any consequence in the areas of literature, culture, and politics, usually as a pioneer of intellectual modes before they became fashionable.

In literature Bahr began as a naturalist, experimented with decadence and art-for-art's sake, and became an impressionist, which he remained essentially for the rest of his life. He admired and affirmed expressionism theoretically but never adopted its techniques in any of his own writings. His political orientation came from a liberal middle-class background, but he turned to German nationalism as a follower of Georg von Schönerer, adopted Marxist socialism under the influence of Viktor Adler, and then in succession was a republican, a monarchist, and finally a supranationalist who envisioned a loose-knit federation of European states with a strong, politically and culturally viable Austria as the unifying center. In religion he was born a Catholic, became an atheist, pleaded no religion upon his marriage to a young Jewish actress, Rosa Jokl, in 1895, and in 1914 rediscovered his Catholic faith with such intensity that he attended church and prayed on his knees daily for the rest of his life.

Bahr remained faithful to each new phenomenon as long as it interested him but yielded just as quickly to each new event, fashion, or trend without the slightest feeling of regret or remorse and certainly without any feeling of guilt. His role was to mediate and to propagandize, not to advocate any particular technique, movement, or program. As a self-appointed critic of his age he considered it his responsibility to remain in the avant-garde and to serve as a guide for the public. He considered it ethically and aesthetically vital not only to be modern but to remain a revolutionary at all times. He has been called in jest but also deservedly "the midwife of modern art." Indisputably he deserves credit for providing the theoretical basis for the advent of modernity in the arts in Austria at the turn of the century.

Bahr was, and remains, controversial, misunderstood, and underrated. Whatever transformation he underwent, whatever cause he espoused, was certain to arouse the ire of various critics. Because he wrote prolifically and could not resist a tendency toward overstatement, the effect of his ideas was diluted. His critical articles, which included "discoveries" of talented new writers and artists, were received suspiciously as attempts at self-aggrandizement. His popular philosophizing and the political ideas presented in his essays and published diaries found no discernible critical echo, although it is impossible to measure his influence on the public, which continued to buy his books and attend his plays. There were ardent supporters like his disciples Willi Handl and Erhard Buschbeck, but they did not match Bahr's detractors in prestige, or influence. However, Bahr was seemingly oblivious to the opinions of others and followed his own inner dictates, unswayed by praise and undeterred by criticism. His major ambition was to feel fulfilled as an individual and to become "a real person," his highest accolade for any individual.

Bahr's frequent changes of direction, his many poses, and his attempts to shock the bourgeoisie made him the despair of his friends and the butt of ridicule by his enemies. Among the many sobriquets coined to describe him are such terms as "quick-change artist," "the great overthrower," "the Proteus of the moderns," "the spirit who always dumbfounds and confuses," and "the man of the day after tomorrow." Bahr preferred to think of himself as "the man who is always present." He also liked to indicate how far ahead of his time he was by quoting Goethe as saying that when people thought he was in Weimar he was already in Erfurt. Bahr felt spiritually akin to Goethe and intensely studied his life and writings.

Beneath the kaleidoscopic external events of Bahr's life, there is a central focus which is usually overlooked. All of Bahr's energies and activities were directed toward the goals of bringing Austria into closer rapprochement with Western Europe, helping it develop into the artistic and political equal of other European nations to guarantee its future, and creating a separate identity for Austrian literature. Regardless of the form they take, all of his writings and activities can be aligned under one or the other of these aims.

Bahr's major role, then, was that of a mediator in several senses. He served as a mediator between the arts and the public, and in a larger context he attempted to mediate between Austria and the rest of Europe. He reported on cultural events from other countries to keep his contemporaries in Austria and Germany aware of the latest European fashions and trends in literature and the arts.

To understand the importance and significance of Bahr's contribution to his age it is necessary to view the full range of his activities. For Bahr was one of those personalities who made his major contribution in his own day largely through the force of his dynamic, almost irresistible personality rather than by creating literary masterpieces. He believed that raising the quality of life for his contemporaries was more important than his posthumous reputation. Not a single one of his approximately 120 books has "survived." However, the totality of his writings—forty dramas, ten novels, six collections of novellas and prose tales, fifty-one volumes of essays, four volumes of theater reviews, and nine volumes of diaries—provides a rich legacy. The sum of all his activities viewed collectively constitutes his importance then and now.

Because of the large number of works and the many activities in which Bahr was engaged, it is not possible to give extended treatment to all facets of his career within the framework of this monograph. Similarly, space does not permit a detailed analysis of specific works to show their intrinsic merits as works of art. Instead, these are examined primarily to reflect the progression of Bahr's ideas, attitudes, and concerns. Because his major impact was made during the first half of his life, this period has been given proportionally greater attention. The book begins with a rapid survey of Bahr's life, followed by detailed chapters devoted to his major endeavors, and concluding with a discussion of his novels and plays. The main intent is to convey an idea of the central role played by this fascinating and engaging personality, to show his influence as the leading theorist and spokesman of his generation, and to document his importance as a major force in the radical change of values at the turn of the century. Only when Bahr has been assigned his proper role can the literary history of this significant period be viewed in its proper perspective.

Only Eduard Castle has attempted a comprehensive view of Bahr's endeavors. Other studies concentrate either on Bahr's early life or on specific aspects of his activities. None of Bahr's works is currently in print. Only a few of his books have ever been translated into English—the last in 1916—and all have long been out of print. Among secondary works in English there are a few articles on Bahr in various encyclopedias and in scholarly journals, and three dissertations have been written; but the present work represents the first attempt to present a comprehensive evaluation of his accomplishments.

As a final word I wish to acknowledge the financial support of this project by the University of California at Riverside and of the American Philosophical Society. I also wish to express my appreciation to my colleagues Jorun B. Johns and Harvey I. Dunkle, who read the manuscript and suggested valuable improvements, and to Ulrich Weisstein for his careful editing of the manuscript. Finally my gratitude goes to Christie J. Hammond, who labored patiently with my handwriting while typing the manuscript through its many drafts.

Donald G. Daviau

University of California, Riverside

Chronology

1863	Hermann Bahr born 19 July in Linz, Austria.
1881	July, passes his *Abitur* in Salzburg with distinction. Valedictorian of his class. October, enters University of Vienna to study classical philology and law. Shifts to *Nationalökonomie*.
1883	March, radical annexationist speech causes dismissal from the University of Vienna. May–August, attempts unsuccessfully to enroll at University of Graz.
1883–1884	Enrolls at University of Czernowitz. Withdraws.
1884	May, enrolls at the Friedrich-Wilhelm Universität in Berlin to study *Nationalökonomie*.
1885	April, delivers message of congratulations from his Austrian fraternity to Bismarck on his seventieth birthday.
1886	April, dissertation rejected by Wagner. Meets Viktor Adler and becomes regular contributor to Adler's weekly newspaper *Die Gleichheit*.
1887	May, in ill health leaves Berlin without completing his degree.
1887–1888	Serves compulsory year of military service.
1888	During year in Paris changes interest from politics to literature.
1889	Travels through Southern France, Spain, and North Africa.
1890	March, returns to Paris. May, returns to Berlin to collaborate with Brahm and Holz in founding the journal *Die freie Bühne für modernes Leben*.
1891	Trip to St. Petersburg with Emanuel Reicher and Lotte Witt. Summer, visits Linz. October, after meeting with Hofmannsthal, Schnitzler, and Beer-Hofmann in Café Griensteidl, remains in Vienna to pursue campaign of modernity.

1892–1894 Theater critic and feuilletonist for the *Deutsche Zeitung*.
1894 Founds the weekly newspaper *Die Zeit* in collaboration with Isidor Singer and Dr. Heinrich Kanner.
1895 Marries minor actress Rosa Joël (also known as Rosalie Jokl).
1897–1900 Major supporter of the Secessionist Art Movement and literary advisor to the art journal *Ver Sacrum*.
1899 October, leaves *Die Zeit* and becomes theater critic for the *Neues Wiener Tagblatt*. Travels to Rome and Naples.
1900 Moves into new home in Ober-Sankt-Veit designed by Joseph Olbrich. Travels to Paris.
1901 Wins lawsuit against Karl Kraus. Speech in Bösendorfersaal in defense of Klimt.
1903 March, operation for appendicitis is nearly fatal.
1903–1904 Extended period of ill health.
1904 September, witnesses performance of Anna Mildenburg as Isolde at Bayreuth and falls in love with her. Travels to Athens.
1905 October, signs contract as director of Schauspielhaus in Munich. Contract withdrawn.
1906 Accepts position as *Regisseur* with Max Reinhardt in Berlin.
1906–1911 One month trip to Venice each summer for five years.
1908 Leaves Reinhardt and returns to Vienna as Burgtheater critic for the *Neues Wiener Journal*.
1909 May, divorces Rosa Joël. July, marries Anna Mildenburg.
1910 Spends winter in London to accompany Mildenburg.
1912 Moves to Salzburg.
1914 Returns to Catholic church.
1916 February, lecture tour in Germany.
1917 February, lectures in Urania. First appearance in Vienna since 1911.

Chronology

1918   September, appointed head of a triumvirate to direct Burgtheater. November, three-man board dissolved and Bahr appointed "Erster Dramaturg" with responsibility for selecting plays.

1919   March, leaves Burgtheater.

1922   Moves to Munich, where Mildenburg teaches at the "Akademie für Tonkunst."

1934   July, Bahr dies and is buried in Salzburg.

Chapter One
Hermann Bahr: A Mirror of his Time

In his autobiography (*Selbstbildnis,* 1923) Hermann Bahr, an impressionist influenced more than most by outside forces, described his turbulent, eventful life: "It was granted to me to encounter decisive people, decisive times, decisive events. If anyone of my generation can say that he was shaped in the maelstrom of life, I may say it of myself. . . . For forty years now I have been participating in the intellectual vicissitudes of the Western world. Whatever truth was the center of struggle during these forty years, I was there!"[1]

Nothing in Bahr's background would have made it possible to predict the unexpected course his life was to take. His parents were descended on both sides from Silesian flax spinners and linen weavers who had migrated to Austria when Bahr's grandfather, Engelbert Bahr, entered the postal service in Vienna, rising ultimately to the position of head postmaster in Prague. After graduating from the University of Vienna, Bahr's father, Dr. Alois Bahr, likewise entered government service, rising to become a leader of the Liberal party and one of the most influential men in Linz. Bahr considered his father a perfect example of the educated bourgeois of his day.

Bahr inherited little of his father's mild nature and almost feminine gentleness but did learn from him the importance of moderation, order, and duty. However, not until his years in Berlin (1884–87) did he decide to practice these virtues. In the meantime, his radical university years were a constant trial for his uncomprehending father. He also resembled his father in his need to esteem and serve some cause greater than himself. This aspect of Bahr's character, coupled with his search for form in art and in life—a realization that came slowly to him after much experimentation and confused searching—led him in 1914 back to God and to his Catholic faith, which he had abandoned in his youth. Like his father, Bahr remained essentially a rationalist but one who put faith above reason.

1

To understand his generation Bahr felt it was important to recognize the narrowly provincial, rationally oriented, and anticlerical atmosphere in which it had been raised: "People will never understand our behavior from 1880 to 1890, unless one knows that we all came from small towns and as children were carefully tended in bright, quiet rooms with white curtains, enveloped in an artificial world of fidelity and honesty. Now, however, suddenly ejected from this intellectual *Biedermeier* style into life, we screamed in horror."[2] Rebellion rather than moderation was the hallmark of Bahr's generation—rebellion not only against the stifling confinement of the small-town atmosphere but also against the intellectual restrictiveness of the prevailing liberalism. These young men wanted to work toward a new and better future which they confidently expected to realize. Their fathers, who had assisted in the Revolution of 1848, were still under the influence of the ideas of that era. Now the sons launched their own revolution—an intellectual, artistic, and political one—to overthrow what they regarded as the outmoded liberalism of their fathers.

Bahr's mother, Wilhelmine Weidlich, was born in Zuckmantel, Silesia, although the roots of her family can be traced back to the Rhineland. She was proud of her family's bureaucratic rank and never overcame the feeling of having married below her social station. She was not temperamentally suited to her husband, and the marriage, though it produced four children, could not be called successful. In character and disposition she afforded a complete contrast to her husband, for she was endowed with a masculine strength of will, extreme stubbornness, and harshness of personality. Bahr described his mother as "a faulty or at least inhibited example of the highest type of person that had stopped developing at some point: a genius crushed by the bureaucratic environment of her youth."[3] Wilhelmine lacked warmth and was unable to display tenderness to her children, generally concealing in satire and ridicule whatever emotions she did not stifle. She possessed a great gift of dialogue, which Bahr inherited. He also learned from her the art of twisting every serious situation in life into comedy.

Bahr was never able to break down the barrier between him and his mother: "We loved each other with inventive hatred."[4] Yet he inherited all of his major characteristics from her: his keen analytic mind, his insatiability, his basic discontentedness, his skepticism—which refused to allow him to accept authority or any fact at face value—and the profound inner loneliness that prevented him from any close relationship with other people. He also owed to her his talent for mimicry and comedy, his extraordinary conversational ability, his gift of penetrating insight, and his ability to express his perceptions in an effective manner.

Hermann Bahr was born on 19 July 1863 in Linz, Upper Austria, then a quiet provincial community situated on the Danube. He attended elementary school in Linz and was regarded as a precocious child. But school taught him to dissemble, for he viewed the whole system as a game that consisted of guessing correctly the type of pupil a particular teacher wanted him to be. In his opinion, the main function of education was to distract the child's attention from the truth of the world that he felt existed beyond the truth of school.[5]

Bahr was always strongly attracted to the theater. His father's recountings of brilliant performances at the Burgtheater remained one of the strongest memories of Hermann's childhood. Long before he saw it, these tales filled him with admiration for Austria's major theater, with which his life was to become closely involved. With his unique talent for mimicry he could imitate the manner of speech, the inflection, and even the walk of another individual. He often entertained his family with his performances and was considered "a complete home theater."[6]

In 1877, at the age of fifteen, Bahr was sent to Salzburg to attend the *Gymnasium*. Salzburg was chosen because his grandparents lived there. Bahr loved Salzburg, which he called the city of his soul, and he returned there to live in 1912 when his situation in Vienna became uncomfortable. In 1922 he moved to Munich, where he died in 1934, but he was buried in Salzburg.[7]

Salzburg exerted a permanent influence on Bahr as a uniquely baroque city that he loved to call the Austrian Rome and the embodiment of Austrian culture. Although he did not discover the historical significance of its baroque tradition until 1912 through Josef Nadler, the city had an immediate effect on his development through the humanistic training he received in the Benedictine *Gymnasium*. The Benedictine philosophy struck a deep chord in him, and filled him with the desire to serve "men or causes."[8] Although he was a good student, he did not enjoy school and later became an outspoken critic of the educational system in Austria. Like many other writers of his generation he felt that school had contributed little to his growth and that it actually proved detrimental to his personal development.

The most notable exception was Bahr's professor of Greek, Josef Steger, whose profound influence was to remain with the young student not only during his university years but for the rest of his life. Steger stirred within Bahr a belief in the eternal values of the beautiful, the good, and the true. He also taught him to understand that these qualities exist regardless of whether they are acknowledged, and that only in them does the individual find ultimate self-realization. The full value of this instruction did not come to fruition for many years, but the lesson had one immediate result: it aroused the desire in the young student to emulate his teacher by becoming a philologist. Bahr later claimed with some justification that he had remained a philologist all his life.

For the graduation ceremonies Bahr was selected by his class to present the valedictory address on the assigned topic "The Value of Work." Bahr created a mild sensation when he concluded his address with the comment that the aristocracy of birth had been replaced by the aristocracy of money, which was now to be replaced by the aristocracy of work.[9] This speech marked the beginning of his socialist orientation which came to full fruition in Vienna in 1886. It is also the first example of his ability to perceive future trends. In later life he still believed that his speech in Salzburg had contained a valid social truth that he continued to endorse.

In October 1881 Bahr entered the University of Vienna to study classical philology and philosophy. The dullness of the classes, however, compared to the excitement of café life, soon caused him to neglect his studies. He was introduced into the Café Scheidl, a popular gathering place for writers and journalists, and in this heady world of pseudocelebrities Bahr believed that he had come face to face with the real truth he had been seeking. Also his association with café life tended to confirm his cynicism and distrust of the world as he knew it. Although wanting desperately to believe in something, Bahr felt he had to negate everything. This conflict between his real inner emotions and the poses he adopted for popular consumption and self-defense remained with him for many years, until he grew secure enough finally to be himself.

Bahr's socialist education in the Café Scheidl led him eventually to the study of *Nationalökonomie,* a blend of political science and economics, at the university. He had tried other faculties, including law, the profession urged on him by his father, without encountering a field that really attracted him. Through *Nationalökonomie* Bahr developed an interest in politics and began looking about for a strong leader. He was introduced to Georg von Schönerer, the radical leader of the German National party, which advocated the overthrow of the Austrian monarchy and the reunification of Austria with Germany. Bahr eventually became Schönerer's right-hand man and was for a few years in the forefront of the pan-German movement.[10]

Bahr's involvement with Schönerer nearly cost him his career, for after his speech on 5 March 1883 at the fraternity commemoration of Wagner's death he was dismissed from the University of Vienna and remained politically suspect. He was refused admittance at Graz because of his record of political activities but studied at Czernowitz until his rowdy behavior and anti-Semitic and antipatriotic actions caused the university to request his voluntary departure to avoid expelling him. Bahr left Austria for Berlin, where he began to mature: "Berlin began with me what Paris later completed. . . . These two cities awakened my conscience."[11]

Bahr continued his study of *Nationalökonomie* with Adolph Wagner and Gustav Schmoller. He never lost his respect for Wagner, who remained after Steger the most influential teacher he ever had. Upon learning of Wagner's death in 1917, Bahr wrote in his diary: "Among the figures in the garden of my youth I scarcely know one that was more important. He influenced me strongly precisely at the time that was decisive for my life."[12]

In Berlin Bahr published his first work, a seminar report entitled *Rodbertus' Theorie der Absatzkrisen* (1884), partly at his own expense. He also published *Die Einsichtslosigkeit des Herrn Schäffle* (1886), a vitriolic attack on the Austrian minister who had predicted the demise of Social Democracy in *Die Aussichtslosigheit der Sozialdemokratie*. The Schäffle book brought him to the attention of Viktor Adler, who invited Bahr to contribute to his weekly newspaper *Die Gleichheit*. Bahr remained an active participant during 1887–88, the year of his voluntary military service in Vienna.

In 1887 Bahr's budding literary interest was stimulated by his admiration for Ibsen as well as his friend Arno Holz, and he wrote the drama *Die neuen Menschen*, which reflected his disillusionment with socialism and politics in general. He began to think about his career and about finishing at the university. In 1886 he had completed a thesis on Karl Marx entitled "Die Entwicklung vom Individualismus zum Sozialismus," but Wagner had rejected it as unsuitable. Bahr, who was still being subsidized by his father, was under constant pressure from home to complete his degree because of the expense involved; yet he refused to suspend his journalistic activities and his literary interests long enough to concentrate on it. Among other things, he engaged in a duel with another student and suffered a head wound. Finally the various pressures became too great even for Bahr's extraordinary constitution and he collapsed. Since there was no possibility of finishing his thesis in this condition, he decided to return home to save his father money. Thus after three highly eventful and formative years he departed from Berlin. He never completed his dissertation and remained the only major figure of the *Jung-Wien* group without a doctorate.

On 1 October 1887, after spending the summer in Salzburg, Bahr reported to the 84th Linz Regiment stationed at the Alserkaserne in Vienna to begin his oft-postponed year of compulsory military training. Since he was still suspect because of his political activities, he was never able to attain the rank of officer but ended his year as a corporal, even though he avoided trouble and was recommended for an officer's commission. It amused and chagrined Bahr that in the eyes of his family his promotion to corporal outweighed all of his literary and journalistic achievements.[13] Because of his son's good conduct his father volunteered to subsidize one final year of education. Without hesitation Bahr opted for Paris.

In November 1888, after stopping along the way to visit Michael Georg Conrad and other writers in Munich, Bahr arrived in Paris and settled in the Latin Quarter at the Hotel Suez, Boulevard St. Michel. He rented an attic room, small and cramped but with a fireplace and a balcony that afforded a beautiful view of the city. One of Bahr's discoveries in Paris that made a deep and lasting impression on his thinking was the role that tradition played in the life of the average French citizen. It later became one of Bahr's major goals in Vienna to restore the role of tradition in Austrian life.

The principal value of his Paris experience was to awaken Bahr's sense of art: "In Paris I was awakened to art for the first time, to art per se, to art as consecration, to art as the meaning and form of life, and also to a certain extent as a substitute for religion."[14] Another important discovery was the utterance by Zola that "A sentence well constructed is a good action." This statement, with its insight into the interconnection between aesthetics and morality, equaled his discovery of tradition in its effect on his life: "On this day a new life began for me. This sentence awakened me. It reminded me of good and evil. Even before we found the formulation in Nietzsche we Germans had been living for a long time beyond good and evil. There was no room in our materialistic view of history for such concepts. But with the distinction between good and evil came also the differentiation between beautiful and ugly."[15] Bahr believed that his return to the Catholic church began on the day he encountered this sentence in Zola, even though it took another twenty years before he made the final decision to accept faith.

Under the impact of his literary awakening in Paris Bahr made his final break with politics. His disaffection formed the basis of his second major drama *Die grosse Sünde* (1888), which, like *Die neuen Menschen,* was strongly influenced by Ibsen. The play served as a catharsis, enabling Bahr to exorcise his political alter ego, so that he himself could freely embark upon the new career to which he was now totally devoted. He tailored his dress and his manner to his newfound interest. He adopted the affected mannerisms of a typical boulevardier, sporting the short Vandyke beard and smart frock coat of the dandy. His final touch was an insouciant curl falling over his forehead. The outer facade corresponded to his interest in literary decadence, which he preferred to naturalism. Indeed, he felt that naturalism was basically misunderstood in Germany and wrote several essays, later collected under the title *Die Überwindung des Naturalismus* (1891), to place the movement in historical perspective as a transitional phase. Bahr's attraction to decadence was partly the result of the strong influence of Karl Joris Huysmans's *A Rebours.* Of even greater and more lasting influence was Maurice Barrès, with whom Bahr felt such a deep inner kinship that he regarded him as a spiritual twin.

Barrès achieved fame with his early series of novels in which he featured a life-style called the *culte du moi*. This was a method for perfecting one's inner being by leading an impressionistic existence, keeping one's ego in a state of continuous development by constantly discarding old attitudes and feelings in favor of new ones. Later, in Goethe's image of human development as a snake shedding skins to grow and in Mach's idea of man as a group of cells in flux, Bahr discovered additional authorities for his philosophy of nerves, sensations, and change. Bahr remained receptive to new experiences as a means of gaining full measure from life. This fundamental attitude, which is the key to any understanding of Bahr, was overlooked by his contemporaries who, irritated by his chameleonlike behavior, unjustly denounced him as a *Verwandlungskünstler*.[16] What critics praised in Goethe as virtuosity and flexibility they condemned in Bahr as inconsistency and instability of character, not understanding that the opposite was true: only a man of solid character with true inner security could venture so many changes. Subsequently Barrès once more influenced Bahr decisively by making him perceive the importance of the provinces to the welfare of a nation.

The frenetic pace of life in Paris filled Bahr with the desire to work. Having resolved that literature would be his chief interest, he wrote prolifically—feuilletons and critical articles for German newspapers and journals, the dramas *Die grosse Sünde* (1889) and *Die Mutter* (1890), the novel *Die gute Schule* (1890), and a collection of short stories and sketches, *Fin de siècle* (1891). His essays were later published in two volumes under the title *Zur Kritik der Moderne* (1890–91). They include some early political essays but for the most part reflect his efforts to introduce to German and Austrian readers the latest literary happenings and the newest writers in France, to confront the issue of literary naturalism, to publicize the French decadent movement, and above all to create in German-speaking lands a receptive atmosphere for a modern twentieth-century viewpoint.

Toward the end of his year in Paris Bahr traveled through southern France to Spain and North Africa. He was greatly impressed by Spain, especially by the painted wooden statues in Valladolid. He interviewed the younger writers, and his interest in Spanish literature remained an element of his literary activities. In 1926 he wrote a short volume entitled *Notizen zur neueren spanischen Literatur*.

Upon his return to Paris Bahr received an urgent summons from Arno Holz to return to Berlin to participate in the founding of the journal *Freie Bühne für modernes Leben*. Bahr, who always remained one of Holz's enthusiastic supporters,[17] responded to this invitation on 1 May 1890 and contributed frequently to the *Freie Bühne* in 1890 and 1891 under various pseudonyms. During these years Bahr was famous in a way that he never experienced again. His decadent novel *Die gute Schule* attracted widespread attention when serialized in the *Freie Bühne*, his drama *Die grosse Sünde* had been successfully performed, and his first volume of essays, *Zur Kritik der Moderne*, received favorable reviews. Moreover, after the collection of decadent short stories and sketches, entitled *Fin de siècle,* was banned and confiscated by the police, the notoriety necessitated a reprinting. His trump card, however, was the drama *Die Mutter,* a work intended to be offensive to bourgeois audiences.

Because of his exaggerated sense of his own prestige and reputation Bahr vainly challenged Otto Brahm, who was proceeding too slowly for him in promoting modernity, for the editorship of the journal *Freie Bühne.* When his bid for control of the journal failed, Bahr had no other recourse except to withdraw with Holz and a few other sympathizers.

Not knowing which way to turn, feeling out of place in the new Berlin, and always in financial difficulties, Bahr accepted an invitation from his friend, the actor Emanuel Reicher, to accompany him to St. Petersburg, where he was to give a guest performance. The experience of the trip became the basis for the travel diary *Russische Reise* (1893), which in style and content reflects the decadent phase that Bahr was passing through.

His Russian experience focused on three individuals: the performers Josef Kainz, Eleonora Duse, and Lotte Witt. Kainz, one of the strong-willed individualists whom Bahr always admired, became a close friend. They shared the same view of art, and Bahr wrote a Napoleon play with Kainz in mind for the leading role.[18] The drama aroused great enthusiasm in Kainz, who even intended to take it on tour to America, but the plan never materialized. After Kainz's premature death Bahr edited a volume of his correspondence.[19]

Lotte Witt, to whom *Russische Reise* is dedicated, inspired Bahr throughout the trip, but the great highlight was the unexpected thrill of seeing Eleonora Duse perform. When Kainz and Bahr attended a production of a small Italian company, they were overwhelmed by Duse's acting, which Bahr ranked among the strongest impressions of his life. In the excitement of his discovery Bahr wrote a glowing account of Duse for the *Frankfurter Zeitung.*[20] A theater agent in Vienna, having confirmed that Bahr's account was accurate, brought Duse to Vienna, where her world renown began. She was the first and most significant of the many "discoveries" that Bahr was to make as a critic.

After the guest performances were over, Bahr had no desire or reason to return to Berlin and went to Vienna temporarily, as he thought. His uncertainty and indirection were behind him. The ideas and impressions gleaned from his student years, his travels, numerous personal contacts, and some literary success gave him the background and self-confidence he needed for the course he was to follow for the next fifteen years. Although the number of refinements were to be added to his basic ideas, Bahr had absorbed by this time almost all of the important influences on his life. All that remained was to develop them.

While still in Paris in 1890 Bahr had received a "stormy letter" from a young publisher in Brünn, E. M. Kafka, who asked his help in "establishing a literature" in Austria. Kafka, a modestly well-to-do young man interested in cultural matters, wished to found a review of Austrian literature under the title *Moderne Dichtung*. His appeal for Bahr's participation serves as some indication of Bahr's reputation. Despite this sign of cultural activity in Austria, Bahr had actually intended his stay in Vienna to be only a short visit before returning "to Europe." However, his meeting with the young prodigy Hofmannsthal, who had astonished him with his mature review of *Die Mutter,* induced Bahr to remain and work to rejuvenate the arts in Austria.

Initially Bahr supported himself partly as a free-lance writer but with continued financial aid from his father. In the fall of 1892 he began writing for Daniel Auspitzer's *Deutsche Zeitung,* and on 1 February 1893 he officially replaced Ludwig Ganghofer as Burgtheater critic. From this position he set about edifying and antagonizing his Viennese contemporaries in equal measure for the next twenty years, until he departed for Salzburg in 1912. Bahr was forced to work as a journalist because he never earned sufficient income from his literary works to support himself as an independent writer. Money was always a problem for him.

Complete maverick that he was, Bahr chafed under editorial control. He became angry when his articles were altered over his objections, and decided to free himself from supervision by founding his own newspaper. Thus was born the weekly *Die Zeit,* established in collaboration with Isidor Singer and Dr. Heinrich Kanner. Through the pages of the belles lettres section, for which he was responsible, Bahr continued his campaign for a transformation of values and for modernity in the arts, which he had begun in Paris.[21]

In Vienna Bahr was the "organizer of Austrian literature," as Peter de Mendelssohn has aptly called him.[22] In addition to his instrumental role in fostering a new literature in Austria and spreading its recognition in Germany, he played a major role in supporting the Secessionist Art Movement, which was established on 1 April 1897 under the leadership of Gustav Klimt. He was also a major contributor to *Ver Sacrum,* the official journal of the Secessionist Movement, and was responsible for enlisting many of the important contributors.

Along with his campaign on behalf of culture and the arts that was continued in the volumes of essays *Studien zur Kritik der Moderne* (1894), *Renaissance* (1897), *Wiener Theater 1893–1898* (1898), *Secession* (1900), and *Bildung* (1900), Bahr pursued his own literary career, producing one or two works a year in a variety of forms. The drama *Der Franzl* (1900) and the comedy *Die Wienerinnen,* like the prose works of the same years, reflect Bahr's turning away from Vienna. In his growing discouragement over the failure of his cultural program Bahr turned to the provinces as a source of strength. This new direction was marked by the series of articles, "Entdeckung der Provinz," that Bahr published in *Die Zeit* just before his departure in 1899. To measure the change in his attitude it is only necessary to compare his hostility toward Vienna in 1899 with his optimistic appraisal of his cultural campaign in an open letter to Hofmannsthal and Andrian in the preface to *Renaissance* (1897): "I founded this weekly *Die Zeit* so that also in our poor country questions of culture would have an advocate. Faithfully I write down there every week what the seekers find; in this way we are approaching the great art. You know that we have been effective; it has not been in vain. From all sides many people have responded to my call, and we may believe that out of our quiet circle many a thought has entered into the great world."[23]

Bahr's animosity toward Vienna also reflected the adversity he was experiencing. He had a falling out with Kanner and Singer, who were happy to see him leave *Die Zeit.* He was involved behind the scenes in an intrigue to oust Adam Müller-Guttenbrunn as director of the Raimundtheater and to replace him with someone more compatible. He was unable to prevent Max Burckard's dismissal as director of the Burgtheater in 1898 and vented his anger in critical jibes at Paul Schlenther, Burckard's successor. The most annoying problem Bahr faced, however, was the increasingly savage attack on him by Karl Kraus, the self-appointed conscience of Vienna, who considered Bahr a social menace exemplifying the corrupt journalistic system he despised.

A high point of this period was Bahr's trip to Greece in 1901, where the sight of the Acropolis became one of his great experiences. Typically he immersed himself in the study of Greek culture and was inspired by the ideas of the Periclean age, which he dreamed of emulating in Vienna. The essays in *Bildung* (1900) and the two dialogues, *Dialog vom Tragischen* (1904) and *Dialog vom Marsyas* (1905), reflect Bahr's Greek interests at this time.

Although Bahr possessed great physical stamina, which enabled him to work beyond ordinary limits, the frenetic pace of his life eventually took its toll as it had earlier in Berlin. The prodigious amount of journalistic and literary work in addition to daily visits with friends and colleagues, an extraordinary correspondence, public lectures, and occasional travels would have overtaxed anyone's strength. He had little personal life that did not involve his work, although for a few years in the mid-1890s he shared the fad of bicycling that all of his friends enjoyed for a time. His favorite recreation throughout his life was hiking.

On 27 January 1903 Bahr almost died after an operation for appendicitis performed by Arthur Schnitzler's brother, Julius, and he remained in ill health throughout the year. This brush with death and the long convalescence sobered Bahr considerably, gave him a new perspective on the relationship between art and life, and marked the beginning of his revitalized Catholicism.

Despite his severe illness Bahr continued to be productive during the year prior to his departure from Vienna in 1906. He wrote the drama *Der Apostel* (1901), the comedies *Der Krampus* (1902) and *Der Meister* (1904), the play *Unter sich* (1904), and *Sanna* (1905), which along with *Der Franzl* (1900) he considered one of his best dramas. He also published two additional volumes of theater criticisms, *Premièren* (1902) and *Rezensionen,* (1903). A collection of novellas entitled *Wirkung in die Ferne* (1902) is significant because it is an early instance of the growing attraction he had for Goethe and also because it reflects Bahr's growing criticism of Vienna.

On the positive side, Bahr in the tale *Der Garten* symbolically portrayed his departure from youthful excesses, a turning point that corresponds chronologically almost exactly with the same transition in Schnitzler and Hofmannsthal. In *Der Garten* a youth thinks he needs to see and experience everything in order to be happy, a reflection of the impressionist credo that the *Jung-Wien* writers portrayed time and again in their early works. Now the adult man realizes, like Voltaire's Candide, that the whole world and all of its wisdom can be found in his garden. This conclusion, however, cannot be construed to mean that Bahr was advocating resignation or withdrawal from society. It was only that with the broader perspective of maturity he viewed the purpose of life in larger terms than simply seeking after sensations of the moment. However, his essays of 1904 on Ernst Mach, whom he called "the philosopher of impressionism," show that he never relented in his attitude that one must remain active and receptive to change in order to keep abreast of constantly changing conditions. It also remained his conviction that intellectuals and artists should be socially responsible and maintain an active interest in the affairs of the nation.

The stories in *Wirkung in die Ferne* reflect a new patience in Bahr and a growing belief that one must live life as it comes. He had shown man as a pawn of fate in *Das Theater, Josephine, Der Athlet,* and *Der Meister,* but here he veered toward reaffirmation of religious faith. This emphasis becomes especially pronounced in the story "Die Menschen" in its stress on love of one's fellowman and the innate goodness of man.[24] During this mellowing period Bahr created two of his most serious and durable works, the *Dialog vom Tragischen* (1904) and *Dialog vom Marsyas* (1905). Using a form that was admirably suited to his style, Bahr discussed the permanent value of drama, the major problems of the artist, and the relationship of art and life.

From 1899 to 1906 Bahr worked as a critic and feuilletonist for the *Neues Wiener Tagblatt*. His discouragement over the lack of public and critical response to his cultural program, along with other personal setbacks and feuds, caused him to grow impatient and angry. He began to escalate his attacks on the Viennese and their characteristics that he felt were hampering progress in Austria. In the process he made himself unpopular with both his editor and the public. He began to cast about for a new position and was offered the post of director at the Schauspielhaus in Munich. He signed a contract on 1 October 1905 only to have the offer withdrawn at the last minute for unspecified reasons. The change of heart by the administration in Munich was doubtless caused by pressure brought against the appointment in the press and behind the scenes. Bahr had been so confident of receiving the position that he had already accepted Schnitzler's play *Der Ruf des Lebens* for its premiere in Munich only to have his recommendation rejected. He wrote to

Schnitzler on 29 January 1906 to reassure him that the difficulties in Munich were part of the effort to force his resignation and did not concern Schnitzler personally. Eventually Bahr sued the theater for breach of contract and was awarded a settlement of 2,400 marks. Singer had been so pleased to see Bahr leave the *Tagblatt* voluntarily that, when Bahr returned to Vienna, he found his position already taken. To reestablish himself in Vienna, where he had "become impossible," was not feasible, and at this point he did not know which way to turn. Max Reinhardt rescued him from his dilemma by employing him as a *Regisseur* at the Deutsches Theater in Berlin. Bahr took a parting shot at Vienna in *Wien* (1907), a "malicious" dissection of the Viennese character, in which he poured out his disgust about the Viennese.

Bahr found it difficult to work for Reinhardt, much as he admired him. Although Bahr had a great capacity for hard work and for maintaining a hectic schedule, he could not stand Reinhardt's frenetic pace and his methods of leaving everything to be resolved at the last minute. During his approximately two years with Reinhardt Bahr directed three plays and also served in a liaison capacity and as tour manager for Reinhardt's company. For reasons that even Bahr could not explain he did not have great success as a director. In a revealing entry in his personal diary on 2 January 1907 he saw in these failures the continuation of a pattern: "Amazing how in every situation I immediately become the *Primus* but without external success. In Wagner's seminar I became his favorite right away and still failed to earn my doctorate. During my volunteer year I was the favorite of the officers without becoming a lieutenant. According to Reinhardt, I am the best *Regisseur* in Berlin, but the plays fail."[25]

Returning to Vienna in 1909, he married the great love of his life, Anna Mildenburg. Bahr had first seen her in 1904 singing the role of Isolde at a performance in Bayreuth. He was enraptured by her performance and regarded this encounter as another of his great experiences. The intensity of his passion is eloquently described in his countless letters as well as in the detailed diaries that he wrote solely for and about her, all of which still remain to be published.[26]

Bahr had been married once before, in 1895, to the attractive aspiring young actress Rosa Joël (Rosalie Jokl). Since she was Jewish, the Catholic Bahr declared himself *konfessionslos* (nondenominational) in order to marry her. His parents objected strenuously to the marriage, but Bahr felt that he had to follow his destiny regardless of the consequences. Very little is known of Rosa or of their relationship except that it was an unhappy one. It is clear that Bahr felt a strong sexual attraction for her and was distressed when she began to ignore him. In his unpublished diaries Bahr often noted that he was taking Rosa to the train station or meeting her there. She seems to have lived apart from him much of the time and to have played no significant role in his life. Yet, despite her treatment of him he remained emotionally attached to her. On 28 February 1904, when he was recovering from his illness in a sanitarium, he wrote in his diary: "My wife is returning to Vienna and leaves me in a remarkably sentimental mood of yearning for her . . . and lying on the sofa, [I] think all evening about how beautiful it would be if the door were to open and she were to walk in with her laughter and goodness and sunshine."[27] They were finally divorced on 14 May 1909 so that Bahr could be free to marry Anna Mildenburg.

Bahr's marriage to Anna Mildenburg, one of the foremost altos of the time and a noted interpreter of Wagner and Richard Strauss, was completely successful and happy. They worked together on various theater productions, particularly *Der Unmensch,* in which she acted under his direction, and he often served as her agent. They also collaborated on a volume entitled *Bayreuth* (1912). Bahr did not have children of either marriage because he was devoted to his work and felt that he would not have the time and energy to be a good father.

During the period 1909–12 Bahr gave many lectures and readings, for his dynamic presence kept him in great demand as a speaker. In 1910 and 1911 he traveled to London with his wife, who was singing at Covent Garden, and they remained there for the entire opera season. They regularly spent at least a month each summer on the Lido, his favorite vacation spot. He wrote prolifically, turning out light dramas, three novels, a collection of novellas, six volumes of essays, and a book of theater criticism. This impressive output was climaxed by *Inventur* (1912), a summation of his views on society and on his own life upon reaching the age of fifty.

It was difficult for Bahr to relate to others; consequently, although he was personally acquainted with numerous individuals, he enjoyed very few close personal friendships. It is doubtful that many people really knew Bahr more than superficially. He always felt rather lonely and regarded this feeling of isolation as an Austrian characteristic.

In 1906 he began to publish his personal diary in the *Neues Wiener Journal* in the hope that his views would serve as a fixed point of reference and thus act as a unifying point for his contemporaries. After 1906 Bahr became more politically oriented than he had been in the first fifteen years in Vienna, but not in the radical way that had characterized his activist involvement in the 1880s. He repeatedly discussed the history of Austria and analyzed Austrian character, which he believed was a major hindrance to progress. He attempted to clarify the role of Austria vis-à-vis Germany as well as toward the other entities of the Habsburg monarchy. For example, in *Dalmatinische Reise* (1909) he attempted to explain the problems and grievances of a province that he loved and enjoyed visiting. Through his essays and diaries as well as through his literary works, Bahr attempted to play a role similar to that of Karl Kraus in *Die Fackel*, except that he was not as interested in uncovering scandals or exposing malefactors; nor was he as humorous or verbally brilliant. Both men worked toward the same goal—a better Austria—but from diametrically opposed positions. Bahr proceeded in a positive way to suggest changes and improvements, while Kraus considered it necessary to destroy the old to make way for the new. Bahr, who always looked forward, encouraged an evolutionary process. Kraus's utopian vision was a return to the past, to the *Ursprung* when the world was pure.

By 1912 Bahr felt persona non grata in Vienna and moved to Salzburg, where he remained until 1922. Although he considered himself the "great helper of Austrian art," nobody in Vienna tried to keep him from leaving, a slight that he felt keenly.[28] During his years in Salzburg his favorite neighbor was Stefan Zweig, with whom he enjoyed conversing. His favorite correspondent and greatest admirer was Josef Redlich, an internationally known professor of law and political science, who was elected to parliament in 1911 and served briefly as minister of finance in 1918. Bahr's home at Schloss Arenberg became a mecca attracting scholars and writers from all over Europe. From his vantage point in Salzburg Bahr ranged freely over the European scene with commentaries on political, literary, and cultural matters. Eight years after the publication of the first volume of his *Tagebuch* (1909), he resumed publishing his diary weekly in the *Neues Wiener Journal* in 1917 and continued to do so until 1933. The diaries appeared annually in book form until 1928. For some reason still unexplained the volumes for 1927 and 1928 were ordered destroyed by the police, although the material is still accessible in the *Neues Wiener Journal.* The remaining years through 1933 have never been collected and are available only in the *Neues Wiener Journal.*

When the war broke out in 1914 Bahr joined the majority of Austrian and German writers in attempting to unify the nation and bolster public morale. In his booklet *Kriegssegen* (1915), written in effusive rhetorical style, he served patriotic interests by viewing the war in positive terms as the means of finally realizing his ambition for Austrian unity. He was not a warmonger, as Kraus alleged, but when confronted with the reality of the situation he tried to present it as favorably as possible. He explained that "There is no happiness that cannot also become a curse, and likewise no misfortune out of which a blessing cannot come. . . . Thus in the same way the word *Kriegssegen* ["blessings of war"] does not mean that war itself is a blessing but that we intend to draw a blessing from it."[29] The benefit that Bahr expected from the war was the unification of the German people, including Austria. Common danger had brought all Germans together once more, and Bahr hoped that this time the union would be permanent. While it is difficult to see how Bahr's clearly enunciated aim could be misconstrued, Kraus maliciously attacked Bahr for glorifying the war.

Another misconception about Bahr spawned by Kraus at this time was the open letter to Hofmannsthal that Bahr published at the outbreak of the war. Although Hofmannsthal and Bahr were close personal friends during the 1890s, they apparently quarreled and terminated their friendship around 1908 for reasons that are still not clear. The break was instigated by Hofmannsthal, and Bahr utilized the opportunity afforded by the outbreak of the war to attempt a reconciliation by means of an open letter, which produced the desired effect. Hofmannsthal responded, and the two former friends resumed their correspondence and their personal relationship, although it never again generated the warmth and enthusiasm of the early years. Both men were close friends of Josef Redlich, and both were greatly interested in the future of Austria. They had both discovered the power of tradition, especially the Austrian baroque tradition, which formed a major topic in their writings. As an offshoot of this interest Hofmannsthal began in 1915 to edit a series of major landmarks of Austrian literature and culture called *Österreichische Bibliothek,* another attempt to create a sense of national unity by calling attention to the country's literary and cultural heritage. He invited Bahr's suggestions, as he had done previously, and Bahr volunteered to contribute a volume on Bishop Rudigier. However, Hofmannsthal, acting upon the advice of Leopold von Andrian and others, took exception to the heavily Catholic slant of *Rudigier* (1915) which Bahr wrote in the initial enthusiasm of his return to the church in 1914, and ultimately rejected it as unacceptable for his series.

In all of the writings produced during the war years Bahr continued to stress the theme of unity. This idea is particularly emphasized in those essays dealing directly with the war, *Das österreichische Wunder* (1915) and *Schwarzgelb* (1917). "The Austrian miracle" was the newly gained unity among all Austrians as well as the unity of Austria and Germany. None of the thoughts is new. The dominant topic is the idea Bahr had acquired in 1884 in Berlin that a strong Austria united solidly with its satellite states and the Balkan countries would constitute the strongest ally of Germany. Bahr cited historical precedents to demonstrate that most of the states comprising the Hapsburg monarchy had been annexed voluntarily. His objective was to prove that all member states of the monarchy were mutually dependent upon each other and that the monarchy should therefore be preserved. He remained a monarchist all his life and never really accepted the republic established in 1918.

Bahr's idealistic view of postwar Europe envisioned Austria as a political center because of its traditional role as an intellectual and geographical crossroad of Europe: "Our mission is to be a bridge. A bridge between North and South . . . and also between East and West. We Austrian Germans have been chosen to become northern southerners and western easterners. We have created one bridge, we are northern southerners, the baroque is our highest intellectual accomplishment. All that is still lacking is the second bridge. We need to accomplish another baroque, this time a westeasterly movement."[30]

In 1914 Bahr's Catholicism, which had been revived in 1903, caused him finally to return to the church of his birth. His friends Schnitzler, Hofmannsthal, and Beer-Hofmann were all extremely skeptical about his sudden outburst of religious fervor, and even his wife expressed serious doubts about his sincerity. Yet he amazed even the most severe skeptics and detractors by maintaining his deeply religious convictions for the rest of his life. From the time of his return to the church he attended mass daily. His conversion was mirrored in the novel *Himmelfahrt* (1916), which depicts an intellectual's path to religious faith, and again in *Die Stimme* (1916), which he regarded as one of his finest dramas. Bahr's subsequent works were all written from the standpoint of a devout but not "dogmatic" believer. He was a Catholic, but one who had gone through the school of Kant and Goethe. He was well aware that critics were suspicious of Catholic authors, but he did not feel that this designation was appropriate in his case. Bahr had repeatedly treated the conflict between intellect and feeling in his writings and continued to analyze the relationship between reason and faith in order to provide a guideline for intellectuals who were unable to accept religious belief. The most cogently argued work on this theme is the essay *Vernunft und Wissenschaft* (1917), which when reprinted in the volume *Sendung des Künstlers* (1923) was retitled *Vernunft und Glaube*.

In 1918 Bahr was granted the fulfillment of a lifelong dream when he was called to the Vienna Burgtheater. He began his duties as director on 1 September 1918 and tried to use the repertory to create an atmosphere of national unity. However, his suggestions went largely unheeded. When internal Burgtheater politics made his position untenable, Bahr returned to Salzburg after only six months. Despite his short tenure Bahr felt that his efforts were successful. He continued to follow the fortunes of the theater and wrote *Burgtheater* (1920), a short history of the theater, as well as *Schauspielkunst* (1923), a monograph on acting, which had always been one of his main interests.

Bahr was still living in Salzburg when Hofmannsthal, Reinhardt, and Richard Strauss joined forces to establish the Salzburg Festival. The idea for an outdoor theater in Salzburg had been suggested by Bahr as early as 1903 in a letter to Reinhardt. However, when the plan was brought to fruition, Bahr was consulted but not invited to participate in the venture.

Bahr never lost his drive to stay abreast of the latest intellectual trends, and in 1916 he wrote *Expressionismus,* in which he tried to explain the significance of this major literary movement that dominated the period 1910–25. Although he felt that he had never personally completed the transition to expressionism, Bahr praised the movement highly. Because of its unique approach to the search for truth and its profound insights into the human spirit he considered it a more important artistic credo than impressionism or naturalism.

In 1922 Bahr's home was uprooted one final time. Anna Mildenburg, who had not been able to obtain a teaching position in Austria, was invited to join the faculty of the Academy of Performing Arts in Munich. Although they both would have preferred to return to Vienna, they agreed that she should take advantage of this opportunity. Despite his friendship with such influential men as Chancellor Ignaz Seipel and Redlich, nothing could be done about procuring her a suitable position in Vienna, to Bahr's extreme annoyance and frustration. His letters to Redlich are filled with suggestions and hopes, but all to no avail. He continued to live in Munich until his death in 1934.

During the last twelve years of his life Bahr continued to write plays, novels, and essays as prolifically as ever. Most notably he published his autobiography *Selbstbildnis* (1923), which may well be his most important and satisfying work. He covered only the period of his life up to his return to Vienna in 1891, for he felt that his writings contained the remainder of his life story. It is unfortunate that he did not continue his chronicle, for Bahr is a fascinating as well as reliable narrator. He has provided one of the best autobiographies of this period, which compares favorably with Schnitzler's *Ein Leben in Wien*, Stefan Zweig's much heralded *Die Welt von gestern*, Siegfried Trebitsch's *Chronik eines Lebens*, and Raoul Auernheimer's *Das Wirtshaus zur verlorenen Zeit*.

In keeping with his role as a mediator Bahr between 1920 and 1927 published a series of letters in the *London Mercury*, in which he provided English readers with an overview of the political mood, the social attitude, and the literary happenings in Germany and Austria in the postwar years. It was an attempt to restore a more positive feeling in England toward Germany and Austria after the bitterness of the war. Bahr was favorably disposed toward the English in general, although atypically he did not write an account of his extended visits in 1910 and 1911 or make any attempt to introduce English culture to Germany and Austria. He could read English and presumably spoke it to some extent. He was a good friend of Wickham Steed and was acquainted with George Bernard Shaw, with whom he was often compared. Once Bahr asked rhetorically why he should be labeled the Austrian Bernard Shaw instead of calling Shaw the English Hermann Bahr. Bahr's interest in England was not deep, and he made no further visits when Mildenburg was no longer performing there.[31]

In his later years Bahr lost his progressive spirit and retreated more and more into the past. He tended to repeat himself frequently and devoted much of his diary to reminiscing about his former exploits and achievements. He continued to survey the European cultural, artistic, and political scene, but increasingly from his readings rather than through direct contact as before. Many of his essays and diary entries were eulogies for friends who had died. During the last three years of his life his health deteriorated seriously. He had long suffered severe hearing problems and also had trouble with his eyes. As his health declined he became more and more nostalgic and was filled with sentimental yearnings for Vienna. In a letter of 17 March 1930 Schnitzler asked why Bahr and his wife did not return to Vienna and chided him for his hypochondria. Bahr replied that economic factors kept them in Munich. Whether this was true or not is unknown, but it seems that finances were a problem for much of his life. His letters to Redlich show him laboring under the burden of deadlines and commissions as well as giving taxing public lectures to stay financially solvent. Bahr died in Munich on 15 January 1934 after a lengthy illness caused by arteriosclerosis. He was buried in his beloved Salzburg. His death not only ended the life of one of the most colorful and prominent personalities of turn-of-the-century Vienna, but it also wrote *finis* to one of the great eras of Austrian cultural history. Hofmannsthal had died in 1929, Schnitzler in 1931, and Karl Kraus's death followed in 1936, while those who survived, such as Beer-Hofmann, were soon driven into exile. Hitler was appointed chancellor of Germany in 1933 and in 1938 set the course of Austria on the corrupt path of the Third Reich. At this moment the world of Bahr had truly become, in Zweig's words, "the world of yesterday."

Chapter Two
Paris: The Decadent Phase

Paris, a city of magic, allure, and sensuality, has been a decisive experience in the lives of many writers and artists from abroad, and the young Hermann Bahr was no exception. His enthusiasm for Paris, developed during his nine-month stay from 16 November 1888 to 18 August 1889 and several additional months in 1890, never faded, and his encounters there shaped his life in important ways: he found the path to his career in literature, which became the main focus of his life; he discovered the importance of form as a cohesive force in society ("That was my Paris experience, decisive for my entire future: the secret of form was disclosed to me, the grand form, through which the sense of our forefathers remained alive in their descendants over the centuries");[1] he played a major role in transmitting the ideas of French decadence to Germany and Austria in the period around 1890;[2] and he conceived his ambitious program of modernity, which became the basic theme of his writings until 1906.

Although Bahr was instrumental in promoting an awareness of French decadent literature in Germany and Austria, he himself was never by artistic conviction, personal inclination, or temperament genuinely committed to the principles of decadence, nor did he seriously adopt decadence as a life-style. If his contemporaries had only heeded Bahr's candid self-appraisal in 1894, they would have been spared much confusion, considerable irritation, and many misconceptions about him: "They do not understand that one can be an enthusiast and Don Juan of all artistic forms, who wants to enjoy and draw out of each what he can and then abandon it again. People are simply mistaken: I do not agitate for any technique. . . . People are deceived by poses that I love, in order to confound the good citizens—*épater les bourgeois,* as one says in my quarter, Pigalle. . . ."[3]

Bahr adopted the outward appearance of a bohemian or dandy at that time, but it was really only one of his many poses. If anyone cared to peer beneath the surface, it could be seen that Bahr not only possessed an iron constitution, but also that he was completely life-oriented.[4] To his own amazement his irrepressibly healthy and in many ways philistine nature asserted itself at the very height of his attempt to feign a decadent posture during his trip to Russia in 1891.[5] It would be impossible to imagine him in the role of the aesthete, des Esseintes, in Karl Joris Huysmans's novel *A Rebours*, the work that Bahr and other critics usually extolled as the prime example of decadence.[6] It was this novel that initially attracted Bahr to literature and to Huysmans, who influenced Bahr's involvement in decadence as art and as a life-style.[7]

Bahr rightly deserves the credit given him for his significant role in the reception of literary decadence in Germany and Austria in the period from 1888 to 1897.[8] Not only was he one of the earliest German critics to comprehend this relatively short-lived but extremely fertile artistic trend, but he was also one of the first German writers to employ the themes and techniques of decadence in his own works. His essays attest to his critical ability to grasp the essence of a new artistic trend and serve as an excellent example of his self-appointed task of informing his contemporaries about cultural and literary phenomena. Through his articles the ideals of decadence were introduced in a positive way, at least initially, as a literary counterweight to naturalism. Just as he felt by 1890 that naturalism had accomplished its purpose and was outmoded, so by 1897 he was convinced that decadence had also outlived its usefulness by degenerating into barrenness and dilettantism. Measured against more recent definitions of decadence, Bahr's grasp of that phenomenon was on the whole perceptive and accurate. Although he never synthesized his views into one totally unified statement—not surprising in view of his impressionistic approach to criticism—all of the characteristics and ideas attributed to decadence in any standard definition of the term are included in one or another of his essays.

Bahr's contribution to decadent literature through his own narrative prose writings and dramas is much less significant than his role in its reception. His works lack the literary quality that would have enabled them to endure. Their value is primarily historical. Such decadent works as his novels *Die gute Schule* (1890) and *Neben der Liebe* (1893), a collection of fifteen prose sketches *Fin de siècle* (1891), the perversely grotesque drama *Die Mutter* (1891), and the fictionalized travel diary *Russische Reise* (1893), together with his volume of impressionistic prose tales *Dora* (1893) and the art-for-art's-sake prose sketches entitled *Caph* (1894), demonstrate the truth of his boast that he could emulate any and every current European literary fashion.[9] At the same time they illustrate the shallowness of his commitment to decadence. These works reflect his literary and technical virtuosity during an experimental period of his life, rather than his innermost artistic convictions.

Bahr's first use of the word *decadent* occurs in a feuilleton on the French writer Villiers de l'Isle-Adam, whom Bahr called "the last romantic and the first 'decadent,' . . . who came from romanticism and proceeded toward 'decadence.' "[10] In both instances Bahr encloses the terms *decadent* and *decadence* in quotation marks, showing either that at this time he did not accept these words as legitimate literary terms or that he was unsure of their precise meaning.

In a subsequent essay, "Salon 1889,"[11] Bahr compared recent developments in painting and literature and highlighted the two major modern literary trends in France: decadence and symbolism. In differentiating between these terms, which were often considered virtually synonymous in contemporary usage, Bahr emulated the French critic Jules Lemaître, whose method of subjective criticism Bahr admired and emulated.[12] In his view the school of the "new lyric" began with Catulle Mendès and passed through the mysticism of Paul Verlaine toward the chaotic yearning of the "decadents" and the symbolists.[13] Not until the essay "Der Buddhismus," in which Bahr described Buddhism as the religion of nerves of the "new lyric" school,[14] did he begin to use the term *decadence* without quotation marks.

In stressing the importance of nervous sensitivity to decadence Bahr touched upon one of the key features of this literary style and of modern literature in general. In an essay that has come to be regarded as one of his most sigificant programmatic statements, "Die Überwindung des Naturalismus,"[15] Bahr emphasized the importance of nerves and of the historical past to decadence: "The content of the new idealism is nerves, nerves, nerves—and costume: decadence continues the rococo and Gothic masquerade, but the form is reality, the daily external reality of the street, the reality of naturalism."[16] Bahr noted the relationship of decadence to naturalism with respect to technique, for both styles are based on exact descriptions of reality except that decadence adds the important dimension of describing states of mind while naturalism restricts itself to depicting external surface details. In a second essay, "Der Naturalismus im Frack," Bahr further demonstrated the relationship between naturalism and decadence using as an example the school of Paul Bourget, whose adherents had started out as decadent writers.[17] Bahr predicted that the combination of the two extreme forms, naturalism and decadence, would result in a synthesis that would form the basis of the future course of literature. This idea became a leitmotiv repeated in many of the essays in *Die Überwindung des Naturalismus*.[18]

The impact of decadence on literary fashion led Bahr to begin predicting the overthrow of naturalism in 1889 before the *Freie Bühne* had even been founded in Berlin and before Gerhart Hauptmann had completed his first naturalistic play, *Vor Sonnenaufgang*. Bahr gave full credit to naturalism for creating the conditions that made the new literature possible, but now it was its turn to be "overthrown" by "a nervous romanticism, a mysticism of nerves."[19] Bahr also proclaimed that the same modern trend would occur in both painting[20] and criticism.[21] As representatives of this new direction in painting Bahr cited Puvis de Chavanne,[22] Degas, and Henri Gervex, in music Bizet, in criticism Lemaître, and in literature the Belgian poet and dramatist Maurice Maeterlinck. Maeterlinck was a key figure in this transition, and Bahr devoted an essay to him in which he traced the derivation of his art from the French decadent and symbolist movements.[23] Maeterlinck's importance resulted from his being the first to bring the principles and aims of decadence to their full realization: "The decadents desire an art that is like themselves, that comes from the nerves and addresses the nerves, that uses every achievement of past art to express nervousness. Decadence was the long heralding of this trend, and Maeterlinck is its final fulfillment."[24]

By 1894 Bahr's understanding of decadence had progressed to the point where he could devote separate essays not only to it but also to symbolism and satanism, which he described as variations of literary decadence.[25] His aim was to refine his definition of decadence, which he felt had gained currency but which was still little understood. In the interim he had experimented with the techniques and themes of decadence in his own writings and consequently was better informed on the subject. Bahr stressed that the concept of decadence was harder to grasp than that of naturalism, because the decadent writers, unlike the naturalists, had no single central idea, followed no common principles, and formed neither a school nor even a group.[26] They were more attuned to their nerves than the older generation, and this caused their estrangement from society and, at the same time, distinguished them from the romantics. Bahr stressed the theory of vowel-color relationships established by René Ghil and called this technique of synaesthesia the "poetics of decadence."[27] With respect to prose technique he indicated that the form of interior monologue was best suited to render the "nerves," that is, the states of mind of the characters.

Until 1894 Bahr's approach to decadence was totally sympathetic, because he viewed this movement as a desired reaction to naturalism and as a trend toward a synthesis that would produce a new, more balanced art form. A noticeable change in Bahr's attitude becomes evident in his essay on Maurice Barrès,[28] the French writer with whom he felt the greatest kinship and to whom he felt the most indebted.[29] Although Barrès at one time was the "master of decadence," he subsequently repudiated this movement, developed a program aimed at reconciling art and life, turned to politics, and was elected as a delegate to parliament from the city of Nancy. Bahr passed through essentially this same evolution, except that he had served his apprenticeship in politics before rather than after his involvement with literature; but he never sought public office.

Bahr's change of attitude culminated in the outright condemnation of decadence in the essays collected in *Renaissance* (1897). The initial essay, "Decadence," discusses two well-known decadents, Count Robert Montesquiou, the model for des Esseintes, and Oscar Wilde. After describing the characteristics of Montesquiou that made him a perfect stereotype, Bahr dismissed him and those like him for "lacking the creative strength of artists."[30] To view Montesquiou and Wilde in equal terms and to deny the artistic talent of Wilde is one of the greatest blunders Bahr ever made. However, such a misconception is further evidence of his eagerness to condemn decadence, even to the point of allowing his tendentious purpose to affect his normally perceptive critical judgment. By this time the predicted synthesis of naturalism and decadence had taken place, and Bahr was again searching for the "art of the future." This he found in Barrès's enthusiastic affirmation of the healthfulness of provincial life in contrast to the decadence of the city. All of Bahr's works written after 1897 repudiate artificiality in every form; similarly, he rejected writers like Sacher-Masoch, whose unhappy, rootless existence served as a warning that one should not become separated from reality.[31]

Bahr's change of heart was not as inconsistent as it might first appear because he had never regarded decadence as more than a transitional phase, a necessary corrective to the extremism of naturalism. For example, he continued to praise Villiers de l'Isle-Adam for his historical importance as one of the pioneers of decadent literature. Changes in literary fashion were necessary, as Bahr noted in a programmatic statement from 1895: "The tradition of art will have to fight just as hard against naturalism and decadence as a few years ago naturalism and decadence fought against the tradition of art. . . . Naturalism accustomed people to measure everything in terms of reason, and Decadence made the moment supreme. But art has nothing to do with reason and with the moment; its concern is to extract the essence out of feeling."[32] Bahr's decadent phase coincided primarily with that period in his literary development when he was experimenting with a range of forms and with linguistic virtuosity. He practiced decadence as he had earlier tried naturalism and would later try impressionism, expressionism, and other trends—political, social, and religious as well as literary—in order to experience them from the inside and thus understand them thoroughly enough to explain them to others. And as a follower of Barrès he delighted in expanding his personality by constantly developing new selves.[33]

Of Bahr's works associated with decadence the novel *Die gute Schule* (1890) is not only the first, but also the most important. Bahr began to write it in Paris on hotel stationery and completed it on his trip through southern France and Spain. The novel represents Bahr's attempt to create, in effect, a German counterpart to *A Rebours*. The plot is largely biographical except that Bahr made his protagonist a painter instead of a writer and changed the name of the woman from Nini to Fifi. The form of the novel was completely new in Germany, and, according to Bahr, *Die gute Schule* created a minor sensation in Berlin when it was published in the *Freie Bühne für modernes Leben*. It was reviewed favorably by, among others, Otto Brahm, who hailed Bahr's work as a *"Grüne Heinrich, fin de siècle."*[34]

Bahr used the stream-of-consciousness technique to trace the states of mind (the subtitle of the novel is *Seelenzustände*) of a poor but idealistic Viennese painter living in bohemian fashion in Paris. His protagonist is both an outsider and an aesthete who feels superior to other people and has dedicated his life to the pursuit of pure color. As an artist he is obsessed by the idea of capturing on canvas the perfect colors that he envisions in his mind's eye without sacrificing truth: "That was therefore his egg of Columbus. They screamed color here and abused the desire for truth; there they screamed truth and abused the desire for color. Color and truth, both, he answered to each side."[35] His mind is obsessed with color, as seen in this description of his feelings about the color red: "It was a lyricism of redness. The redness contained within it his entire soul, all his feelings, his intentions, his wishes, in sorrowful and yearning sonnets; it was an absolutely complete biography of red that transpired within him and could occur absolutely only within him—or it was a psychology of red, as one might call it."[36] On another occasion the sight of green sauce on his plate at a restaurant gave him transports of inner delight and frantic torment as he tried to burn the color ineradicably into his brain so that he could secure it there for later reproduction.

When he fails to capture on canvas the conception of pure color in his mind's eye, the painter seeks to intensify his sense perception through an erotic encounter that descends into brutality and sadomasochistic perversity, including Nietzsche's whip: "With his whip he tried to destroy her completely, beat her flesh to nothingness, until not a trace of her remained and he could find release. Not until he saw blood streaming from her did he feel good. Then he forced her to make love and scourged her with kisses, while she beat at him, dribbled saliva, and gnashed her teeth, until they lost consciousness, as if fading into death."[37]

When even these extremes of cruelty and lust still fail to produce the desired artistic breakthrough, the painter capitulates and becomes "respectable," that is to say, a pragmatic, crassly materialistic bourgeois. The school of love, *Die gute Schule,* has led him away from his fruitless quest as an artist into a mundane existence based on material security and personal comfort. Most of his time is devoted to playing tarok, a favorite Austrian card game. His dedication to aestheticism and art-for-art's-sake has been replaced by the cynical business of churning out hack paintings, most of which are purchased by his ex-mistress Fifi, who has married a millionaire.

With its powerful emotional scenes and richly detailed psychological descriptions the novel shows Bahr's skill at utilizing or imitating the decadent formula: elitism, aestheticism, eroticism, perversity, and alienation from the bourgeois world with its materialistic values and belief in progress. However, the cynicism of the abrupt ending[38] demonstrates that Bahr, despite his facility in exploiting the techniques of decadence, lacked any genuine commitment to decadent principles. By the humorous conclusion Bahr revealed his true attitude toward decadence, the glorified romantic idea of the artistic quest, and art-for-art's-sake.

Die gute Schule exemplifies Bahr's aesthetic stance at this time, subordinating plot to style and technique. He uses a blend of precise naturalistic detail combined with minute descriptions of the artist's though processes. The language is especially rich in dynamic verbs and colorful adjectives. The senses are stressed, particularly visual and olfactory sensations. In the preface to the second edition in 1898, after he had rejected decadence, Bahr admitted the heavily descriptive nature of the novel. While he affirmed the work in general, he felt he could now compress it into a third of the space in his new style: "Words say more to me now than they did then, and therefore I have acquired more respect for them. Formerly I only heard their sound and their glitter, now for the first time I know their value. . . . It was our misfortune to have grown up among words without value. We were surrounded by words which we had not yet experienced. . . . We had language before life; then life came along, and we had to invent another language for it."[39]

In his second novel, *Neben der Liebe* (1893), Bahr employed the same technique as in *Die gute Schule* except that the earlier overheated style was now replaced by a cooler narrative manner. Whereas *Die gute Schule* stressed the colors red and green, *Neben der Liebe* features gray tones. In this short novel, which he always held in high regard, Bahr deals with a group of Viennese aesthetes and bon vivants who live a half-life of passivity and self-indulgence without genuine feelings. Against a richly described setting, including all of the modish fashions of the day such as Japanese decorations, Bahr relates a bizarre and tragic love story. A married woman, Margit von Rhon, whose husband has been away for an extended period of time taking a cure for his weak physical condition, commits suicide in self-loathing after having spent the night with a crude Prussian named

Strass, whom she does not love. This situation resulted because she cannot bring herself to surrender to Rudi Lederer, the man who loves her and whom she desires. She is a victim of repressed sensuality with which she cannot cope. Women are still victims of the double standard, and men show no comprehension of their needs and drives. This psychological tale, told in a stream-of-consciousness technique to render the complex and subtle psychological nuances of feeling and thinking, shows that love and erotic desire rarely coincide completely, a situation that causes people to live their lives *Neben der Liebe*. The novel concludes with the fatalistic view that the fate of human beings is controlled by outer forces, not from within.

A more important work for spreading the ideas of decadence—not because of its intrinsic literary merit but because of the notoriety it aroused—was *Fin de siècle* (1891), a collection of sketches and short prose narratives. Biographically the volume is noteworthy, for it displays the shift in Bahr's thinking from politics to literature, particularly in "Niklaus, der Verräter."[40] Several of the tales seem left over from Bahr's political days and involve discussions of Marxist theory and social and political criticism. Most of the sketches, however, treat states of mind, aestheticism, erotic sensuality, and various types of sexual perversion. For example, "Der verständige Herr" extolls the protagonist's denial of sexual fulfillment, which he terms "perverse modesty," as the true art of love. In each instance the plot is minimal and serves mainly as a framework to show Bahr's linguistic virtuosity. Bahr's aim seems to have been to shock the bourgeoisie, and he was delighted when the work was banned and confiscated by the police, because the book received publicity that it would not have gained otherwise and went into a second printing.[41]

Artistically the volume was intended to put into practice the dictum of Zola that had fascinated Bahr since he first encountered it: "Une phrase bien faite est une bonne action."[42] His idea was to keep the plot as minimal as possible and to make the work effective solely through linguistic means. In fact, Bahr achieved a simple but elegant style that he rarely matched again. There is the same stress on nerves, color, sound association, and olfactory sensations as in the novels. Also as in *Die gute Schule* Bahr could not refrain from concluding each of the vignettes with a pointed moral or by satirizing his own characters, showing that this book was for him primarily a series of finger exercises, mere practice to develop skill in the virtuoso use of language. The tales involving politics are overly tendentious and explicit, while the remaining narratives dealing with sexual themes are anecdotal in nature, ending usually with an O. Henry–like surprise twist.

The title *Fin de siècle* shows how Bahr, with his keen sense for popular trends, employed a currently fashionable word to capitalize on the latest artistic craze. Koppen, in fact, claims without supporting evidence that Bahr introduced the term to Germany through this work.[43] While this point remains to be established conclusively, it seems evident that Bahr, who was not a *Kulturpessimist* but regarded the 1890s as a period of great promise for the future, did not intend his use of the term to be programmatic. "Fin de siècle" is not completely synonymous with decadence, although it contains many of the same connotations of dissolution, decline, neurosis, and eroticism. In employing the term in the title, Bahr was exploiting its topicalness. Three years later in 1894 he still admitted that he had no clear idea of its meaning: "Fin de siècle was a catchy phrase in general use all over Europe. Only no matter how many people liked it, nobody really knew what it meant. Everyone interpreted it differently, as it suited his needs, and there was much confusion."[44]

In 1891, the year in which *Fin de siècle* was published, Bahr tried to carry the perverse ideas of decadence to an extreme in his drama *Die Mutter,* which was intended as a "purely artistic work, as an act of defiance, as an insult to dull, petty bourgeois naturalism, abysmally common but almost great in the heightening of its commonness."[45] *Die Mutter* treats the theme "love ruins the man" or "all women are murderers of man." The plot concerns the fears of a dominating mother, an opera singer named Fredegonde, who believes that she had literally loved her husband to a premature death. To save her physically frail son from the same fate she overprotects him. She seeks counsel and support from her friend and confidant, a homosexual circus clown,[46] and she wishes her son would emulate the clown's sexual life-style as a protection against suffering his father's fate. However, the son is already in love with a woman who is revealed subsequently as his mother's former lesbian partner. When Fredegonde proves unable to rescue her son from his mistress's clutches she kills the other woman in a desperate effort to save him. Her gesture is in vain, for she brings him home only to watch him die. This tale of unrestrained demonic passions and deviant sex is presented in a highly colorful (purple and gold, the favorite colors of decadence, are stressed), sensuous setting.

Among Bahr's works utilizing decadent themes *Die Mutter* is the most consistent in technique, style, and form. Bahr always admired this play for its uninhibitedness. It represents the major instance where the decadent atmosphere is maintained throughout and is not undercut by moralizing, cynicism, satire, or irony. Bahr called this work "evidence, even if despicable, of my impulse to go to the extreme in everything I undertake, to be what I am completely, even if it leads to self-destruction."[47] He also noted that he had not written any single work in which others could find him as he really was, and only one "where I at least find and satisfy myself: *Die Mutter.*"[48] At the time he finished the play he was convinced of its literary importance. Yet when a student group requested permission to perform it in the early 1920s, Bahr declined, stating that it was a product of special circumstances and he could see no purpose in reviving it.

The first indications of Bahr's break with decadence appeared in *Russische Reise* (1893), a fictionalized diary of his experiences during his trip to St. Petersburg. It is an important work in tracing Bahr's association with decadence both as a literary mode and as a lifestyle, for it shows how his philistinism kept breaking through the veneer of his superficial pose. From the first sentence *Russische Reise* displays the overheated, precious, "nervous" style that is maintained throughout the catalog of descriptions of Bahr's various states of mind during his Russian experience: "I must travel again. There is no more fodder for my nerves. . . . Travel. To botanize for a new sensation. In the first place it is a pleasure; in the second place it is my actual occupation. One has as many personae in oneself as one has experienced different worlds; each time something new is added to one's spirit. It is the cheapest and most comfortable enrichment."[49] Yet his attitude began to turn more and more critical as he recognized the deficiencies and limitations of decadence, specifically its rejection of everything human.[50] Finally, through the wholesome presence of the actress Lotte Witt, to whom the book is dedicated, Bahr shed his decadent posturing and was restored to reality.[51] However, despite this early disavowal he continued to experiment with decadent themes and art-for-art's-sake until his final break with them in *Renaissance* (1897).

Dora (1893), a collection of three prose tales ("Dora," "Die Schneiderin," "Jeanette"), further displays some features of decadence, but in a mannered fashion that borders on parody. Like *Neben der Liebe* the title story explores the constantly changing psyche of an aging aesthete involved in a love triangle. After exploring all the psychological ramifications of the affair the tale concludes with the protagonist's ironic comment: "Things are never the way one would like them to be. One never likes things the way they are."[52] In contrast to *Die gute Schule,* "Dora" is told in a simple, straightforward, unpretentious style without excessive use of adjectives or descriptive details.

Most pertinent to the theme of decadence are the descriptions of the aesthete, whose cultivated manner and sensitive nerves place him in the tradition of the dilettante. The emphasis on nerves and states of mind, his refined esoteric tastes, reflected in the description of his apartment with its Japanese decor and collection of women's boots, his disgust with the inelegant, inartistic bourgeois furnishings of Dora's home, and his annoyance over her lack of sensitivity to his moods, all reflect decadent motifs. However, these features are included only in an incidental manner, and the humorous use of decadent characteristics, style, and technique in "Dora" indicates that Bahr was moving away from his decadent phase.

At this point in his career, form mattered more than content, and Bahr wrote primarily for his own experience and not necessarily to convey ideas: "It was an attempt to transform even the content back into form. Indeed, even more: form itself gradually became for me a mere stimulus; the snake of my aesthetics rolled itself together in such a way that it slowly ate its own tail and finally bit into its own head. Art for me finally was nothing more than a suggestion of sensations. At just about this time a comrade acquainted me with the use of cocaine. I discovered that what I received from art could actually be gotten from cocaine with much less fuss. It was fortunate that it was so expensive and I was as poor as could be."[53]

If *Russische Reise* provided the theory behind the idea that form mattered more than content, the collection of prose tales, *Caph* (1894), represents the extreme example of this tendency in practice. *Caph,* bearing the appropriate motto taken from Barrès, "Rien ne vaut que par la forme de dire," is virtually devoid of content.[54] The tales comprising this collection are related to decadence only in the emphasis on art-for-art's-sake and in the stress on beauty of language, on nerves, and on inner moods. Unfortunately, Bahr's disregard of content is not redeemed by his style. Most of the tales are little more than superficial anecdotes that are not even on a level of interest or quality with those in *Fin de siècle*. On the whole, this work shows that Bahr was moving away from some tendencies of decadence toward a final exploration of pure art, before he also abandoned that direction.

In the perspective of Bahr's career the decadent phase was a significant aspect of his program of modernity which dominated his writings and activities until 1905. His leading role in introducing decadent literary principles to Germany and Austria documents his critical judgment and his venturesomeness. He was never afraid to challenge the status quo or to take a position contrary to the prevailing trends. It is impossible to document with certainty, but it is at least conceivable, that Bahr's attacks on naturalism and his advocacy of decadence as a necessary corrective leading to symbolism as the artistic trend of the future may have substantially shortened the life of the naturalist movement in Germany. Bahr's interest in decadence stemmed primarily from his belief that it was a necessary stage in modern literary development. His interest in decadence faded as soon as he was confident that he had mastered it, had utilized it in his works, and had explained it to the public, satisfying what he considered to be his obligation as a critic. Bahr was forever seeking the new and the exciting, and he rarely stayed with any particular technique very long, at least before 1905. By 1894 he was already discussing decadence from a historical perspective as a phenomenon that was no longer in the forefront of literary trends. This interest had been replaced by his new mission of modernizing the arts in Austria.

Chapter Three
Catalyst of Modernity and Cultural Mediator

The Hermann Bahr who returned to Vienna in 1891 was a radically transformed individual. On the basis of his experience in Paris, he was convinced that the arts rather than politics signified the path of the future and held out the greatest promise for the development of the new man, the new society, and the new humanity. His goal of improving the world had not changed, only the choice of means to accomplish it.

Except for his year of compulsory military service in Vienna (1887–88), Bahr had not been in Austria, except for brief vacations, since 1884 when he had departed to study in Berlin. He found the country relatively little affected by the discoveries in the natural sciences and innovations in art and literature that were occurring in other European countries. Far from reflecting these new developments, Vienna languished in a state of comfortable stagnation that Stefan Zweig described as the "golden age of security." Despite the lack of enterprise Bahr discovered that it virtually abounded in talent. In addition to Peter Rosegger, Richard von Kralik, Marie von Ebner-Eschenbach, and the esteemed Ferdinand von Saar, who played a transitional role in Austria similar to that of Theodor Fontane in Germany, a new generation of writers and artists had appeared. Those were the years

> when Hugo Wolf was still living, Burckhard renewed the Burgtheater and Mahler the Opera, Hofmannsthal and Schnitzler were young, Klimt reached maturity, the Secession began, Otto Wagner founded his school, Roller introduced his concept of painting into the theater, Olbrich, Hoffmann and Moser created the Austrian school of applied art, Adolf Loos appeared, Arnold Schönberg arose, Reinhardt walked unknown in quiet streets dreaming of the future, Kainz returned home, Weininger expired in flames, Ernst Mach held his popular scientific lectures, Joseph Popper

his *Phantasies of a Realist,* and Chamberlain, having fled to our kindly city from the distracting world, wrote the *Foundations of the Nineteenth Century*. . . .[1]

Bahr, who at this time considered himself a "good European" in the sense of Barrès, had no desire to remain in Vienna because he did not encounter there the stimulating new ideas that had captivated him in Berlin, Paris, and Madrid. However, his discovery of Hofmannsthal quickly changed his view and was the principal reason why he remained in Vienna.[2] To Bahr Hofmannsthal signified the vision and the hope of Austria. He believed that the youthful genius foretold the dawn of a new era and began to formulate his dream of a glorious future for Austria, an ideal that he worked for the next fifteen years to achieve. It does not detract from the merits of Bahr's accomplishments that he later had to confess that what he had considered to be a sacred spring turned out to be an Indian summer.

In Vienna Bahr consulted with E. M. Kafka about their plan to create a literature in Austria that would appeal to the public and thus unify artists and readers: "They [the young writers] wanted to awaken, to summon, to unite; art was no longer to be produced by individual eccentrics but out of the mutual effort of the entire nation."[3] Bahr greeted the arrival of Kafka's new journal *Moderne Rundschau* in January 1890 as the "heralding of a new literature in our country." He contributed the essay "Die Moderne," but this programmatic statement was a plea for a new art in general and had little connection with the present purpose, for it was written in Paris before he had had any thoughts of returning to Vienna.

Because of his visibility and volubility, Bahr is often credited with having founded the so-called *Jung-Wien* group, an impression to which he himself contributed:

It is now thirty years since I returned to Vienna—having in the meantime roamed around Berlin, Paris, Madrid, Tangiers, Paris again, Berlin again, and finally also St. Petersburg—urgently invited by E. M. Kafka, a young man from Brünn, the editor of *Moderne Dichtung* to found "Young Vienna." The material was already at hand: a young physician, Dr. Arthur Schnitzler, the city celebrity, Richard Beer-Hofmann who was famous because of the splendor of his neckties, and a young schoolboy who wrote under the name Loris—Hugo von Hofmannsthal. I looked them over, ventured the "founding," and since then have taken advantage of every opportunity for thirty years to annoy the Viennese.[4]

In fact, Bahr did not found *Jung-Wien,* nor did he really believe that he had done so, as he indicated in his autobiography: "For years the cynics regarded [Jung-Wien] as one of my inventions. They do me too much honor; it was not I who stood god-father to young Austria, young Vienna, but Henrik Ibsen. . . . I received it from the hands of Ibsen."[5] Bahr was referring here to the visit of Ibsen to Vienna in April 1891 to attend the performance of his play *The Pretenders* at the Burgtheater. Afterwards Kafka, Joachim, and Kulka, the publishers of *Moderne Dichtung,* gave a banquet in Ibsen's honor to which most of the young writers were invited. Bahr was not yet in Vienna.

Not only did Bahr not found *Jung-Wien,* but no group by this name ever existed. The term was coined retrospectively by journalists and critics as a convenient label for the circle of writers around Bahr. Although these young men were brought together by mutual literary interests and by personal friendships, they never considered themselves part of any formal organization. They had no charter, no officers, and did not write any manifestos. Although their works did display a certain thematic similarity in the early years, they had gone in different directions by 1900. A convenient terminal date for the *Jung-Wien* group, insofar as it existed at all, is Karl Kraus's satirical pamphlet *Die demolirte Literatur,* which celebrates the demolition in 1896 of the Café Griensteidl, the favorite meeting place of the young artists, to make room for a bank.

Insofar as any mutual feeling existed at all, it was primarily as a circle of friends who shared similar backgrounds and interests. When Bahr tried in 1894 to clarify some of the misconceptions about the group, which was so frequently discussed, he referred to it as "Das junge Österreich" and not as *Jung-Wien:*

Therefore, "Young Austria" does not imitate the Berlin model, and it does not follow the Paris design; it is not revolutionary, and it is not naturalistic—indeed, what terms can one use to define "Young Austria," since it does regard itself as a renewal. The young men have no formula, they have no program, they have no aesthetics. They only repeat that they want to be modern . . . it is their answer to every question.[6]

Bahr included within the group Karl Baron Torresani, Schnitzler, Loris (Hofmannsthal), Felix Dörmann, Arnold Korff, Richard Specht, and himself.

Only once did the group act together in an attempt to establish a Viennese equivalent of the *Freie Bühne* in Berlin and the *Théâtre Libre* in Paris. A committee composed of Kafka, Joachim, Bahr, Beer-Hofmann, Schnitzler, and Salten rented the *Theater in der Josefstadt* in January 1892 for performances of Maeterlinck's *L'Intruse* and *Les Aveugles*. The police commissioner, however, forbade the performances because Salten had forgotten to present the books to the censor for approval. Once this oversight was corrected the performances took place before a full house, "after Hermann Bahr delivered a raging speech dripping with rebellious irony against the authorities."[7] This one venture marked the beginning and the end of a *Freie Bühne* in Vienna.

Because of his flamboyant and aggressive manner Bahr easily stood out in this circle of budding authors, but to call him the leader unqualifiedly in a spiritual or intellectual sense would be inaccurate. Hofmannsthal's letters show that he considered Bahr merely a good friend. The acquaintance of Schnitzler and Bahr ripened only slowly into friendship on both sides. Schnitzler did not quite trust Bahr, who "became completely fair toward the rich talent of Schnitzler only after years of hesitation."[8] Salten, whom Bahr claimed to have defended "against all the world," assigned Bahr a rather minor role in the affairs of the group. On the other hand, to a group of lesser talents such as Willi Handl, Arthur Kahane, and Adalbert von Goldschmidt, Bahr served as the leader they had awaited. His bold plans, aggressive spirit, and sparkling orations in the Café Griensteidl won these younger men over to him. According to Handl, Bahr consolidated and gave direction to ideas which, until he arrived, had remained but vague, isolated stirrings.[9]

Bahr became the catalyst for the arts in Vienna, and on the basis of his extraordinary drive, organizational talent, and literary connections all over Europe, he energized and gave the needed direction and, above all, encouragement to the young artists in all disciplines. Through his many articles in newspapers and journals Bahr served as the major theoretician of his generation and in this manner played a leading role in determining the course of the arts in Austria in the 1890s. With his boundless enthusiasm and indefatigable activity he enlivened, enriched, and influenced the cultural scene in Vienna more than any other single individual of his time.

It is not surprising that Bahr took charge of the situation in Vienna, because he had a penchant for leadership and a genuine talent for organization. Whether the need was to arrange a performance of a Maeterlinck play, a reading for a charity, or a bicycle outing, he oversaw the details. Similarly, if one had a manuscript to evaluate or place, needed an introduction, or desired an intermediary in seeking a favor or a job, Bahr was the man to see. He became the nominal leader by making himself indispensable. Moreover, he believed that he merited such a position because at this time he had stronger credentials than any of his colleagues. Not only had he traveled widely and spent considerable time in Paris, Berlin, and Madrid, but he also possessed a literary reputation. He saw little reason for modesty among the writers of his own age group, who by 1891 had published little beyond a few lyric poems. In addition, he was known in the major capitals of Europe, particularly in Berlin, whereas the other writers were still not even familiar to the Viennese public. In his self-assessment published in 1894 in the article "Das junge Österreich" Bahr best conveys the self-assurance verging on arrogance that characterized his attitude at the time:

One forgets that in one sense I am different from the others and unique unto myself. The others represent their nature in a single note. . . . But I am driven to give form to the total abundance of notes. . . . None of these notes will penetrate to the essence, but I would like to grasp the entire surface of this extensive period and experience the full intoxication of all of its upheavals on my nerves and senses. That is my fate. In me everyone finds more than himself. . . ."[10]

Another example of Bahr's extreme self-confidence is the motto of the volume *Studien zur Kritik der Moderne* borrowed from Hofmannsthal's *Gestern:* "No one has gone away from my door who has not at least received understanding." Bahr boasted that there was nothing on the European scene in the realm of the arts that he could not understand or shape into a literary work; hence his extreme confidence and the sense of conviction that animated his activities as cultural mediator.

Once he decided to stay and work in Vienna rather than "return to Europe," Bahr threw himself into literary life with complete dedication and with total optimism about the eventual success of his program. He became the dominating force of the new spirit of modernity that refused to be restrained by the chains of tradition, inhibited by the atmosphere of resignation, or deterred by opposition. At the time he began his work in Vienna, Bahr's program consisted primarily of furthering the idea of modernity in life so that Austria could catch up with the newest European developments: the central theme of his two volumes of essays *Zur Kritik der Moderne* and *Die Überwindung des Naturalismus.*

Although Bahr did not originate the idea of modernity, he became its most articulate spokesman and vociferous champion, to such a degree that he has often been credited with having coined the term *Die Moderne.* Actually the precise origin of the word remains to be documented, but it was used in 1884 by Wilhelm Arendt in the title of the lyric anthology *Moderne Dichtercharaktere.* Arno Holz also included the poem "Modern" in *Buch der Zeit: Lieder eines Modernen* (1885) in precisely Bahr's sense of progressiveness and total transformation. Most importantly, however, Eugen Wolff defined the term in his essay "Zehn Charakteristiken,"[11] stressing exactly those features that became essential ingredients in Bahr's program: a modern spirit, the rejection of classical antiquity as the ideal of art, and the need for art to portray human beings in all their passions with unflinching truthfulness. Wolff also indicated that modern literature should be a reaction against the epigonic authors of the time, such as Paul Heyse and the Munich group, and should represent the national German spirit. This emphasis on nationalism in literature is an important idea that was reemphasized in 1890 by Julius Langbehn's influential book *Rembrandt als Erzieher.*

Bahr's borrowing and promoting of the term *modern* reflects his general procedure as a cultural critic. He was not a profound original thinker but was and remained a gifted journalist who reacted to the events of his day. His talent lay in his keen perceptiveness of future trends, which, like a seismograph, he was able to detect earlier and more clearly than other critics. These newest and most rewarding tendencies he promoted in his various publications. Since he took most of his ideas in this period from his experiences in Paris, he was considered ahead of his time in Germany and Austria, a fact that earned him the nickname of "the man of the day after tomorrow." In truth, however, Bahr was usually following rather than leading, mediating rather than innovating. This perspective detracts nothing from the importance of his contribution, for an idea is worth little until it is utilized. Bahr deserves credit not only for publicizing, but also for promoting the ideas of modernity in art and life and helping them to gain a more rapid acceptance in German-speaking countries than they would have had without his aggressive campaign.

Although he did not coin the phrase *Die Moderne,* Bahr expanded the concept into a full-scale program, provided its theoretical basis, and publicized the necessity of modern thinking in the arts until these ideas gained general acceptance. Because he was often groping for direction and feeling his way more by intuition than reason, he developed his program gradually in various essays. Consequently, his theories, which have proved correct in retrospect, did not have the impact they might have had if they had been presented as one unified statement. Just as Bahr refined his understanding of decadence until he could dismiss the movement, he followed the same procedure in all his theoretical writings. As a critic he was excited by every new manifestation in the arts, which he sought to comprehend and make part of himself. Then he was ready to move on to newer ideas. This personal dimension of Bahr's role as a critic is often overlooked, but it is essential to any real understanding of his goals and critical approach.

Bahr's program in Vienna unfolded through the following distinct stages: (1) introducing the concept of modernity as a flexible lifestyle based on nerves; (2) introducing modernity in all of the arts to overcome the dichotomy between art and life; (3) promoting the development of all artists in Austria; (4) educating the public to a greater awareness, understanding, and acceptance of the arts, so that they would become transformed into meaningful culture, that is, art that was experienced by the public and made part of its life; (5) fostering indigenous Austrian, as opposed to German, art equal to the quality of other leading European nations; (6) publicizing European artists in Austria and Germany and Austrian artists in Europe in order to effect a closer rapprochement between Austria and the countries of Western Europe; (7) shifting from an exclusively Viennese to a total Austrian orientation with the program "discovery of the provinces" in 1899; (8) envisioning the arts as playing a central role in Austrian life similar to that played by them in Periclean Greece, which became his model after 1900. The progression of Bahr's thought during the 1890s ranged from economics and politics through aestheticism and decadence to general cultural problems. An examination of the evolution of his thinking through these various stages reveals his significant contribution as the "midwife of modern art" in assisting the intellectual and cultural transition of Austria into the twentieth century by a complete transformation of values.

In "Die Herkunft der Weltanschauungen," an extract from Bahr's rejected doctoral dissertation that formed the first essay of *Zur Kritik der Moderne,* Bahr posits as his premise a belief in the economic process as the objective correlative for modern *Weltanschauungen.* However, more important than his emphasis on economics is his emphasis on contemporaneity, and the rejection of all outdated ideas: "The only principle on which all ethical systems agree is to be modern. However, not merely to be modern once but to remain modern; and because the quality of that correlate changes unceasingly, that means to be a revolutionary at all times."[12] Even at this early stage Bahr saw that his ideas would have to be taught in school to be accepted, and he frequently discussed the school system as the means to educate the next generation to the goals and principles he was espousing. Children particularly had to be taught to remain aware of the constantly changing nature of society: "The highest command of school to every individual cannot be anything else except to be nervous to one's very fingertips."[13]

Bahr continued his stress on the basic importance of the economic process and on the necessity of viewing history from a Marxist perspective in his second essay "Die Geschichte der modernen Malerei" as well as in "Die Weltanschauung des Individualismus." All of this material with its economic basis may have come from Bahr's dissertation on Marx. This economic viewpoint persists in Bahr's first literary essay, "Henrik Ibsen," which represents a turning away from economics to literature. Here for the first time Bahr established the polar opposites of romanticism and naturalism and postulated as the goal of modern literature the need to synthesize these two contrasting tendencies. Bahr views Ibsen's Brand as the first modern man,[14] as a free personality who struggles to unite life and will or nature and intellect. Although Bahr said of Ibsen what he later said of himself, namely, that his artistic power was not equal to his literary intentions, he nevertheless called him "a literary Johannes who preaches the turning away from the present and shows the path which the redeemer of the future will travel. That is his imperishable service which will make his name unforgettable in the history of world literature. . . ."[15]

This essay on Ibsen illustrates Bahr's Hegelian thinking, which presents conflicting tendencies in the form of a dialectic and then seeks a synthesis. The reconciliation of opposing ideas is the dominant task of the present, as Bahr repeats throughout the essays of *Zur Kritik der Moderne* and *Die Überwindung des Naturalismus:* the merging of individualism and socialism in politics, the combining of practical experience and theoretical thought in science, and the synthesis of naturalism and romanticism in art.

In his search for truth, which was the banner under which the campaign of modernity was conducted, Bahr utilized a system of relative standards as opposed to belief in eternal truth and absolute values. This was reflected in the essay "Die Krisis im Burgtheater," where Bahr disputed the claim of Ludwig Speidel, the dean of theater critics in Vienna, that since the new drama did not suit the old Burgtheater style it should be rejected. Bahr drew the opposite conclusion: that the Burgtheater should change. There were no eternal truths and hence one must change with the times: "I admit a single eternal truth, namely, constant change, as a result of which all art as well as all nature rejuvenates itself in every new phenomenon."[16]

Modernity, then, as Bahr defined it, meant acceptance of the idea that life remains in constant flux and that the individual as well as all human manifestations, including art, must remain sensitive to change in order to keep abreast of the current social reality. Bahr was influenced here by Ibsen and his fight against the *Lebenslüge* ("the lie of life"). There are overtones in Bahr's essays of a break with tradition, of new beginnings not burdened by the weight of past practices.

Bahr's major essay on the subject, "Die Moderne" (1891), served as the opening piece of *Die Überwindung des Naturalismus*. The very title of the book shows that Bahr had now gained sufficient confidence to predict flatly the future course of art: the goal was a new humanity, the motto was to strive for truth, and the means to this end was to overcome the dichotomy between art and life. Art must become wedded again to reality as its source, and it must reflect the true condition of contemporary life, not flee into idealized, romantic flights of fantasy.

"Die Moderne," which was written in the stylized prose of Bahr's Paris period, provided a summary definition of modernity that was distilled from all of his previous essays, stressing primarily the need for a new art to keep pace with the changing times: "The idea of modernity exists only in our wishes and outside in the world around us. It is not in our spirit. But that is the torment and the feverish and choking illness of the century that life has outrun the spirit. Life has been changed to its very core and continues to be transformed ever anew, every day, restlessly and continuously. But the spirit remained old and inflexible and was not animated and did not change, and now it suffers helplessly because it is isolated and abandoned by life."[17] To overcome this schism between the spirit and life a rejuvenated truthful art was necessary: "We want to become true. . . . We want to become what our environment is. We want to discard the foul past, which, long faded, stifles our soul in withered foliage. We want to become present."[18]

The new art was to be based on contemporary reality and written in the spirit of the times, with the main stress placed on the senses and the nerves. "We have no other law except truth as each individual experiences it. . . . This will be the new art . . . , and it will be the new religion. For art, science, and religion are the same."[19] The thrust of the essays in *Die Überwindung des Naturalismus,* which were written prior to his return to Vienna, was consistent with those in *Zur Kritik der Moderne:* to achieve and maintain a modern posture, to be receptive to life through the senses, and to maintain an open attitude permitting, if not actually seeking, constant change. They clearly document his role as the major theoretician of his generation as well as a catalyst, organizer, and cultural mediator.

The main difference in Bahr's approach, once he began to work in Vienna, lay in his change of attitude from that of a European to an "Austropean," a term applied to him by the English critic J. Middleton Murray and one that Bahr personally found most appropriate. Although his activities in Austria from 1891 to 1896 may at first seem diffuse because of the many projects in which he became involved, his direction was not random but was centered on specific aims which Bahr never lost sight of: to raise the cultural level of Austria by elevating the status of the arts to a position of primacy in the life of the nation; to create an identifiable Austrian literature as unique and separable from German literature; and to bring Austria, which he like Ferdinand von Kürnberger called "Halbasien" because it was more oriented toward the East than the West, into closer rapprochement with European nations.

These aims are clearly reflected in the third volume of essays, *Studien zur Kritik der Moderne* (1894), in which Bahr encouraged the young talents of Austria while at the same time informing Austrians about the literary developments in the other European countries he had visited. *Studien zur Kritik der Moderne* illustrates Bahr's versatility as well as his programmatic aims. The ideas are basically repeated from the earlier essays, now organized in four categories: criticism, literature, painting, and theater, the areas of Bahr's major concern. He was also interested in renewing music, but, based on superficial knowledge, his contribution in this area remained quite general. In "Kritik" Bahr emphasized again that he followed the critical model of Jules Lemaître, practicing subjective criticism based on the concept of constant change and relative values. In "Die Zukunft der Literatur" he reiterated the idea that naturalism had been overthrown. While there was no consensus about the future direction of literature, whether it would be a new idealism, a synthesis of idealism and realism, or whether it would be symbolic, everyone was agreed that it would not be naturalism.[20] In "Die Decadenz," "Die Symbolisten," and "Satanismus" Bahr described what he felt were the three major trends of current literature that would replace naturalism. After groping for direction for several years, he now felt on solid ground, as can be seen from the historical dimension of these essays as well as the more authoritative tone, the greater organization, sense of progression, and unity of the volume.

In the section on literature Bahr provided a lengthy five-part survey of the German scene in "Das jüngste Deutschland," reinforcing the idea that he was motivated by a sense of historical purpose. His coverage is comprehensive, including "Das junge Österreich," "Vom jüngsten Frankreich," and "Vom jüngsten Spanien." These general overviews are followed by essays on individual writers from each nation. As representatives from Austria, for example, he featured "Ferdinand von Saar," the transitional figure between the older and younger generations, "Adalbert von Goldschmidt," whom he had tried to champion, and "Loris," whom he held in the highest regard as the hope for the future Austrian literature. Regardless of the individual discussed, the basic themes remain constant until they become an overpowering litany: naturalism is over, the tendency now is toward symbolism and an art of nerves. Apart from this general shift, Bahr does not advocate any particular style; in fact, throughout his criticism he pointedly avoids acting as an advocate of any particular technique or manner—critics were supposed to learn from writers, not try to teach them—but to emphasize that every individual artist should present his personal view of the world.

This mandate for personal integrity and conviction in art runs consistently throughout his early critical essays. Bahr praised both Hermann Conradi and Detlev von Liliencron among his German contemporaries precisely because each had his personal new style through which he expressed his own inner being. However, Austrian art still lacked this individuality, as he noted in the lengthy essay "Bildende Kunst in Österreich": "The personal element at any price is the great passion of our age. Never did other [nations] possess so abundantly what we lack."[21] Bahr also stressed the personal note as the greatest feature of acting and praised Eleonora Duse for this quality: "Thus she always appears as a unique personality, and this quality works where other performers would fail. That is her secret."[22] This emphasis on personal integrity also coincides with Bahr's search for real human beings *(wirkliche Menschen)*.

The final section of the book, "Der neue Stil," is devoted to acting and consists of a series of personal interviews with fourteen leading performers to discuss the naturalistic style. All of the actors repudiated naturalism and like Bahr desired a modern, flexible technique.

A new dimension of Bahr's critical approach evident in *Studien* is the emphasis on morality, which fits his search for the purpose of art. Bahr had been influenced by Nietzsche and Zola to equate morality and art. Initially he had interpreted this relationship to mean that form alone justified literature and that meaningful content was superfluous, as he tried to show in *Caph*. Now he returned to the more traditional view that it is the function of literature to confront the major problems of life. Bahr makes the point most clearly in his essay on Hofmannsthal, whose importance lies in his concern with moral questions, who "probes the relationship of man to the world, seeks the meaning and significance of things, searches for certainty on the path of life."[23] If other critics had heeded Bahr's lead, the world would have been spared the mistaken view of Hofmannsthal as an unworldly aesthete that has persisted to the present day.

In *Studien* Bahr adumbrates positions that he was to bring to final form in *Inventur* (1912), which marks a major turning point in his life. He describes the literature of his day as being technically superior to anything written in the past. Modern writers, according to him, were endowed with genuine capability and excellent knowledge of their craft, but despite their rich powers, their talent and technique, they were at a loss for subject matter. They were plundering every corner of life to find new themes, but the emphasis on the worldly, the transitory, prevented them from finding what Bahr called the eternal, the Wilhelm Meister quality. Just as Bahr had inaugurated *Die Zeit* on 6 October 1894 with *Herr Fridolin und sein Glück* by Ferdinand von Saar to show the public that he respected the Austrian literary tradition, now he reestablished connections with the ideas and values of Goethe, who had been repudiated by writers at the turn of the century.

Bahr could praise the minor Swiss writer Edouard Rod because his latest book, *Les Idées morales du temps present,* subordinated the aesthetic quality to the moral.[24] The same view was presented in the essay on Ferdinand von Saar, whom Bahr praised for his treatment of contemporary problems and for the uniquely Austrian quality of his writings. However, Saar's major achievement lay in his moral stance: "I would like to call it almost a moral beauty. One senses in every word that an honorable artist is talking. That sounds like very little, but it is a great deal today."[25] Bahr also praised Saar for his independence of mind: "Thus he is perceived as a moral model, whom one gladly follows and entrusts oneself to in matters of art. The temptations are great today, when art is carried on as business and trade."[26]

In all his essays Bahr utilized a subjective approach, partly because it best suited his nature and partly because he believed that impressionistic criticism was preferable to rigid dogmatic criticism based on absolute standards: "I became completely uncritical and precisely in this way a critic of special uniqueness. . . . To understand the artist and his art, to emphasize, to learn to re-create his feelings, seems to me more important than the question about his value or whether I like him. . . . The attempt at such a rebirth in the being of every artist whose works I encountered was my criticism."[27] By applying relative standards Bahr was able to praise all artists on their own level. If art was the major path to the future, as he believed, then it behooved a nation to have as many artists as possible. He felt that all talented people in Austria must contribute, and he therefore frequently "discovered" young writers and artists.

Bahr claimed to have helped thousands through his kind of criticism, which he called "Animierkritik" or criticism of encouragement. In his autobiography, musing about whether he should have written less with a corresponding increase in the value of each of his works, Bahr concluded that he had, after all, followed the right course: "I would then have foregone this part of my life: I would not have been able to help thousands. I would not wish to renounce the feeling of having been the great helper of Austrian art and gladly bear the ingratitude with which this office is rewarded."[28]

Bahr continued to publicize his program of modernity through his columns in *Die Zeit*, the newspaper he had jointly founded in 1894. A number of these essays were subsequently collected in the volumes *Renaissance* (1897), *Bildung* (1900), and *Secession* (1900) as well as in his four volumes of theater reviews: *Wiener Theater* (1898), *Premièren* (1902), *Rezensionen* (1903), and *Glossen zum Wiener Theater* (1906). Throughout these works Bahr repeated his call for a modern literature in tune with conditions of contemporary life as well as modern painting, modern theater, modern criticism, modern acting, and a totally modern *Weltanschauung*. He also provided the theoretical basis for Viennese impressionism and broached the tentative beginnings of the transition to expressionism. It is impossible to overstate the importance of Bahr's writings and activities calling for a total renewal of intellectual and artistic life and for its acceptance by the general public.

By 1897 Bahr felt that his cultural campaign was working so effectively that he used the title *Renaissance* for his next collection of essays from *Die Zeit*. His preface, an open letter to Hofmannsthal and Leopold von Andrian, brimmed with optimism over the widespread response to his cultural efforts. *Renaissance* represented an important turning point, for it marked Bahr's final break with decadence and his turn to a new definition of art, which now had to be not only individual, moral, and nationalistic, but also life-oriented and a contribution to culture.[29] Bahr's new cultural orientaion, which makes cultural value the basis for determining the quality of art, coincides with the repudiation of decadence in *Renaissance* beginning with the first essay "Decadence." Through his restless fascination for constant change Bahr has been led to the hidden essence of true art that concerns itself with eternal truths. The antithesis of the eternal and the momentary runs like a leitmotiv throughout the essays of *Renaissance* and serves as the litmus test to distinguish the true artist from the dilettante. Bahr's view of art is most clearly stated in his defense of Hubert von Heyden's painting *Schweine:* "All things are representations of the eternal in the temporal; to eliminate the temporal and to extract the pure essence of the eternal from objects is the task of art."[30]

Another tendency evident in *Renaissance* is Bahr's turn from the ephemeral and the fragmentary to unity and totality. This shift was expressed most clearly in his analysis of Leopold von Andrian's tale *Der Garten der Erkenntnis,* in which a questing young prince finds religious faith, and through it acquires a true sense of reality: "Thus he gradually reached the point of no longer searching for the meaning of life in individuality but in its totality, and began to sense the unity of things."[31] The prince still has to learn that he also belongs to life, that the things of the world outside are the same as those within him, and that there is nothing in the world except what happens within him. With this realization he has reached his goal in life and must die; "for life is ultimately the separation of the individual from totality, and whoever attains this insight and through it rejoins totality has fulfilled his destiny."[32] This emphasis on the unity of all phenomena in life, of the visible and the invisible worlds, became as important a theme for Bahr as it was for Hofmannsthal. It led him to Goethe, who became his mentor and intellectual guide in the years ahead.

Another tendency evident in *Renaissance* was Bahr's growing weariness with Vienna and the attraction to the wholesomeness and healthfulness of the provinces. Bahr praised Johanna Ambrosius, a young peasant poet, whose poems he described as true art in the sense of William Blake's comment: "I am the secretary, the authors are in eternity."[33] While Ambrosius was not a great poet, she expressed true humanity and served as a "consoling reminder in this confused and hypocritical age."[34] One of the main reasons why Bahr appreciated folk art was that it could not be falsified. He also praised groups, such as the Franz Stelzhamer society in Linz, that were being founded in the provinces for the furtherance of regional literature: "They have the merit of directing the attention of the public away from the shapeless and worthless literature of the big cities, which is surrendering more and more to journalism and business, toward simple and honest men who 'sing like the birds,' hence toward the eternal significance of song as a voice from the soul of nature."[35]

Bahr followed the same path in his four volumes of theater reviews that covered the period from 1892 to 1906. As in his other essays, his aim was to prepare the public for the reception of new trends in the theater and for dramatic experiments. The reviews formed part of his effort to create a fertile soil for modern plays and to minimize audience resistance to change. He paid considerable attention to performers and analyzed their various acting styles to help create a better informed public. His investigations led him to discover the importance of the actor as a model for life. In addition, Bahr discussed a wide variety of theoretical topics in his reviews such as the nature of art, the need for modern indigenous Austrian art, and for a stronger, more progressive Austrian character, along with all of the themes discussed in connection with his other essays. He touched upon all the major problems of his time and brought wider horizons, greater depth of understanding, a heightened sense of national cultural goals, and more personal flair to his role as critic than did any other reviewer of his day.

In 1899 Bahr's growing dissatisfaction with Vienna led to a correspondingly stronger interest in the provinces. Here again he was following rather than leading, for Barrès had become an advocate of regionalism in his novel *Les Déracinés* (1897), depicting the tragedy of young people who left their native soil for life in Paris. Also in 1899 the German regionalist writer Fritz Lienhard sent out the rallying cry "Away from Berlin!," while in Austria Hugo Greinz and Heinrich von Schullern edited a poetry anthology entitled *Jung-Tirol*. Bahr, who had already written favorably about the provinces in *Renaissance,* greeted this new trend and published a series in *Die Zeit* to publicize artistic life in the provinces. The initial essay was written by Peter Rosegger under the title "Die Entdeckung der Provinz" (25 March 1899), followed by Urs Jenny's "Jung Tirol" (26 March 1899) and Hugo Greinz's "Aus Linz" (30 March 1899).

The important aspect of this new campaign was that Bahr now expanded his view to include all of Austria rather than restricting his attention to Vienna. He had already suggested in *Renaissance* that it was impossible to speak of an Austrian literature as long as one focused only on Viennese figures, problems, and moods. He felt it would be beneficial for Viennese literature to face competition from the provinces: "It is our belief that we must leave the circle of the few literate and dilettants and go into the country to the people if the great dream of a new Austrian art is to be fulfilled."[36]

Bahr still considered the split between the intellect and nature to be the major problem of his generation. In all the novels and dramas he wrote up to 1912 this conflict served as the major theme. He hoped that writers from the provinces, where people still lived at one with themselves, with each other, and with nature, might help overcome this dichotomy. Bahr's expansion of his cultural program to encompass all of Austrian art was but part of his major goal of improving the general level of culture throughout the country.

The essays in *Bildung* (1900) reinforce and further clarify the themes of art and culture while placing greater emphasis on nationalism: the need to support Austrian artists, the importance of national culture, and the necessity of developing a total Austrian rather than exclusively Viennese art to help unify the country. Bahr, who repudiated the nineteenth-century liberal tradition of education, offers his conception of how a modern person should be raised and taught. In his laudatory introduction to the Grand Duke of Hesse for supporting Olbrich's efforts to establish an artists' colony in Darmstadt, he states: "We have projected an educational plan, which would make it possible to raise the whole of life to the level of our highest moments when we feel fully alive. Knowledge of noble things and of great activities are no longer sufficient for us; we will only be satisfied by a full existence in goodness and beauty, to which every happy moment will attach new wings."[37]

The initial essay of the volume, "Cultur," contains a definition of culture that shows how Bahr had finally organized his ideas into a unified conception: "We will be able to speak of culture in a country when everyone unconsciously expresses the living connection of his race to the eternal in everything that he does every day. Whoever lives in the reflection of his sensual world and accepts this literally without perceiving that the truth only begins behind this surface, lives in a state of nonculture. . . . [Culture] arises when a whole nation connects its sensual existence to the eternal, has found an interpretation that can satisfy it, and now lets each one practice this interpretation within his own circle."[38] It is perhaps a sign of Bahr's growing disillusionment with the results of his cultural program that after a decade of trying to raise the cultural level of Austria by enlightening the public, he now insisted that culture could not be achieved unless it was imposed from above: "We can attain culture only when a wise man recognizes our appropriate relationship to eternity, when artists let us perceive it in their works, and when powerful heroes, whom the nation trusts, command us to respect these representations. If we want culture, we must first have wise men, artists, and heroes again."[39]

The model for the cultural state Bahr now envisioned was Periclean Greece. What the Greeks transmitted to the people via their statues, the artists of Vienna must convey to the people in their works. Goethe, whose influence on Bahr continued to grow, is held up as a model of the Apollonian *Weltanschauung:* "Whoever can live without Goethe may try it; he may even believe that he is very modern—one can grant him that. We here in Vienna are of the opinion that the demonic is not such a great thing; we prefer to devote ourselves to Apollo. To be able to serve Goethe we see as the highest ideal; we would like a ray from him to fall on us. . . . It is not in our power to determine whether we shall become great or small, but we would like to achieve order."[40]

All of the essays in the first part of *Bildung* deal with the question of culture and stress the Apollonian values of Periclean Greece: calmness, order, moderation, and inner harmony. Bahr's aim was to make art an integral, vital part of everyday life. This idea is especially pronounced in "Volksbildung," where he describes the value of culture as the means to connect present society with the illustrious beauty of his country: "it has always been the meaning of all culture to generalize the particular, to cause the beautiful work or the great deed of a noble man to continue to live in the hearts of all the people and thus enable the individual to have an effect on the masses."[41]

Through his analysis of Greek culture Bahr demonstrated the need for a new form of education that would no longer concentrate on the acquisition of positivistic facts but would awaken a receptiveness to the manifold richness of life. Bahr cited Goethe, Schopenhauer, Nietzsche, Paul de Lagarde, and Moritz von Egidy as exponents of this new concept of education. He wholeheartedly endorsed Edigy's view that art and science should no longer exist adjacent to life but should be life: "Only this concept is worthy of being called *Bildung,* both of the individual and of the nation."[42] Bahr expressed his view of culture even more concisely and directly in the essay "Die plastische Kraft": "This is what we mean when we say so often that it is now our duty to unite all arts in order finally to establish culture. Culture is experienced art."[43] Bahr's idea of applied art formed part of his idea of culture. If the artists of his generation could make it possible for the people to have better living accommodations and more beautifully bound books, "then we would have what I regard as more than art, we would have a culture."[44]

Bahr's ideal of culture was intended to produce a race of inwardly free, independent, and harmoniously adjusted people. In "Die Haupstadt Europa," he described in utopian terms the radically new kind of school that it would take to produce such people.[45] In *Studien* Bahr had emphasized that the people needed to be educated to appreciate the arts and had suggested that the state assume the responsibility for achieving this goal through the school system. He believed that if people were not attracted to the arts, it was mainly because they failed to understand them. It was the responsibility of the state to educate them so that they could appreciate the arts and the arts could flourish. Bahr did not wait for the state to take action but attempted on his own initiative to fill the role of an educator and mediator. All of his essays from the time he returned to Vienna were motivated by this ambition.

The second section of *Bildung* was devoted to specifically Austrian themes. This national interest continued to grow in importance in Bahr's discussions, as he tried to awaken pride in Austrian accomplishments, artists, and tradition, particularly in the baroque heritage. He began with a discussion of the first volume of Nagl, Zeidler, and Castle's *Deutsch-Österreichische Literatur-Geschichte* and faulted the inclusion of the word *German* in the title. Bahr accepted the idea that there was an indigenous Austrian literature distinct from German and encouraged Germanists to document this thesis. Without waiting for outside help he projected the idea throughout his career. "The idea that there is an Austrian art, as Grillparzer, Feuchtersleben, and Stifter knew at firsthand but which gradually had been concealed and effaced by the omnipresent liberalism, not merely as a pendant in some corner of German literature but from earliest times sui juris, indigenous, autonomous, nationalistic, unique, and independent, could be perceived everywhere. To announce it loudly took my courage, my boldness, my delight in paradoxes. . . ."[46]

In addition to writing these general articles Bahr also discussed specific writers: Ferdinand von Saar, Ludwig Speidel, Peter Altenberg, and Beer-Hofmann, names that show how he now concentrated on major figures and no longer discovered and promoted minor authors. In "Zehn Jahre" Bahr provides a retrospective summary of what he believed his efforts in Vienna over a decade had accomplished. He believed that he had made some concrete gains particularly in promoting the *Jung-Wien* writers in Austria and in creating an identity for Austrian literature in other countries: "Whenever people anywhere speak of Vienna they no longer merely think of this or that author who by chance writes in Vienna but of a very specific Viennese type of writing . . . today one knows the 'Wiener Stück,' a [dramatic] form which is not associated with any individual but is the expression of a general essence, of a city. We have also brought it about that there is again such a thing as Austrian art."[47] Bahr failed to mention that the *Wiener Roman* also became a recognized designation for a novel that was written by a Viennese author about Viennese life. Bahr had subtitled *Neben der Liebe,* for example, a *Wiener Roman*. Both the *Wiener Stück* and *Wiener Roman* were generic terms recognized in Berlin by 1900.

This nationalistic emphasis was reflected also in the relationships of the modern Austrian writers to tradition. It is a hallmark of the Austrian, as opposed to the German, modern generation that the young writers manifested no desire to break with the past. Bahr's choice of a story by Saar to introduce *Die Zeit* is a clear expression of this esteem for the older generation. The turn-of-the-century writers all stressed modernity, but they respected and wanted to continue the Austrian tradition in tune with their own times. In Bahr's terms, they desired "to retain the old form of tradition but fill it with our new poetry."[48]

The final section of *Bildung* is devoted to advice to young authors. One recurring theme is Bahr's criticism of the pragmatism of contemporary artists, a topic that grows in intensity until *Inventur* in 1912. In "Erleben" he warned young artists against creating works that were not based on experience, for such art was without value. In "Ein Amt der Entdeckung" Bahr presented the imaginative idea that the government should subsidize young talent since it bore the responsibility for the cultural education of the nation. The plan called for establishing offices in the provinces with a headquarters in Vienna to judge works of art and support the artists according to their merits. Since the country would benefit greatly from the project, the government should be willing to bear the expense. This idea was undoubtedly motivated by the fact that Bahr's desk was overflowing with manuscripts of hopeful young writers seeking his help and advice. Bahr concluded with heavy irony that nothing would come of his suggestion because it was too practical. However, in the post–World War II period the Austrian government has made an effort to stimulate the arts by a program of subsidies and awards similar to Bahr's proposal.

By 1900 the battle of modernity had been won, and its ideas were now taken for granted. Yet Bahr was still dissatisfied, for his grandiose dream of a new Periclean age had not been fulfilled. When the public's desire for art was not as widespread and compelling as he had imagined and when his ideas failed to arouse the enthusiastic response that he had anticipated, Bahr grew discouraged despite his successes and finally abandoned both his cultural plans and Vienna in 1906. Before then, however, he waged his important campaign on behalf of the Viennese painters of the Secession, one of the most significant phases of his modernization program.

Chapter Four
The Modernization of Art: Secessionism

Bahr greeted with elation the formal establishment of the Secession in Vienna on 3 April 1897, for the aims and principles of the seceding artists coincided with the cultural program he had been advocating in Austria since 1891. His role in assisting the breakthrough of Secessionism is one of the most important facets of his critical activity between 1891 and 1906. Bahr's participation is particularly noteworthy, for through his essays he provides a firsthand sympathetic insider's view both of the development of what is generally considered the most important movement in Austrian art in more than a hundred years, and subsequently of the "Wiener Werkstätte."[1] In addition, this episode provides an excellent explanation for Bahr's role in the breakthrough of modernity in Austria, of his nationalistic cultural program, his views on art and the artist, and his concept of criticism. As in everything Bahr undertook, his writings about the Secession reveal as much about him as about the subject. Yet the corroboration of his judgments by recent art critics shows how accurate and perceptive a critic he actually was despite his subjectivity.

Bahr's documented interest in art stems from 1888 and coincides with his "discovery" of literature during his year in Paris. In fact, since 1888, nine years before the Secession was officially established in Vienna, he had been advocating what became the Secessionists' goal in painting. His models were the newest developments he had witnessed in other countries, for example, the innovative techniques of the impressionist and symbolist painters in France, Belgium, and England, and later the Secessionist Art Movement in Munich in 1892 headed by Franz von Stuck.

Bahr's early essays on art and artists were primarily based on exhibits he attended. His interest in art is also reflected in his novel *Die gute Schule* (1890). Whether Bahr had any training in art or in art history is unknown, but it is certain that his formal background was minimal at best. He certainly had no native skill or talent, and he neither sketched nor painted. He was, however, a prodigious reader, and his essays show him to be well informed about the historical development of European art in the nineteenth century and about the newest trends at the turn of the century. To Bahr (as to Hofmannsthal and Max Burckhard) it was of no consequence that he was not a qualified expert in art, music, or in any field, for he viewed his role as a critic to be one of creating an atmosphere of empathy rather than of engaging in technical analysis, a task that would clearly have surpassed his ability and training. For a more scholarly approach Bahr recommended Richard Muther's *Geschichte der Malerei im neunzehnten Jahrhundert:* "a valuable book that one cannot praise enough, nor recommend enough, to cognoscenti for pleasure, to laymen for information."[2]

From his earliest essays Bahr stressed that modernity demanded a break with historical academic art. In Vienna he chided the ultraconservative attitudes of the "Künstlerhaus Genossenschaft," the official organization of artists in Austria founded in 1861 for cultivating and preserving historicism and preventing a change to new techniques and styles.[3] Similarly Bahr attacked the *Ringstrasse,* "the pride of the nineteenth-century liberals," because of its eclectic architecture that displayed a variety of historical styles including classical, Gothic, and Renaissance. Like the architect Adolf Loos in his essays "Die potemkinsche Stadt" (1898) and "Ornament und Verbrechen" (1908), Bahr remained a lifelong foe of the pretentiousness of the "Ringstrasse" and the veneer of pseudoculture it represented.

The Secession seemed to Bahr to be the fulfillment of his wish to see a genuine modern Austrian art. With his customary enthusiasm and aggressiveness he devoted his energies and journalistic efforts to help the movement succeed, both through the pages of his own newspaper, *Die Zeit,* and through his editorial and critical contributions to the official journal of the Secession, *Ver Sacrum.* His commitment to the Secession dominated his activities during the period 1897–1901. As he remarked in a letter to his father on 5 April 1898: "Now I am only painting."[4] In a subsequent letter of 25 April 1898 he expressed his great expectation that this movement would assist him in creating an Austrian style in painting and in applied art, as he had done earlier in literature through *Jung-Wien:* "In the fall, when the Secession will have its own house that is now being built, I will show on Sunday afternoons to manual workers, furniture makers, book binders, etc. the works of the English and Belgians in their specialty and hope in this way to produce something in a few years that can be regarded as an 'Austrian style.' I want to do for our applied art what I succeeded in doing for literature."[5] As can be seen from the reference to "applied art," Bahr was anticipating the direction that the "Wiener Werkstätte" would take upon its formation five years later in 1903. Clearly, in this instance "the man of the day after tomorrow" once again demonstrated his forward thinking.

It is difficult to document accurately how effective Bahr's activities on behalf of the Secessionists were, but the critical consensus is that he played a fundamental role. The critic Ludwig Hevesi, who is credited with a major role in promoting the movement, acknowledges Bahr's efforts and also his critical acumen. However, he also notes that Bahr's aggressive approach and his tendency toward overstatement kept the public from taking him as seriously as it should have.[6] Bahr was driven by a strong impulse to shock the bourgeoisie as well as by a desire to support the underdog and attack the establishment. He was also afraid of appearing boring; hence his tendency to wax emotional, to overstate, to exaggerate. There is no doubt that these features of his writings alienated intellectuals and kept Bahr the critic from being fully recognized.

Nevertheless, critics today generally acknowledge that Bahr and Hevesi made the most significant contribution to the success of Secessionism.[7] In addition, Nebehay credits Bahr's "great influence and extensive participation" for the high quality of *Ver Sacrum*.[8] Gustav Klimt, the first president of the Secession, approached Bahr in 1897 to solicit an article for the first issue of the new journal, and Bahr responded with a programmatic essay entitled "Ver Sacrum," in which he encouraged the young painters to become rebels for their cause: "The Viennese painters will have to show whether they understand how to be agitators: that is the meaning of our Secession. If they do, then they cannot fail."[9] In 1898 Bahr became officially associated with the journal as "Literary Consultant," and he remained affiliated in this capacity until 1901.

Bahr felt that he merited credit for goading the Secessionists to secede from the Künstlerhaus and form their own group. In a letter to his father of 5 April 1898, gloating over the success of the first exhibition, he boasted: "To be sure, the exhibit of the Secession has cost me a great deal of work, struggle, and agitation, but its tremendous success now brings me enormous pleasure. For when I urged the young painters to leave the Genossenschaft a year ago, I was called a fool by all Vienna, and when this exhibit was announced my enemies hoped I would make a real fool of myself. And now it is such a success. To be bold is after all a beautiful quality—one only needs a little luck along with it."[10]

A catalyst for the *Jung-Wien* movement in literature, Bahr also served as a catalyst for the Secession. One means was to praise the independent-minded artists in Vienna who attempted to rebel against the prevailing system, for example, the painter Theodor von Hörmann, whom Bahr called the first Secessionist.[11] Hörmann died embittered, and Bahr used him as an example of the isolated artist, who could accomplish little against the entrenched interests.

Thus Bahr's early essays on art were directed as much toward arousing the artists as toward informing the public. His efforts to encourage the young painters to assert themselves were clearly evident. He argued that the sole model for art must be truth, not that of mimetic naturalism but tha of the artist's world, including the world of fantasy. To follow the dictates of his own integrity and talent is the artist's only proper course. It is this individuality that sets the real artist apart from the epigones: "Let the artist show his world, the beauty that is born with him, that never was before, that never will be again."[12] This quote from Bahr was used as a motto by Koloman Moser in a decorative window (later destroyed) he designed for the Secession building. It was also used by Olbrich over the entrance of the Ernst-Ludwig house in the artist's colony on the Mathildenhöhe in Darmstadt. Bahr's concept of art was further reflected in the motto by Ludwig Hevesi that still stands over the main entrance to the Secession building: "To each age its art; to art its freedom."

Throughout his early essays, usually reviews of art exhibits, Bahr condemned historicism in art and accepted naturalism and even impressionism only as necessary transitional phases leading to symbolism, which was the direction of the future. As models Bahr pointed to Puvis de Chavanne, Whistler, and Ferdinand Khnopff, whom Bahr called the counterpart in art of Maeterlinck. Others whom Bahr praised at various times for their originality were Giovanni Segantini, Arnold Böcklin, Edvard Munch, Max Klinger, Felicien Rops, Theo van Rysselberghe, and Walter Crane.

Bahr was actually less insistent on the kind of art to be produced than on its genuineness. In 1894 Bahr reported that he had viewed approximately 16,000 examples of contemporary painting at exhibits in Vienna, Paris, Munich, and Brussels. His reaction to the state of art on the basis of this broad sampling was horror at the number of copyists at work. Everyone was an imitator: the younger painters imitated the masters, and the masters were imitating themselves.[13] Like the writers, the painters possessed greater technical skill than ever before; but Bahr questioned the value of this superior technique when no genuine feeling animated the brush. This view, repeated like a leitmotiv, motivates his praise of such independent artists as Jean-François Millet, who stated he would rather be a mason than paint against his convictions, as well as minor artists like Theodor von Hörmann, Herbert von Heyden, and Ludwig von Hofmann. Heyden's picture *Schweine* and Hofmann's *Rothe Bäume* were attacked by the public and the critics, but Bahr defended both works on aesthetic grounds as well as with his standard argument that the true artist must follow his own convictions.[14] The same idea also features prominently in the art criticism of Hofmannsthal, who was unquestionably influenced by Bahr's views. One of Bahr's important themes was that painting should return to the original idea of being nothing but painting, and not a representative of morality, philosophy, or politics, among other things.[15] Again Bahr was ahead of his time in foreshadowing nonrepresentational art as early as 1894.

Bahr's approach to art embraces several notions that he reiterated in all his essays: art is important to the culture of Austria; Austrian artists must become aware of the latest developments in art in other Western countries and modernize their approach; the art academy must allow real talent to develop in its own way and not restrict students to traditional techniques; the state must support art by educating its citizens to an appreciation of art; talent in the provinces must be developed; and critics must play a role in preparing a climate for art in Austria.[16] A receptive public was lacking for both literature and art in Austria, and Bahr was motivated to develop this necessary audience by means of his self-appointed role as a critical mediator between the artists and the public. In his essays up to 1895 it is evident that he was attempting to stimulate the incipient Secessionists to take action. Once this aim was fulfilled, he directed his essays mainly at the public, until he found it necessary to chide the artists for betraying the original ideals of Secessionism by falling prey to empty mannerism and materialism.

Although the official founding of the Secession took place on 3 April 1897, Bahr considered the important breakthrough to have been accomplished at the end of 1895 when young painters seized control of the "Künstlerhaus Genossenschaft."[17] The enthusiasm with which Bahr greeted this self-assertion by the progressive members of the association is entirely symptomatic. However, Bahr noted realistically that it was one thing to conquer and another to rule. The difficult question facing the young dissidents was whether they truly wanted to achieve something for art or whether they had merely substituted one clique for another. He praised their first exhibit (the twenty-fourth annual exhibit of the "Künstlerhaus"), which reflected their willingness to accept tradition while being innovative, for they did not suppress the old guard as it had formerly suppressed them.[18]

Bahr's feeling of triumph was somewhat premature, for despite their bold stand in 1895 the young painters lost control of the "Künstlerhaus" again at the end of 1896. Bahr was incensed by this turn of events and wondered whether it was true that the Viennese could not change. His anger at this setback, at this return to art as business, was vented in an intemperate attack on the "Künstlerhaus" and its president Eugen Felix in December 1896. Bahr suggested that the few real artists rent facilities and hold independent exhibits so that the Viennese would have at least some opportunity to keep abreast of the latest European developments. His proposal was not immediately accepted. Instead, the dissident artists, after losing the leadership, formed their own club, the "Vereinigung der bildenden Künstler Österreichs," within the framework of the "Künstlerhaus Genossenschaft." The justification advanced by Klimt for this step parallels precisely the views held by Bahr.[19]

There was a precedent for such affiliated organizations in the "Hagengesellschaft" founded in 1876 and in the "Siebenerclub," both offshoots of the "Künstlerhaus Genossenschaft." However, because of a dispute with Felix over exhibition rights, the dissidents, nineteen in number, led by Josef Hoffmann and Klimt, officially severed all connections with the "Künstlerhaus" and founded the Secession. They were joined by other artists to bring the total to forty members plus auxiliary members from other countries. To show that the issue was not youth versus age, the eighty-six-year-old Rudolf von Alt was named honorary president while Gustav Klimt became president.[20]

Bahr was quick to point out that the reasons behind Viennese Secessionism were different from those behind similar movements in other countries, where the conflict arose over matters of style and technique. In Vienna the conflict centered around the fundamental issue of art versus business.[21] Since the Secessionists put art before financial considerations, it came as a pleasant surprise to everyone that the public not only came in numbers (57,000) to the first Secessionist exhibit—26 March to 15 June 1898 in the "Gartenbaugesellschaft"—but also bought eagerly (218 of 534 works).[22] Contrary to all expectations, the new movement became a financial as well as an artistic success, which Endler explains by noting that Vienna was still in a stage of growth and that consequently there were many patrons seeking art to decorate their homes.[23] Bahr was rhapsodic to see his efforts succeed, and he felt that his view of the public's eagerness for art was vindicated. All the public needed in order to appreciate the arts was a little education such as he had tried to provide. Among other things, Bahr actually did serve as a tour guide for workers, but his gesture was probably not entirely altruistic; for by talking with the public and hearing their questions he gained information that he used as the basis of articles in which he explained the new art and the new artists. As he remarked: "Let us simply confess, we critics really have nothing to give to the artist. It is up to us to educate the laymen for the artists."[24]

According to Bahr, this first exhibit answered the public's question about what constituted Secessionist style: the moderns did not advocate or endorse any particular style; they simply followed their own artistic dictates. Although art historians have come to associate *Jugendstil* with the Secession, Bahr never used the term. This is not surprising, for the name, based on Georg Hirth's journal *Jugend*, founded in Munich in 1896, did not gain currency until 1900, after Bahr had written most of his essays. But the main reason was that Bahr consistently denied that there was any Secessionist style. A Secessionist, he says, "has his own sense of life, and he has found a form that is the necessary, complete, and unchangeable expression of his feeling. That is all that 'Secessionist' means, if one absolutely insists on using the foolish word."[25] The architect Joseph Olbrich, one of the prime sources for Bahr's outlook, emphasized the same point: "Style! English! Secession! What kind of silly words are those?

The Modernization of Art: Secessionism

Let everyone do what he feels, as he feels it—time will demonstrate what it is worth."[26]

Despite the attitude of Olbrich and the other Secessionists as reported by Bahr, "Jugendstil" or "art nouveau" is now universally considered synonymous with the Secession. Bahr used the term "art nouveau" only to refer to the kind of applied art that in 1903 was produced by the "Wiener Werkstätte." It would seem, from the present-day usage of these terms, that art historians have ignored basic distinctions perceived by the artists and have overlooked the original aims of the Secessionists.

Whatever the style, it is indicative of the financial success of the first exhibits and also of the amount of government and private support the Secessionists received that they were able to build their own exhibition gallery in 1898, only one year after the founding of the group. The young architect who received the commission to design the building was Joseph Olbrich, the talented student of Vienna's leading architect, Otto Wagner. Bahr was a good friend of Olbrich, who designed and built Bahr's villa in Ober St. Veit. in 1898. He held Olbrich in the highest personal esteem and dedicated the volume *Secession* to "Master Olbrich in joyful admiration."

The work on the Secession building progressed rapidly, and the opening was set for 4 November 1898. According to Powell, Olbrich's building is "anti-historicist and intentionally contrasts with the *Ringstrassenstil* of the Künstlerhaus across the Karlsplatz."[27] In typical fashion Bahr tried to prepare the public for what it would see, for he feared that the unadorned architectural style would be misunderstood. He emphasized that function rather than appearance determined the design. The building was not intended "to boast or to dazzle. It is no temple or palace but a room that is capable of allowing works of art to be shown to their maximum effectiveness."[28] Bahr expected that the public, its taste spoiled by the decorative art it had always known, would find the building monotonous, because there was no color and because people had lost the ability to appreciate the noble effect of large flat surfaces.

Despite his attempts to forestall criticism of Olbrich's building, it became the object of ridicule because of the large decorative grill on the roof, which was dubbed "Das goldene Krauthappel" ("the golden cabbage"). According to Endler, few people recognized that this ironwork was supposed to represent a laurel wreath crown for art.[29] In subsequent essays Bahr continued to defend Olbrich and tried to make the Viennese understand his courage to trust his own convictions.[30]

For his part Olbrich was so sorely wounded by the antagonism toward his building that in 1899 he left Vienna to accept an invitation from the Grand Duke of Hesse to design and build an artist's colony in Darmstadt, in which everything from the facades of the houses to the tableware would be artistically coordinated and harmonious. He completed part of this project on the Mathildenhöhe, including several houses, a tower, and a theater.[31] After a visit in 1901 Bahr used the occasion to vindicate Olbrich as an architect and also to remind the Secessionists of their early ideals, which by 1901 were slipping: "Here one of us has shown clearly and with greatness what in others is still in confusion. He serves as an example that not he who renounces, not he who resigns himself, but only he who has the strength to remain true to himself can become mature."[32] Unfortunately Olbrich died on 18 August 1908 before he could carry out his grandiose plan to achieve the ideal of the "Gesamtkunstwerk" ("total work of art"). Bahr's eulogy reminded the Viennese of how they had mistreated their best artists by ridiculing them and driving them into exile.[33] Eventually Bahr himself shared what he termed "the Austrian fate" when he was forced to leave Vienna in 1906.

Despite the early loss of Olbrich to Darmstadt, the Secessionist movement continued to gain support and popularity, so much so that after the second successful exhibit, the first in the new Secessionist building, that opened on 12 November 1898, Bahr felt impelled to warn the Secessionists against succumbing to success. They had to remain artists and not betray the ideals of the Secession by painting routine decorative works just for financial gain.[34] Another danger for the Secessionists lay in the pressure to try to continue to surprise and dazzle the public, as happened in the first two exhibitions, because art in Austria was far behind the times. The artists should not worry whether their work pleased the public; they themselves were their only judges. A later period would determine the value of their work and recognize that they had fulfilled their promise to create an Austrian art.[35]

Only four months later, in March 1899, Bahr reported that Secessionism had won the day and was now accepted. His views on the complete success of the Secession echoed those of Otto Wagner, whose book *Architektur* (1895), appearing in a second printing in

1898, described the changes resulting in the complete triumph of modernity. Bahr fully agreed with Wagner's assessment that the coming change in architecture would be so radical that one would no longer speak of a renaissance but of "a complete new birth, a naissance."[36]

Bahr believed that Wagner's prophecy was fulfilled in the fourth exhibition of the Secession held in March 1899. This exhibition, one of the most notable ever held by the Secessionists, realized Bahr's goal of Austrian art—especially the works of Klimt, Josef Engelhart, and Karl Moll, which could stand comparison with the best paintings in the rest of Europe.[37] Among the paintings displayed was Klimt's *Nuda Veritas* with the motto from Schiller: "If you cannot please everyone by your deed and work of art, make it right for the few; to please many is bad." Bahr, whose rallying cry since his first essay on Ibsen in 1886 had been the call for truth, was greatly attracted by the theme of this picture and also by the inscription expressing his own viewpoint. He acquired the painting and made it the centerpiece of the study in his villa.

The triumph of the fourth exhibition was Klimt's *Schubert*, which Bahr called "the most beautiful picture an Austrian ever painted."[38] Bahr used the painting to try to convey the uniqueness of Austria:

I only know that I become angry whenever anyone asks me whether I am a German. No, I answer, I am not a German, I am an Austrian. But that is not a nation, one replies. It has become a nation, I say, only we are different from the Germans, something unique unto ourselves. Define that! Indeed, how is one to "define" it? But one can see it in [Klimt's] *Schubert*. This stillness, this mildness, this reflective glow over bourgeois modesty—that is our Austrian character! Here we have our Austrian feeling; that the human being, no matter how insignificant he may be, has a flame within him that is never extinguished in any storm of life. Each of us has his sacredness within him that cannot be violated by fate. Let it storm, nothing can happen to us. The tiny flame does not go out. Nobody can take our ultimate value away from us. This is what I would like to call the Viennese sense of life.[39]

On the basis of this fourth exhibition Bahr apologized for the fears he had expressed about the danger that the Secessionists might fall into mannerism. Yet, only eight months later, in November 1899, in an essay entitled "Die falsche Secession" he deplored the imitative tendencies of many members. In his customary blunt manner he stated sarcastically that the Secessionists could have saved themselves the trouble of their revolt, for the movement had been subverted and had come full circle from creating art to producing clichés. The problem was its great popularity, which had become a fad exploited as the latest fashion. Bahr redefined the original aims of the movement and declared that Secessionism had to return to its basic principles or would cease to exist.

The leading Secessionists such as Klimt, Josef Hoffmann, and Koloman Moser were aware of this trivialization and commercialization but were unable to combat it effectively. There was also a split into two factions over the importance of applied art. As a result they, along with Emil Orlik, Alfred Roller, and Karl Moll, left the Secession in 1905 to join the "Wiener Werkstätte," which had been established in 1903 by the young entrepreneur Fritz Wärndorfer. With the defection of its most prestigious members, the movement lost its impetus. The "Wiener Werkstätte" henceforth replaced it as the most significant art movement in Vienna.

Before Klimt shifted allegiance to the "Wiener Werkstätte" he came under severe attack in 1901 over the three allegorical paintings of the disciplines *Medizin, Philosophie,* and *Jurisprudenz,* which had been commissioned for the "Aula" ("Great Hall") at the University of Vienna. Eighty-seven professors signed a petition to reject them, and even Karl Kraus, who normally showed sober judgment, joined the attack against Klimt, almost certainly because Bahr was Klimt's avid supporter. Only a short time before this incident Kraus had lost a lawsuit against Bahr and was eager to discredit his archenemy at any cost. As it turned out, the price was high, for his fanatical polemic against Bahr over a forty-year period belied Kraus's reputation for uncompromising honesty and integrity. The Klimt episode, as Hans Weigel has noted, is a case in point.[40]

When the scandal first broke in 1900 over the display of *Philosophie* in the Secession, Bahr remained silent. However, after a second scandal over *Medizin,* which caused Klimt's government contract to be debated in parliament on 20 March 1901, Bahr delivered a lecture in the "Bösendorfersaal" on 24 March sponsored by the writers' organization Concordia. Bahr started out by saying that it was not his intention to defend Klimt, whose reputation and art needed no defense. Rather his concern was that the shameless attacks on him made Austria look ridiculous to the rest of the world. *Philosophie,* which was castigated in Vienna, was awarded the *Grand Prix* when shown in Paris. Formerly the mediocrities in the arts had kept Austria cut off from developments in Europe. Now they were endangering the recent progress in the arts that had spread recognition of Austria through Europe. The issue in the Klimt affair was freedom of art and the protection of the artist, a cause every educated person should support against the mob.[41]

Klimt's tribulations did not end in 1901. In 1902, when he was recommended for the third time for a professorship at the Akademie der bildenden Künste, his detractors mounted a whispering campaign that he had gone insane. Again Bahr came to the defense of his beleaguered friend. In this instance, he limited himself to publishing a collection of the articles written about Klimt, partly for historical purposes and partly as "a document of the human spirit."[42] In his preface, Bahr stressed the maliciousness of the attack and noted how Klimt's enemies hoped to break his spirit with the rumors.[43] Under such continued pressure Klimt resigned his commission for the university paintings in 1905 and returned his advance payment. Nevertheless, he was forced to sue the state to obtain the return of his three pictures. They were later lost in the destruction of the Immendorf Castle in Lower Austria by the retreating Nazis.

After 1901 Bahr no longer followed the fortunes of the Secession closely, and he failed to rekindle his interest in the "Wiener Werkstätte" upon its establishment in 1903, even though Klimt later joined the group. However, Bahr had been one of the early advocates of applied art, for after his decadent phase he came to believe like Otto Wagner that only the practical could be beautiful. His favorite example was a chair, which should be comfortable as well as attractive.[44] In the "Kunstgewerbe," which applied artistic design to functional objects, particularly to artifacts of the home such as furniture and other appointments, Bahr saw the fulfillment of his dream of culture as a basic aspect of life. The ideals of functional art coincided with his aesthetic goal of the "Gesamtkunstwerk."

As with Secessionism, Bahr's essays on functional art trace its development in Austria. The influence came from America to English artists such as William Morris, Dante Gabriel Rossetti, Edward Burne Jones, and Walter Crane, who were not ashamed to design chairs or bind books. Another impetus came from Samuel Bing in Paris who in 1895 opened his gallery of art nouveau to show that artists are capable of incorporating art into daily life.[45] The movement spread to Germany, where it found supporters in Berlin,

Hamburg, and Munich. At the first exhibition of the Secession in March and April 1898, Josef Hoffmann designed a room for *Ver Sacrum* that was devoted to functional art. Through this display Bahr recognized the need for the artisan to become an artist, for the artist to become an artisan, and for harmony in decoration.[46]

Bahr had experienced this idea of stylistic harmony at firsthand in the villa built and furnished for him by Olbrich, whose style Bahr was anxious to maintain. Once he found a chair of different manufacture that he admired and sent it to Olbrich to have him build one like it in order to preserve the interior unity of his home.[47] Olbrich's design for Bahr's villa faithfully realized the latter's ideas on architecture. Bahr's essay "Das Landhaus"[48] corroborates how the house reflected his ideal of unadorned, simple, functional architecture, in short, the style espoused by Otto Wagner and later by Adolf Loos. By contrasting the honesty and peacefulness of a provincial "Landhaus" to the artificial and shrill architecture of the "Ringstrasse" Bahr expressed the pro-province, anti-Vienna bias that culminated in his malicious book *Wien* in 1907.

With respect to art Bahr continued to propagandize the idea of the "Gesamtkunstwerk" to be achieved by the collaboration of artisans and artists. The talent of both was available and all that was lacking was organization.[49] The ideal of the "Gesamtkunstwerk," of creating architecture as a totally integrated artistic entity, was carried to its furthest extremes by Olbrich at Darmstadt. However, the most famous and most successful attempt is the Palais Stoclet in Brussels (1905–11), designed and built in Vienna under the supervision of Josef Hoffmann and then reassembled in Brussels. It was the greatest triumph of the "Wiener Werkstätte," which had been given financial carte blanche by the Stoclets. To this day the cost of the project is unknown.

Bahr's final association with the "Wiener Werkstätte" came in 1907, when Wärndorfer sponsored the building of the theater and cabaret "Die Fledermaus" on Kärntnerstrasse. Josef Hoffmann designed the project, and Bahr, Altenberg, Blei, and Ewers participated in the venture. Bahr's involvement must have been limited to an advisory role, for at the time he was working for Max Reinhardt as director and "Regisseur" in Berlin. "Die Fledermaus" failed to attract the public and closed in 1910.

By 1906 Bahr's interest had shifted completely away from the Secessionists, for, as happened with all of the individuals and causes he supported, he no longer promoted or espoused them after they had become established. Thus it had been with *Jung-Wien,* and so it was with the Secessionists. With Olbrich well situated in Darmstadt, Klimt relatively free of controversy in Vienna, and the "Wiener Werkstätte" successful, Bahr could shift the focus of his activities to other fields, secure in the knowledge that he had contributed significantly to the success of this important breakthrough of modern art and architecture in Austria.

Chapter Five
Theater and Burgtheater

The theater remained a major interest of Bahr throughout his life, and he became one of the most versatile and knowledgeable theater people of his time. In addition to writing thirty-four dramas Bahr was involved in the theater in a variety of other ways: as a reviewer, as a critic and theoretician, as a consultant for the Deutsches Volkstheater in Vienna around 1900, as a director for Max Reinhardt in Berlin in 1906–7, and finally as director of the Burgtheater in 1918. Because of its prominence as a cultural institution in Austria renewal of the theater was a major aspect of Bahr's program of modernity. Through his essays and reviews he tried to educate the public not only to a greater understanding of new trends in the theater, but also about the history and nature of the theater itself. He particularly attempted to influence the course of the Burgtheater in order to enable that institution to fulfill its role as a cultural force in the life of the nation.

Like his overall cultural program, Bahr's attitude toward the theater also went through definite stages of evolution, as his study and experience brought greater understanding of its nature, workings, and significance. He himself indicated, in his preface dedicating *Wiener Theater* to Ludwig Speidel, that the following reviews would show how he had proceeded gradually from an uncertain idea of beauty to a pure concept of dramatic art, as he came to recognize the essential nature of the theater.[1] Initially Bahr's attention was directed toward the dramatist and the aesthetic problems of writing modern plays for the theater. Through his reviews and his work as a consultant for the Deutsches Volkstheater, his interest was gradually diverted to the actor as the primary force in the theater and to an analysis of the nature of acting. Above all of these considerations hovered his constant preoccupation with the Burgtheater, which had held a fascination for him since his boyhood days, when he had listened eagerly to his father's enthusiastic accounts of performances seen on his trips to Vienna.

In his four volumes of theater reviews—*Wiener Theater* (1898), *Premièren* (1902), *Rezensionen* (1903), and *Glossen zum Wiener Theater* (1906)—Bahr continued his "criticism of encouragement" and utilized the same impressionistic approach found in his other essays. While he readily pointed out weaknesses of plays, performers, and productions, his reviews were generally positive appreciations and his approach was one of empathetic understanding rather than of critical judgments based on absolute aesthetic standards. During the impressionistic period of the 1890s when all values were relativized Bahr was less concerned about artistic quality than about encouraging all talent to contribute to his program of modernity. He was also more interested in interpreting theater works as expressions of ideas useful to his own age and to the development of the new humanity than in judging them from the standpoint of their literary quality: "As one born to affirm, I withheld my own judgments about artists and their works, for in my opinion it seemed unimportant to them. It was not my ambition to be a judge of art like a pontificating critic; I was satisfied to extract from their work the 'demands of the time.' "[2]

Bahr summarized his attitude toward theater criticism in 1890 in the following statement that established the approach and the tone for the entire body of his theater criticism:

It is no longer the task of criticism to proclaim to the artist what is eternally beautiful, but instead its role is to confirm from the artist's work what is regarded as beautiful at the time. It is not the task of criticism to teach the artists but to learn from them . . . and to impart this understanding, formulated in a comprehensive manner, to other artists, and finally to broadcast it among the people.[3]

The actress Eleonora Duse characterized Bahr's theater reviews succinctly and accurately when she remarked: "You are not a critic, you are our good comrade!"[4] Despite their subjectivity, his reviews are not ephemeral opinions intended merely to inform the public about whether a given play was worth its time and money but valid and important theoretical documents that partly reflect the tendencies of the time and, more importantly, chart the course of the theater in Vienna during the critical transition period at the turn of the century.

Bahr defined his purpose as follows: "It is usually not my method to recommend plays. I think that whoever knows them does not need a recommendation, and even after a recommendation the others do not know anything really essential. I prefer to report whether and how a play has affected me, to seek the reasons for my pleasure or annoyance, and if I succeed in deducing a dramatic law or what appears to be such from the play, I am very happy."[5]

As a reviewer Bahr accepted it as his responsibility to help those who were creating, and in this way he served as a productive force to a degree not achieved by any other reviewer of his time. It is impossible to measure the actual influence he exerted on the artists and public of his day, but it can be shown that the theater did follow the direction he recommended. Bahr was primarily responsible for Burgtheater reviews, but he also covered the Deutsches Volkstheater, the Theater in der Josefstadt, the Raimundtheater, and even the Carl-Theater, when there were guest performances by the Berlin ensembles of Brahm and Reinhardt. From 1892 until 1906 no event of significance occurred in the Viennese theater that escaped Bahr's attention.

Because of the central importance of the Burgtheater, Bahr considered it a matter of urgent priority to modernize its repertory. He strongly defended the directorship of Max Burckhard, who also wished to introduce Hauptmann, Ibsen, Sudermann, Schnitzler, and Wedekind. Through his support of Burckhard, Bahr exerted a major influence on the Burgtheater. Burckhard remained under attack for implementing Bahr's recommendations, and in "Direktion Burckhard," the first essay of *Wiener Theater*, Bahr rehearsed the arguments against his friend and refuted them one by one. He concluded that Burckhard might not be the most qualified director of his day, but he was the best man for the Burgtheater at that particular time. In "Fünf Jahre," Bahr once again defended Burckhard, describing the progress he had made in various areas over the past five years. Burckhard had introduced a modern repertoire while at the same time keeping the best traditional dramas. It was not necessary to perform only recent plays, for when presented in a new style, the older works would suddenly appear new.[6] Bahr concluded that Burckhard had shown administrative and critical talent and had prepared all of the ingredients necessary for progress. Now it was his task to show his talent as a director who could bring all the individual entities together into a unified whole. Such candid evaluation shows that Bahr did not allow personal friendship to influence his judgment.

Despite Bahr's support, Burckhard was forced to resign on 18 January 1898 to be replaced by Paul Schlenther, a critic for the *Vossische Zeitung* in Berlin. Bahr was furious over Burckhard's ouster and wrote a blistering exposé, in which he accused the critic Hugo Wittmann, the actress Bebette Reinhold, and the actor Anton Bettelheim of intriguing to have Burckhard removed.[7] Although Bahr's charges were not refuted (most probably because they were true), it was still impossible to save Burckhard.

Bahr's reviews, which were motivated by the highest ideals, were intended to elevate the level of the theater in Vienna and develop it into a strong, effective social force. To achieve these goals he dispensed lavish praise and showed great understanding, but at the same time did not spare the feelings of anyone who he felt was opposing his plans or was not contributing to progress according to his capabilities. For example, in his reviews Bahr consistently attacked Paul Schlenther, whose appointment he resented, considering him not only an outsider, but also lacking in theatrical experience. Schlenther's positive achievements were attributed by Bahr to the benefits he reaped from Burckhard's innovative efforts; when Schlenther erred, Bahr was waiting to discredit him. Some of Schlenther's dubious practices furnished Bahr with ample opportunity for criticism, such as in 1898 when Schnitzler became embroiled in a controversy over his play *Der grüne Kakadu,* which the Burgtheater director had accepted and then failed to stage. When Bahr expressed his intention to publish an appeal drawn up by Burckhard, who was an attorney, Schlenther decided to produce it (premiere 1 March 1899). Schlenther behaved the same way toward Schnitzler's *Der Schleier der Beatrice,* which again he accepted and disregarded. This tactic prevented Schnitzler from negotiating with another theater, forcing him finally to withdraw the play. To defend Schnitzler and other artists against such unfair treatment Bahr published a statement protesting Schlenther's unfair practices.

In his reviews, Bahr not only acted as the unofficial director of the Burgtheater, but he also lectured authors on their responsibility toward their audiences. He believed that whoever wrote for the stage had an obligation to try to please the public. A literary play often did not make good theater, and therefore a dramatist who created a purely artistic work had to be prepared to renounce success on the stage.[8] Bahr's definition of a good play, particularly important because it formed the basis of his own dramas, was one that had the power to make the audience laugh or cry as the playwright desired. In short, theatrical effectiveness was the sole valid criterion.[9]

Bahr also lectured the public on its obligation to be receptive to what was being presented on the stage. In a review of *Niobe* by Oscar Blumenthal, which had been subjected to unmannerly behavior by the audience, Bahr put the relationship of the artist and the public into perspective: "One does not need to tell any artist that the public is stupid and hostile to art. The public has all kinds of merits: it does not disturb morality and it serves the state; but it is the sworn enemy of art and the artist must hate it."[10] The Burgtheater audience reacted negatively to *Niobe* because it refused to change with the times and "will not tolerate a play in the Burgtheater that has not already been performed for twenty years under twenty different names."[11] In "An das Publikum" Bahr addressed the public directly, stating that the dramatist had the duty to serve its taste but that the public also had an obligation to have taste. He lectured the public not to vent its irritation on the performers because it disliked the play.

Bahr devoted many reviews to individual performers in an effort to explain the refinements of their acting technique. It is not surprising that he was a favorite with actors and numbered many of them among his personal friends, such as Eleonora Duse, Adele Sandrock, Friedrich Mitterwurzer, Charlotte Wolter, Joseph Kainz, Alexander Girardi, Ferdinand Novelli, Lotte Witt, and Otto Tressler. To each of these performers Bahr devoted individual essays in which he tried to capture their special style and technique. His protectiveness toward actors shows in his suggestion that new performers should not be required to make their debut in roles that were associated with established actors but should begin in new roles, so that the public would judge them on their performance rather than through a comparison with their predecessors.

Bahr often used his reviews as vehicles for his ideas of the moment. For example, his review of Adele Sandrock's Burgtheater debut in Schiller's *Maria Stuart* incorporated a theoretical discussion that illustrates his program of modernity, and shows how he maintained a consistent viewpoint in all his writings at a given period. Sandrock, who had built her reputation as an actress in modern roles, portraying women who were depraved or disturbed, living in the intoxication of sensations, yielding to every stimulus from the outside, and driven by impulses, had now turned to classical parts. In the same way, literature, after using naturalism to break with the past, had progressed through an art of the senses and nerves to classical calmness:

One need only think of the beginnings of Barrès or of our writers who depicted sensations. Lemaître could speak of a *folie sensationniste*. Such art was called impressionism, it was called decadence. The whole of painting, all of literature only played Sandrock roles. That is what we called art at that time. We were wrong and yet we were right because epigones could not come to their own art in any other way. We first had to have our blissful hour with life in order to understand those signs of the old art, to be able to form others of a new and yet of the same kind of art.[12]

Sandrock's shift to classical roles was symbolic of the general move of art away from the excesses of decadence to classical values. Another sign of this trend was the revival of Goethe as evidenced in Gerhart Hauptmann's speech for the opening of the Berlin Deutsches Theater and Otto Erich Hartleben's Goethe reader. (Bahr eventually published a volume of essays, *Um Goethe* [1917].) This acceptance of Goethe and Schiller did not imply the end of Bahr's program of modernity but merely indicated that he and other writers of his generation had grown secure enough to be able to accept the best from the past. This ability and willingness to see the value and strength of tradition grew in importance for all of the Viennese writers but particularly for Bahr and Hofmannsthal. As Bahr noted: "Sandrock is not the only one to become classical. We are all now at the point of discovering the old art, the great art, the eternal art for the first time. Only now that we know how to interpret life, to trace it to its elements, to feel its meaning, do Goethe and Dante speak to us."[13]

This article is an excellent example of how Bahr incorporated in his theater reviews the same ideas found in his essays. It is possible to extract the entire aesthetics of his day from Bahr's reviews and essays and to follow its progression through all of its modulations up to expressionism and beyond. Among authors, he must be considered the major theoretical voice of his generation. Another unique feature of his reviews was that they had a European rather than a local Viennese perspective because of his broad background of travel and because he attended most productions of foreign plays as well as guest performances by visiting companies.

Through his exploration of the inner workings and social dynamics of the theater Bahr came to elevate the performer to a position of primacy. This trend is most clearly evidenced in his attempts at writing pantomimes around 1900.[14] Bahr had first written on pantomime as early as 1891 when he reviewed the pantomime *L'enfant prodigue* by Michel Carrès and praised this return of fantasy to the theater which had been fundamentally ruined by naturalism. He urged German authors to imitate the French by utilizing the pantomime form, which alone satisfied the current hunger for fantasy created by the overemphasis on naturalism.[15]

Bahr, Schnitzler, Hofmannsthal, and Beer-Hofmann were all experimenting with pantomimes in 1892 at the very height of naturalism. These experiments were a reaction not only against naturalism, but also against the tyranny of rationality, against language, against excessive psychology, and against static lyric drama with its emphasis on states of mind. Bahr turned to pantomime in an attempt to convey the immediacy of feeling in the most direct and universal manner. Pantomime replaced naturalistic description with universal symbols, detailed analysis of psychological states of mind with actions, and words with mime, gestures, and body movements. It served as another reflection of the return to eternal values in art. It also represented a major transition from the aestheticism of the 1890s to art that was primarily life-oriented. In Bahr this change can be traced from the essays of *Renaissance* to its culmination in *Dialog vom Marsyas* (1905). For Hofmannsthal the essay *Ein Brief* in 1902 marks a turning point, for Schnitzler *Der einsame Weg* (1904), and for Beer-Hofmann *Der Tod Georgs* (1900).

In developing his theory of the actor's primacy in the theater Bahr was strongly influenced by the performance of a Japanese troupe featuring the actress Sada Yacco, which he reviewed at length. In Europe the theater remained weak, Bahr wrote, because of its individuality; Japanese theater derived its strength from its use of tradition. In Japan actors learn to move as living puppets. The goal of Japanese theater is not to re-create life but to project a heroic idea. It is a moral institution aimed at instructing the individual how to act in all basic social situations. The actor reflects Japanese life, which "appears to eliminate everything accidental, capricious, and personal in order to penetrate to the essential, the necessary, and the typical."[16] The Japanese actor, therefore, is trained in universal gestures and selects the one that is most appropriate in a given situation.

It was the universality of pantomime as well as its ability to stimulate fantasy that attracted Bahr. Language individualizes, gestures universalize. He felt that pantomimes could render the most delicate nuances that were not accessible to the other arts. Also important was the fact that pantomime made an equal impact on the connoisseur and on the ordinary theatergoer and created a common bond of taste. This universal appeal adumbrates an important feature of Bahr's later view of art as a unifying force in the life of the nation. Since in Bahr's view the aim of the theater was to affect the audience emotionally, that is, since he was an advocate of Reinhardt's theater of illusion as opposed to Brahm's naturalistic theater, he felt that words were expendable. Pantomimes used all the usual dramatic means except words, but nevertheless they had a more powerful effect. It was therefore possible to conclude that language had become a hindrance to dramatic effect. Bahr believed that the theater was not intended as a forum for rational analysis but as a means of influencing the spectator emotionally, thereby producing an inner transformation. Already in the 1890s Bahr was pointing ahead to expressionism.

Bahr wrote three pantomimes—*Pantomime vom braven Manne* (1901), *Der Minister* (1902), and *Der liebe Augustin* (1902). None of these works has ever been set to music or performed, and it is evident that the form was too restrictive for him despite his enthusiasm for its potential. Yet the techniques of pantomime—placing the actor in the center, stressing universal symbols and the eternal values of a living tradition, creating a theater based on symbols and direct emotional reaction, and utilizing the ideas of the Wagnerian *Gesamtkunstwerk*—were features of his subsequent dramas and of his later writings on the theater. In terms of their implications for Bahr's later ideas, these experiments, minor as they were, possessed significance far beyond their intrinsic merit as works of art.

In 1907, after two years as director in Berlin with Reinhardt, Bahr remained convinced that the actor must dominate in the theater: "Acting must cease to be sculpture or literature or any other art and must be developed to the greatest possible effectiveness."[17] Once acting is sovereign it can unite with all the other arts to represent beauty in the most perfect way possible. Bahr's endorsement of the *Gesamtkunstwerk* helps explain his fascination with the baroque stage. As early as 1903 he had adumbrated the idea of the Salzburg festival by proposing the idea of performing outdoors during the summer in Salzburg. In such a setting the actor could fulfill his role as a model for life and the theater its function as a *Vorschule zur Nation.*

One of the aspects of acting that especially fascinated Bahr was the ability of performers to "transform" into their role, to become the part they are playing. Bahr featured this idea in his novels *Theater* and *Die Rahl* as well as in his dramas *Der Star* and *Die gelbe Nachtigall.* Initially he was fascinated by the idea of using the human potential for transformation as a way of life in accordance with his theory of remaining modern by staying flexible and in tune with one's time. His ideas were confirmed by Ernst Mach,[18] by Théodule Ribot's *Les Maladies de la Personnalité* (1887), and by Goethe, who constantly shed personalities as a snake sheds its skin in order to develop and grow. The culmination of Bahr's analysis of acting resulted in the volume *Schauspielkunst* (1923), where he divided actors into two types, those who "transformed" into their role like Charlotte Wolter or Eleonora Duse, and those like Sarah Bernhardt, who always played only themselves. The capability of the human being for transformation intrigued Bahr for most of his life and fueled his optimism about the hope for the future of society; for before 1900 he believed that social progress could be accomplished only by changing the attitudes of individuals.

Bahr used his reviews not only to analyze the theater, but also to comment on general trends. For example, in his review of *Jugend von heute* by Otto Ernst he introduced his newest phase that was publicized under the catchword "discovery of the provinces." The people of the provinces sought a literature that would show how the fate of man assumed a different shading in each separate village.[19]

Another topic that recurs throughout the reviews is Bahr's interest in Spanish literature. In a review of Calderon's *Hombre pobre todo es trazas (Zwei Eisen im Feur),* Bahr utilized a historical perspective to remind the director of the Burgtheater that Goethe as well as E. T. A. Hoffmann, the romanticists, Grillparzer, Schreyvogl, and Halm all favored Spanish literature: "This is not a matter of chance nor can it be interpreted as merely a romantic caprice, but if one will examine our literature sometime and analyze in terms of our uniquely complicated Austrian culture, one will discover how strongly it has retained the Spanish element: and even in our day one can show in Otto Wagner that a universal Catholic feeling still lives among us—his manner of ornamentation and splendor is the same as in the architecture of Spanish dramas."[20] Because of the cultural ties with Spain Bahr recommended that the Burgtheater include more Spanish plays in its repertory. The review of Calderon demonstrates how Bahr used the production of a single play to deduce a larger principle. He always retained his belief in the importance of the Spanish heritage in Austria, and although he did not stage any Spanish plays while he was director of the Burgtheater because other ideas took precedence, he returned to this interest in *Notizen zur spanischen Literatur* (1926).

These examples show some of the variety and richness of Bahr's theater criticism, and also why he stood out in his day as the drama critic par excellence. The reviews demonstrate Bahr's technical expertise about the theater, reflect his European scope, and serve as part of his overall cultural program. None of the other reviewers from this period—Speidel, Wittmann, Hevesi, Hermann Kienzl, or later Raoul Auernheimer—could match the breadth, range, depth, and above all the theoretical thrust of Bahr's reviews. In general, Bahr's dramatic judgments have survived the test of time and must be considered among his most durable works. Those which are no longer valid do not usually reflect lack of discernment but rather his eagerness to "promote tendencies" that he wished to support at the moment, regardless of how he might distort the play or subject in other respects.

Bahr received his first opportunity to put his theoretical ideas into practice through his association with Emmerich von Bukowics, with whom he had developed a personal friendship. Since plays by Bahr were also performed at the Volkstheater, Kraus viewed the practice as a conflict of interest and attacked it severely in *Die Fackel*, charging that one should not serve as a critic for a theater where one's own plays were being performed and where one had such close ties with the management.[21] It is true, as Kraus alleged, that a crony system existed in Vienna, where reviewers, many of whom also dabbled in playwriting because of the prestige it brought, gave polite reviews to each other's productions. Kraus further accused Bahr of originally criticizing Volkstheater performers and productions as a means of blackmailing Bukowics into accepting his plays. When Bahr later published his reviews in book form, Kraus alleged that he altered them to reflect a more favorable opinion.[22] Kraus also alleged that Bahr's reviews of guest performances by the Berlin Deutsches Theater had been overly critical in order to favor the Deutsches Volkstheater. Finally Kraus went so far as to charge Bahr with accepting a choice piece of land in Ober Sankt Veit from Bukowics as a bribe for his favorable reviews. Bahr and Bukowics sued Kraus and won—the only suit that Kraus ever lost in court.

One of Bahr's major theoretical works on the theater is the *Dialog vom Tragischen* (1904), in which he investigates the concept of the tragic, the continued importance of the theater, and the function of the actor. He demonstrates that tragedy and drama are expendable in themselves in the modern world, but shows that the theater retains its validity because of the actor, who can teach people how to live. Henceforth Bahr's commentaries on the actor proceeded along two separate lines: he continued his earlier interest in the purely technical aspects of acting—how an actor actually performs and achieves his effects—and at the same time he emphasized the performance as a symbol of how one should approach reality in order to lead an authentic existence. Bahr felt that the confusion between role playing and reality was a major problem of the Viennese. Through the model of the actor, who knows how to distinguish between the two states, people could apply the lesson to their own lives.

The attempt of the Viennese to avoid reality was one of the reasons why Bahr reevaluated his position in Vienna in 1905. His attitude had become openly hostile because of the lack of popular response and government support for his cultural program. To escape what had become an unpleasant situation he signed a contract on 27 October 1905 to become director of the *Schauspielhaus* in Munich for two years beginning 1 August 1906. When that offer was withdrawn because of unexpected opposition, Bahr was rescued by Max Reinhardt, who engaged him as a *Regisseur* for the Deutsches Theater in Berlin. Bahr was grateful for the opportunity but found it difficult to adapt to Reinhardt's frenetic pace and his method of working according to a plan known only to himself. Although this approach should have appealed to Bahr's flexible nature, it upset his sense of organization, and he complained constantly in his letters and in diary notes about how intolerable he found the working conditions in Berlin. In addition, Bahr was disturbed by the subordination of art to business, for Edmund Reinhardt, who controlled the finances, also wielded authority over the productions. His inability to work with Reinhardt personally did not blind Bahr to his greatness as a director, and he always held Reinhardt in high esteem. Bahr dedicated his comedy *Die gelbe Nachtigall,* a persiflage of actors and directors, to "My dear friend Max Reinhardt in cordial admiration and esteem."

During his first year with Reinhardt Bahr staged three plays, his own comedy *Ringelspiel* and two Ibsen plays, *Hedda Gabler* and *Die Komödie der Liebe.*[23] None of these productions was a success. *Ringelspiel* closed after only three performances, partly because the leading lady Waser had to withdraw from her role. However, the results he achieved convinced Bahr that he was a born director. On the eve of the premiere he wrote: "I do not have confidence in a success. This question interests me least of all. The main thing for me is that I have worked well and joyfully at the rehearsals and now know within myself that I am a *Regisseur* with heart and soul and that Reinhardt as well as the actors believe in me."[24]

During his second season with Reinhardt Bahr served as a consultant and advance man for guest performances in other cities rather than as a director. While in Salzburg on such an assignment he once again raised the idea to Reinhardt on 4 April 1908 of performing plays in an outdoor theater before the church. He wrote also to Anna on 20 December 1906 that he was considering building a *Festspielhaus* "where Reinhardt, Sorma, and I will perform plays, while you and I stage operas (annually from the middle of June to the middle of August) and we all earn a great deal of money."[25] Bahr cautioned Mildenburg that the undertaking was still only a plan but mentioned that Harry Graf Kessler was attempting to raise the necessary funds. Kessler was unsuccessful in locating backers, and the project failed to materialize.

On 4 April 1907 Bahr mentioned the Salzburg idea again in a letter to Reinhardt.[26] This time the suggestion was more modest in scope, since it involved an existing theater and excluded opera. Bahr presented Reinhardt with a list of stipulations to be met, showing that the plan had been carefully throught out in advance, but again nothing resulted. However, Bahr's intent was clear. He wanted to establish in Salzburg a summer theater on the model of Bayreuth, a theater of the people in the manner of the former baroque theater. Although Bahr himself was unable to bring this important concept to fruition, he deserves credit for its conception. As Joseph Gregor states: "Not until ten years after this first very commonsensical proposal of Bahr's was the Salzburg Festspiel society founded and even then not for three more years could the first *Everyman* be performed. On this point Bahr definitely has priority."[27] Bahr's interest in the festival theater idea was given substantial impetus by the literary critic Josef Nadler, who awakened Bahr's understanding of the Austrian baroque heritage. The concept of the baroque theater, unifying all of the arts and all levels of society, became henceforth one of Bahr's dominant themes.

Following the completion of his two-year contract with Reinhardt and his return to Vienna in 1908, Bahr's attention shifted from the theater to the broader horizons of cultural, social, and political commentary on a European scale. He continued to follow the fortunes of the Burgtheater and always regarded himself as its secret director until circumstances at the end of World War I finally gave him the opportunity to put his theories into practice.

Bahr's opportunity arrived when the resignation of director Max von Millenkovich on 3 July 1918 precipitated a crisis in the Burgtheater. Both Bahr and Hofmannsthal, who shared the view of the importance of Austria's leading theater as a social force, published statements stressing the necessity of filling the position of Generalintendant, which had been left vacant for years. Hofmannsthal's statement appeared on the front page of the *Neue Freie Presse* on 4 July 1918, and Bahr's two days later. It is clear that they had coordinated their efforts in order to make their point forcefully. Although their mutual friend Leopold von Andrian was not mentioned by name, the description of the type of man needed for the position was tailored to his qualifications. Andrian was appointed Generalintendant on 18 July 1918. Although he knew little about the technical side of the theater, he was similarly devoted to the idea of using the influence of the Burgtheater to promote the concept of *Grossösterreich,* as he made clear in his initial statement to the press.[28]

The selection of Bahr as director of the Burgtheater was made not only because he was an advocate of *Grossösterreich* or out of friendship on the part of Andrian but also because of his excellent credentials as a theater man. On 1 September 1918 he was appointed senior member of a triumvirate along with the actor Max Devrient, who had served as producer under Millenkovich, and the soldier-poet Major Robert Michel. Bahr was given the responsibility of chairing the meetings of the board and of representing the administration to the members and employees of the Burgtheater as well as to the public. The expedient of a three-man board was adopted when Bahr refused to accept the directorship alone on the grounds that he did not want to be hampered by the administrative details. Through his intimate knowledge of the workings of the Burgtheater from his association with Max Burckhard he recognized the potential problems and pitfalls and from the outset tried to free himself from one of the principal causes of difficulty: an administration that usurped the powers of the director. Despite his precautions he succumbed to this very problem. The triumvirate did not function well and lasted only two months. On 2 November 1918 Andrian replaced it by appointing the actor Albert Heine as director. Heine gladly retained Bahr's services for the additional four months he was willing to remain. Andrian himself resigned on 24 November 1918 after three months in office.

Because of the great love of the Viennese for the theater, the Burgtheater that Bahr entered enjoyed a position of eminence in Vienna equal if not superior to that of any other theater in the world. As Laube once remarked: "Acting is the center of Viennese life, the pride and pleasure of the Viennese. . . . If the theater were not yet invented, the Austrians would invent it."[29] In addition, the Burgtheater possessed the added prestige of being the court theater. Next to the *Neue Freie Presse* the Burgtheater was probably the most influential institution in Vienna, and Bahr hoped to put its influence to work for the cause of Austria and the Monarchy. Unfortunately, when he undertook this task, it was too late to serve the cause of unity among the states of the monarchy and too early to be of assistance to the floundering republic during the first months of postwar reconstruction. In view of the chaotic situation during the last months of 1918, it is not surprising that Bahr's ambitious and highly idealistic plans could not be realized. In October a cholera epidemic forced the closing of the theater for ten days. The shortage of coal permitted only five performances in December, sixteen in January, and only half the normal schedule in February and March.

During the few months of his directorship Bahr presented the Burgtheater premiere of Goethe's *Die natürliche Tochter* and revived such classical works as Sophocles' *Antigone* and Racine's *Phèdre* in Schiller's translation. He also gave the premiere of Wildgans's *Dies Irae,* Beer-Hofmann's *Jaákobs Traum,* and secured the rights to introduce Kornfeld's *Himmel und Hölle.* He left the Burgtheater convinced that he had accomplished more in his short tenure than many directors managed in five years. Commenting on this period later, he found solace in the success of the Austrian plays: "I had the undeserved luck of being permitted to introduce *Dies Irae* and *Jaákobs Traum*. They rewarded me richly for those seven [*sic*] months of work, vexation, and patience."[30]

How seriously Bahr took his mission in the Burgtheater can be seen in his rejection of Schnitzler's play *Casanova in Spa*. Despite their many years of friendship and common effort, Bahr still felt justified in refusing the erotic comedy on the grounds that its theme did not fit into the image he was trying to convey. The fact that Bahr was now a strong Catholic and that Prelate Seipel, who later became chancellor of Austria, objected to the play undoubtedly played a substantial role in Bahr's decision. The play was later accepted by Albert Heine, but Schnitzler never forgot the incident. On 17 March 1930 he jestingly wrote to Bahr, who had lamented his homesickness for Vienna, that if it were within his power he would recall Bahr to the Burgtheater, even at the risk that Bahr might reject another of his plays.[31]

As director, Bahr, who had believed since the late 1890s that his age needed the wisdom of Goethe to learn the meaning of humanity, considered the introduction of *Die natürliche Tochter* into the repertoire as his single most important achievement, both because of the appropriateness of its theme of unity to the conditions in Austria and because of its style, which he felt should be a model to follow. In a review written in 1906 Bahr argued that Goethe's art was misunderstood. It was not "marble smooth and cold" but communicated its intensity through the performers rather than through the action. Goethe's aim was "to calm excitement by portraying it. He turned to art at times of extreme conditions of mortal rebellion in order to calm them."[32] Goethe used distance and restraint to enable us to view the dangers of life without having to experience them personally and suffer the consequences. To convey this ideal the actor must perform the play with passion, not coolly. At the time Bahr had no inkling that fate would decree that he himself would be given the opportunity to direct the play. Nor did he when in *Kriegssegen* (1915) he noted that if he were Reinhardt he would perform *Die natürliche Tochter:* "For it could be that finally the moment for it has come now when our heroes return from the field."[33]

The premiere of *Die natürliche Tochter* took place on 16 November 1918, less than a week after Austria had been proclaimed a republic. The audience seemed confused and did not know how to react. A contemporary reviewer reported: "The work was greeted by many with respect and even with reflection, but only after the fourth act did the applause, which had only been weak up to that point, resound in a more lively manner."[34] Although Bahr had intended to present the play as a warning against anarchy and a plea for unity, events moved faster than his scheduling, so that when the play was performed it ironically confirmed the fact that the monarchy had ended. Yet Bahr remained proud of his effort.[35]

Although he could no longer work on behalf of the monarchy or for *Grossösterreich,* Bahr continued to strive to maintain the unity of the country. He redirected his goals to try to establish a tradition of the Burgtheater that would elevate it from its recent doldrums because of wartime restrictions and reinstate it in its former glory; for a flourishing Burgtheater would have represented a significant contribution to Austrian life. The purpose of his revival of *Antigone* and *Phèdre* along with *Die natürliche Tochter* was to test whether the acting tradition that evolved under Burckhard in the 1890s and continued in Reinhardt's theater had produced a style that would enable Western classical drama, the heritage of the baroque, to be revived again.[36] Bahr felt it was time to go beyond Reinhardt, but his own few experiments were insufficient to be of any real influence.

Bahr claimed to have found his mature ideal of art and the principles that he attempted to incorporate into the Burgtheater in expressionism, in Nietzsche's *Menschliches allzu Menschliches,* in late Goethe, and in classical antiquity: "Not individuals, but more or less ideal masks; not reality but an allegorical generalization; . . . no new subjects and characters, but the old long-accustomed ones in ever-new styles and forms."[37]

It can be seen that Bahr's ideas had not changed substantially from his earliest essays opposing naturalism and advocating symbolism. The emphasis on the general instead of the specific, on the universal instead of the individual, was the result of his discovery of the importance of tradition to the life of the nation. Hence the emphasis on the mature Goethe: "who found the strength to lead our literature back from the isolation of vain individualism to the great Western tradition."[38] All the major plays that Bahr introduced exemplify this theory of art. Nor by such a program was he being untrue to his belief in the importance of baroque both for the Burgtheater and for his time, for in his opinion both the Goethe of *Faust II* and modern expressionism belonged to the baroque tradition. "Our entire classical literature is only an attempt of the word to control the baroque through speech. All romanticism is baroque, often misunderstood even by itself, German music from Bach to Mahler is baroque, and the result of all intellectual accomplishments of my generation is that the first baroque was no longer sufficient, that is, it was only a prelude to the second that is now being fought for under the new name of expressionism."[39]

Bahr deemed it Austria's historical mission, by virtue of its geographical location and character, to act as the mediator in this unification of Europe into a loose-knit federation of states, even if it might mean the sacrifice of Austria's individuality.[40] From this it can be seen how Bahr's view of the actor and the theater broadened through his concept of the baroque in ever-widening circles to embrace finally the political unity of Europe.

Revival of the baroque tradition held for Bahr not only artistic and political but also religious implications. Since his reentry into the Catholic church in 1914, his writings revealed a preoccupation with the need of the age for a heightened sense of Christianity. The religious aspect of the baroque is allied with the importance of the theater, for one of the major benefits to be gained by the spectator was the insight into the actor's "innermost secret," namely, that he was merely acting. After the performance he removed his makeup and the spectators "see in him the poor sinners they are: the day will come when they too will stand there in similar fashion."[41]

In *Burgtheater* (1920) Bahr provided a historical survey of the Burgtheater and the importance of the baroque tradition to its development. Since he views the baroque theater as all things to all men, finding ultimate harmony through extreme diversity, one can see why he felt it could accomplish all of the functions he attributed to it: "The baroque theater appealing by all of the arts to the entire man through all his senses, at the same time church play, consecration play, festival play, court play, folk play, artist's play, and children's play, . . . theater as intoxication for the senses, food for the intellect and consolation for the heart, theater of miracles, theater of magic, puppet theater, theater away from God and to God."[42] The spectator is drawn into the action on the stage and identifies with the performers. Just as the actor "transforms" into the character he is playing, the spectators also become transformed, lose their individual personality, and at least temporarily become one united group.[43] This unification of the audience is the effect Bahr was seeking, for the need of unity—unity of Austrians and Germans, unity of Austrians and Slavs, and first and foremost unity of the Austrians themselves—was a theme that Bahr never tired of reiterating. In this respect the theater assumed political importance for Austrians as a "Vorschule zur Nation" ("preschool for becoming a nation").

The secret of the success of the baroque theater came from its ability to accomplish this ideal of unity. This was also the secret of Bayreuth, as well as of Reinhardt's theater, both of which followed the baroque tradition. Reinhardt employed every possible effect—music, dancing, lighting, and elaborate stage settings—for the purpose of drawing the spectator into the play. It was Bahr's conviction, therefore, that the Burgtheater must return to the baroque manner, which had been employed by its greatest directors. According to Bahr the Burgtheater was founded as a protest and a reaction—as a protest of eighteenth-century Enlightenment against the baroque *Hanswurst* and as a reaction by a few non-Austrian intellectuals against the spirit of the Austrian tradition. Because the Burgtheater represented a breach of faith with everything by which Austria had become great, because it was untrue to the spirit and tradition of Austria, it was able to attain greatness only when it belied its own origins. Unfortunately, not enough evidence is available to determine how much of Bahr's thinking remained theory and how much of it he put into practice. His program met with little success, and Bahr later confessed: "Nobody understood the sign that I gave."[44] However, at least some of Bahr's ideas with regard to baroque theater were brought to fruition three years later in 1921 by Reinhardt and Hofmannsthal with the performance of *Jedermann* in Salzburg.

Although Bahr had been engaged for a year with an option for renewal of his contract, he failed to endure the pressures of the task for more than six months. It is obvious from the outset that such an ambitious scheme as his would require years for its realization, and thus the briefness of his tenure stands first and foremost among the reasons why Bahr was unable to establish his program. Laube, for example, one of the greatest Burgtheater directors, had demanded a five-year contract before he would accept the office, insisting that he needed at least this much time to accomplish anything. Bahr had only a few months, and he did not have the free hand and the autonomy which had been granted Laube. Andrian became disenchanted with Bahr and complained about him constantly to Schnitzler and Hofmannsthal. In addition, as Bahr indicated to Hofmannsthal, he had no one to support him in the press, as he himself had previously done for Burckhard.[45] Finally, the unsettled conditions prevailing in Vienna were not propitious for such an experiment as Bahr was making. He was unable to convince either his colleagues or his audiences of the soundness of his views; while the premieres of the modern Austrian plays were well-received, audiences were apathetic to the classical performances. Heine promptly dropped all three classical plays from the repertoire.

Bahr's greatest handicap, and the major reason for his leaving so prematurely, was internal dissension. He later claimed with biting irony that "the entire staff had fallen victim to the same mental illness: everyone suffered from the persecution complex of being the Burgtheater director."[46] According to Bahr, the appointed director was not supposed to direct but was considered merely the executor of the will of the accountants. Bahr warned that the Burgtheater would continue in its state of crisis until the system was abolished. The truth of this was seen in the rapidity with which Heine, Wildgans, and Paulsen succeeded one another as directors.

After his experience as Burgtheater director, Bahr retreated again to Salzburg. He continued to follow the progress of the Burgtheater and summarized his views in *Burgtheater* (1920), which was dedicated "to Professor Josef Nadler, the Schliemann of our baroque culture, in thankful gratitude." He wrote a similar survey and analysis of acting in *Schauspielkunst* (1923), in which he repeated the idea that the actor alone legitimized the continued existence of the theater. Since he had always considered the performer the central figure in the theater, *Schauspielkunst* represented a fitting conclusion to Bahr's concern for the problems of the theater. Henceforth his interest became increasingly absorbed by politics and other topical events. Nevertheless, even during his later years he liked to attend rehearsals from time to time, because he claimed in his paradoxical manner that the world of madeup actors still provided him with the only opportunity to see unadorned humanity.[47]

Bahr's activity as director, though it did not achieve either his artistic aspirations for the Burgtheater or his political hopes for the country, is nevertheless of significance within the framework of his own life. The period as director of one of the world's greatest theaters formed the climax of a life rich in theatrical experience and study. His willingness to undertake the assignment proved that he had not been simply an idle theorist with regard to his artistic and political suggestions, for, in line with his belief that the artist should be a responsible member of society, he accepted the challenge to present his ideas in concrete form. His attempt to use the Burgtheater to create unity among the Austrians and to promote European unity by means of a new baroque tradition is the logical result of his artistic, political, and religious views. In essence this interlude serves as the focal point of his thinking after 1906. His aspirations further close the circle of Bahr's life and striving around the central theme of the mature period: his ideal of a strong nation based firmly on the traditions of old Austria. However, the Burgtheater proved to be another instance where there was no resonance for his ideas. The lack of response and success, however, does not detract from the dedication, sincerity, and integrity which motivated his ambitious and idealistic program.

Chapter Six
The Creative Mirror: The Novels

After approximately twenty years of intensive observation and direct involvement in the artistic, cultural, and social life of Austria, Bahr conceived the idea of writing a series of twelve novels to give form to his personal image of Austria, or, in his words, to recite his "inner alphabet."[1] In rapid succession he wrote *Die Rahl* (1980), *Drut* (1909), and *O Mensch* (1910) in Vienna. He continued the series in Salzburg with *Himmelfahrt* (1916) and *Die Rotte Korahs* (1919). The final two novels, *Der inwendige Garten* (1927) and *Österreich in Ewigkeit* (1928), which appeared in Munich, reveal the increasing difficulty Bahr was experiencing in shaping his ideas as his artistic powers faded. Only seven novels were completed, and we have no information concerning his plans for the remaining novels, if indeed they were planned at all.

Bahr denied any intention of trying to create an Austrian *Comédie Humaine*. His ambition was more modest: to depict Austria, its people, and its inner workings not objectively but strictly from his own point of view and out of his unique vision. These novels were intended to be his personal analysis of conditions in Austria as he had perceived and experienced them. His use of the novel accords with his definition of that form as a "creative mirror" and was not intended to reflect reality but to refract it in such a way that its hidden significance was rendered visible. While the novels are not great works of literature, they are rewarding documents of their time and merit consideration by anyone interested in Austrian cultural history. Because of Bahr's subjective approach they possess enormous value for tracing and examining the evolution of his thinking about the major problems of his day.

Bahr's early novels—*Die gute Schule* (1890), *Neben der Liebe* (1893), and *Das Theater* (1897)—do not belong to the Austrian cycle, but *Theater* moves closer in that direction as a precursor of *Die Rahl*. *Theater* utilizes a frame technique with the outer narrative written in the first person. Bahr serves as the narrator and incorporates biographical elements, such as his experiences in Berlin, without troubling to transform them into fiction. As in all of his novels, the plot is minimal and distinctly secondary to the psychological portrayal of characters and the description of theater life. Not only is Bahr truly gifted in creating well-rounded characters, he is also able to write brilliant individual scenes. What he lacks is the ultimate talent for combining plot and characters into a unified whole in which every aspect of the novel blends together. Instead of presenting his ideas and conflicts from a multiple perspective, Bahr's novels remain two-dimensional and unilinear. As a result, they lack polyvalence and invariably end with a clear-cut resolution. They are thus no greater than the sum of their parts. They are all tendentious and explore ideas about which Bahr wishes to express a point of view. The fictional world of the novel never leads an autonomous life, but Bahr is ever present and in control as the omniscient author. The novels all display an essayistic quality, and at times there is little difference between the novels and the essays even in wording. In *Das Theater* Bahr sought primarily to explore and to some degree expose the make-believe world of the theater with its "comedians, speculators, enthusiasts, and satanists." Although he usually only draws one or two characters in each work as totally rounded figures, he was so fascinated by the entire gallery of theater types that he portrayed each one fully. He treats the details of the milieu in the same painstaking way. Significantly, despite its exposélike quality, the novel presents a generally positive view of the theater as a valuable institution.

Bahr traces the fate of Dr. Maurus Mohr, a man controlled by his reason, who by sheer luck writes a hit play and becomes an instant success. The novel covers his ensuing association with the theater to the abysmal failure of his second drama and his subsequent disillusionment with the world of art. Discovering that he has no genuine talent and betrayed by the actress Mascha, Mohr returns to his understanding wife, Lotte, who takes him back without question in a scene of great warmth and tact. His tale demonstrates the power of fate, against which the human being is helpless. Reason cannot compete with chance, which dominates life: "Nothing happens the way one imagines; everything happens differently. The theater is a lottery. The whole of life is only a lottery. One cannot do anything about it."[2] Through Mohr's experience Bahr illustrates that rationality and the vaunted education *(Bildung)* so prized by the nineteenth-century liberals was really a false way of approaching life. Mohr also echoes one of the major motifs of Bahr's cultural campaign, the lament that poetry and life were separated and needed to be united: "I would like to have art more lively, and I would like to see life become more artistic, so that they finally become the same thing" *(T,* 68–69). Finally, through the actress Mascha, Bahr treated the theme of how a performer could be transformed into the role she was playing.

As a novelist and dramatist Bahr's problem was not a shortage of ideas but rather insufficient creative power to shape the material adequately. Like most of the authors of his generation he was a victim of inspiration that faltered. When he encountered these barren spots in his creativeness, he tried to fill them in as well as he could, not always successfully. Bahr was always in the mainstream in choice of themes but failed to develop them with the degree of sophistication, complexity, and intensity that would have invested his works with more than contemporary appeal. In this respect *Das Theater* fares well because the theater is a universal subject. Moreover, the excellence of the characterizations, the quality of the style, and the unity of the plot make it one of his most successful novels.

In 1908 Bahr published *Die Rahl* as the first novel of the Austrian cycle. Because of the importance of the theater in his life, it is not surprising that the initial work would be devoted to this world that fascinated him and that he knew so intimately. However, whereas in *Das Theater* Bahr had attempted to depict a cross section of theater life, here he specifically concentrates on portraying the actress, Rahl, who is possibly modeled on Charlotte Wolter. *Die Rahl* treats again the mystery of the transformation of the actress into her role and the empty life of the performer when not on stage. Bahr also describes the deficiencies of the nineteenth-century liberal concept of education. Through the theme of education and the maturing of the schoolboy Franz Heitlinger to independence of mind, there is a clear connection between the novel and the essays in *Buch der Jugend,* published the same year. Finally, *Die Rahl* reveals a significant change of attitude toward the aristocracy in Bahr's sympathetic portrayal of the count, Rahl's tolerant, patient, and understanding husband. Up to this point Bahr had always depicted aristocrats negatively as useless remnants of a bygone era, typified by Prince

Adolar, who appeared in the play *Der Klub der Erlöser* (1907) and in several novels.

As in all of Bahr's novels, the plot of *Die Rahl* is simple and straightforward, serving only as a scaffolding for the descriptions of Austrian life and, above all, for the examination of various Austrian archetypes. It is spring in Vienna, and Franz Heitlinger, a student at the *Gymnasium,* is in love with Rahl, the prima donna of the Viennese theater. On the evening of the celebration of her one-hundredth performance of Melitta in Grillparzer's *Sappho,* she impulsively takes him home with her for the night. Life now assumes new meaning for Franz, who has been transformed by the experience. Even the pedantic schoolmaster, Professor Samon, no longer fills him with fear, and Franz openly defies him in class. The resulting expulsion from school does not disturb him in his euphoria. However, his happiness is short-lived; the count with great sensitivity tells him that Rahl has no intention of ever seeing him again. Franz was only a whim of the moment. With the resilience of youth Franz recovers, recognizing that the situation could not have ended any other way. Wiser and with greater self-assurance, he plans to return to school. Rahl meanwhile continues her empty existence off stage, coming gloriously alive only when she has a role to play.

From his earliest essays on the theater Bahr had emphasized that the actor should be the dominant force in the theater to serve as a model to show people how to live and how to elevate their existence to a higher level of intensity and meaning. Despite the emptiness of the performer's existence, the function as a model is not impaired. On the basis of his Greek studies Bahr had described the importance of reaching beyond oneself, of living to the hilt, of achieving periods of ecstasy even at the cost of subsequent emptiness and depression.[3] In the novel, the characters who recognize the actress's importance in these terms are Rahl herself, Franz Heitlinger, and Adolf Beer, the radical Jewish classmate of Franz, who understands the necessity of accumulating one's powers in order to accomplish a purpose: "Tension, tension, that is what matters. To become tense, to charge oneself! To charge oneself with yearning, with desires, with determination and not to dissipate the tension but to collect it until the time comes for the deed to spring forth out of it."[4] Rahl follows this process, lying fallow for days collecting her inner strength in order to rise to greatness beyond herself during her performances.

Beer recognizes the symbolic value of art, which is "a guarantee that a higher existence is possible for man and a sign of how high man can rise if only he does not resign himself to mediocrity and let himself be content with the ordinary" (R, 63). Rahl expresses the same thought in her own way by stating that it is a question of whether the fire burns within. Even her husband, the count, an unimaginative dilettante of science, senses the potential greatness of man without being able to define it: "Through all sciences and all arts one can ultimately only knock on the door . . ." (R, 165).

A central chapter of the novel reveals the sequence of Rahl's thoughts during her performance in an attempt to capture the elusive mystery of transformation. Previously Bahr had only characterized performers through their actions or through descriptions of other characters. Rahl was the first female character he had attempted to develop from the inside by analyzing the psychological workings of her mind. Nevertheless, the conclusions are the same as in *Das Theater:* a performer is an empty vessel without the identity of a role to play. The disgruntled painter Höfelind, who has some of Klimt's characteristics, best attests to the emptiness of Rahl offstage, for he finds it impossible to capture her on canvas: "Nothing remains of her, nothing, nothing! And now paint that! Paint the woman, who, while you are painting her, suddenly is not there anymore! . . . And there sits a small, fat person with watery eyes, who smokes cigarettes and constantly sniffs her perfume bottle and always has cold feet" (R, 92).

Through Franz Bahr explores the school system, which he, like other writers of his generation, felt had injured his spirit. Bahr describes the classroom as a battlefield, but he does not caricature Professor Samon in the manner of Heinrich Mann's *Professor Unrat*. Samon is a dedicated man; if he has a distorted outlook, it is from his training more than his character. He is misguided in his ideals and attitudes and believes that to allow his students any personal freedom is harmful. It is his aim to break their will so that they will become obedient servants of the state. He will not tolerate any spark of originality or freedom of thought. Samon too is a tragic character, for, although he pursues questionable objectives, he is acting out of full conviction and is motivated only by what he thinks is in the best interest of his students. At times he wonders whether he is right, but to acknowledge any other viewpoint but the school's would nullify his entire life's work. Here Bahr is attempting to depict the dreary educational conditions in Austria, which he attacked at the same time in *Buch der Jugend*. The blame is placed on the system more than on Samon, who is victimized just as much as the students are. On another level Samon is a counterpart of Rahl in the sense that he has no life outside of the classroom, just as Rahl loses her human identity when she is not on stage. Samon is simply a robot guided by rules, a dedicated servant of the state, but in Bahr's view the antithesis of what a human being should be.

Bahr liked to work in terms of sharp contrasts: Samon, who would like to marry Franz Heitlinger's widowed mother, is diametrically opposed in character and nature to Franz's father, whom Samon had hated because of his carefree spirit and self-confidence. Bahr presents the conflict of spirit and nature in new terminology, stating that the world is divided into two groups, sun-and-air people and city-and-dust people. Franz's father and Samon, respectively, represent the opposing qualities of individualism and submissiveness, imagination and passivity, originality and sterility, progress and convention, feeling and reason. Bahr continued to stress these contrasts throughout his remaining works.

Like Franz young Beer also has an optimistic view of the future. In terms echoing *Buch der Jugend* the latter exults: "A new era is dawning, it will bring a new humanity, and we are this new era!" (*R,* 56). Beer, who is determined to improve social conditions, is a totally positive character showing how far Bahr had outdistanced his youthful anti-Semitism. In the friendship of the two boys he portrays the unity that is needed for progress. Bahr leaves no doubt that they will succeed in life. Through Rahl they have discovered an ideal and have sensed the greatness one can achieve. The novel concludes with Franz's uttering "softly to himself, as if saying farewell to many things: Rahl" (*R,* 292). Bahr used Rahl in a doubly symbolic way as both actress and woman, not only providing the young people with a glimpse of greatness through her acting, but also leading and uplifting them in the spirit of Goethe's "eternal feminine."

In *Drut* (1909) Bahr opposed the optimism of *Die Rahl* with a gloomy portrait of how bureaucracy functions in Austria. Since this is the system with which Heitlinger and Beer will have to cope, there is a sequential pattern to the two works. To reinforce this idea Bahr included some of the characters from *Die Rahl* and from the drama *Sanna,* a practice he continued in the subsequent novels. He had attacked the bureaucratic system in *Wien* (1907), *Buch der Jugend* (1908), *Dalmatinische Reise* (1909), *Tagebuch* (1909), and *Austriaca* (1911). *Drut* represented the attempt to provide a literary version of the ideas he had developed, specifically the notion that Austria was controlled by a small number of titled families who refused to admit any outsiders, no matter how capable, into positions of power. The higher echelons of the bureaucracy existed for the nobility, who used their government posts to serve themselves, not the state.

Along with this autonomous bureaucracy there is the institution of the *Hofrat,* a figure Bahr satirized in *Der Krampus* (1902) and *Sanna* (1905) and considered a menace to the country until he changed his attitude in the 1920s. The *Hofrat* is not an individualized being but a type. The little *Drut* is symbolic, for it refers to the Upper Austrian superstition of the *Drut* or *Trud,* a malicious witch, who comes during the night and sits on one's heart until one can no longer breathe and suffocates miserably. Bahr was attracted to this figure as the perfect symbol of Austrian bureaucracy. Just as Bahr in *Sanna* had shown the *Hofrat* sitting like a *Trud* on his own family, suppressing all freedom of spirit and emotion, in *Drut* he portrays bureaucracy as a *Trud* suffocating the whole country. Bahr's view of bureaucracy as the enemy was shared by his Upper Austrian compatriots, who were suspicious of all officials and anything that came from Vienna.

The novel is based on an actual incident: a young district commissioner (Bezirkshauptmann) from Upper Austria was driven to ruin by a woman named Drut. From this situation Bahr fashioned the story of Baron Klemens Furnian, the son of an impoverished nobleman and the nephew of Domherr Zingerl. The baron receives an appointment as a district commissioner in Ischl from the powerful and calculating Minister Doltsch, who is personally fond of him and would like to make him one of his protégés. The position represents a major opportunity for the baron to launch his political career by demonstrating his worth to the system. The baron seems well suited to be a bureaucrat, for he has been raised in obedience by an ambitious father, who resembles Professor Samon in his faith in the system. The baron has never been allowed to develop his individuality, and his new position also allows him no latitude to do so. He is anxious to serve his district well, but he is and remains an outsider, confronted everywhere with mistrust if not hostility.

One day he meets in the woods the young Prussian baroness, Gertrude Scharrn, who has a checkered past and comes from a disreputable family. Although she tries to warn him away, Klemens refuses to relinquish his love. When she becomes pregnant and cannot obtain an abortion, he insists on marrying her despite her forebodings. Because her papers are not in order, Klemens must use the influence of his position to force a priest to perform the ceremony. The information is revealed to the press, which runs a story about her past and about the illegal wedding. Klemens's fellow bureaucrats, who are competing for Minister Doltsch's favor, seize the opportunity to destroy him. Even his uncle, Domherr Zingerl, contributes to his downfall by trying to capitalize on the knowledge that Doltsch regarded Klemens as a favorite to obtain a tax dispensation on factories owned by the church. However, the minister refuses to be blackmailed for anyone and in a callous, pragmatic manner coldly dismisses Klemens, who shoots himself in disgrace. Drut is arrested on the suspicion of bigamy before she can leave town, because her former husband is found alive in an English prison. While being escorted to jail she is stoned and killed. The novel concludes on a mollifying note that is filled with irony. Instead of regarding themselves as murderers, his people feel virtuous for having protected society against an injustice. They are not bad, only very conservative people who are unforgiving toward any encroachment upon their autonomy or any breach of their customs and manners. The deaths of the baron and Drut were tragic, but the curative powers of nature will soon efface any harmful effects: "Sometimes in the winter in Vienna I have very bad hours! However, as soon as I am back here once again in this dear tiny place with its calm, good, peace-loving people, . . . then everything is suddenly all right again! That happens only in Austria, doesn't it?"[5]

Bahr shows not only how the coalition of bureaucrats and priests controls society, but also that behavior permissible in Vienna is not tolerated in the provinces. The quixotic nature of justice, the system of protection and connections, and the ruthless competition of young administrators trying to curry favor with superiors are all represented. Klemens is trapped between the stern ambition of his father and the equally relentless system headed by Minister Doltsch, whose one ambition is to survive. Thus to keep peace with the church, his rival for power, he willingly sacrifices the baron, as he would anyone else. Survival in this system becomes a matter of chance. In a foreshadowing speech Doltsch warns Klemens, who has been raised to live by his reason: "You must not always make a plan, Klemens; it never works out for you then. For life is planless" (*D*, 268). And yet Klemens is destroyed not by his plan but by trying to break through the fetters of his rational life to become a real person, to be free, to allow himself to love and be loved. Heitlinger and Beer at the end of *Die Rahl* had optimistically believed that they could change the system. The fate of Klemens demonstrates what an enormous task this will be.

In *O Mensch* (1910) the emphasis shifts from politics to religion, although not the religion of the church, which is to Bahr at this time still the enemy, but a free, open, all-embracing natural religiosity that believes in the essential goodness of all human beings. The novel, with its message of universal love, has no plot but consists of a series of encounters. Bahr uses this means to exemplify one of his major themes: the isolation of people in Austria. As Hofrat Stelzer explains: "To carry on a conversation one needs a common area of concepts or at least of feelings. . . . A dog could sooner talk to a horse than an Austrian of one party with someone of the other. Austria is a country where one can only hold monologues."[6] To engage in monologues is basically all that the characters do in this static, highly subjective novel. Bahr was so concerned with expressing his precepts on life that he devoted all of his attention to the message and none to the form. As a result, the characters merely enunciate, often in aphoristic fashion, their views on life, happiness, and religious spirit, but they do not interact. Even though another person is present, each individual is talking to himself and to the reader about topics that can be correlated with Bahr's dramas and essays from this period.

The action takes place at the Upper Austrian estate of the Wagnerian singer Fiechl, who lives with his sister Annalis in a relationship of love and friendly disagreement. Prince Adolar, the misfit from the drama *Der Klub der Erlöser*, reappears, searching unsuccessfully for a purpose in life, a symbol of an aristocracy that no longer plays a role in the modern world. The most interesting character in the novel is the *Nussmensch*, a stylized free spirit who is more an idealized allegorical figure than a man. The *Nussmensch* is Bahr's major spokesman for the ethical message of the novel: the need for people to draw together in love and compassion. The *Nussmensch* is capricious in his behavior and is surrounded by an aura of mystery to capture the imagination of the reader. He represents the realization of Bahr's ideal of an independent, genuine, purehearted person, such as he had postulated as an ideal in *Buch der Jugend.* The *Nussmensch* is made the brother of the baronness in *Drut* not only to emphasize the unity of the series, but also to show that the attainment of goodness in life is a matter of individual will rather than of heredity and environment. Everyone is capable of realizing the *Nussmensch's* love of nature and man.

In an ironical twist, and as a means of showing Bahr's lingering hostile attitude toward organized religion, the *Nussmensch* lectures the local priest on the goodness of man through the image that was responsible for his name:

But now comes my discovery: this inner man, who is the same in all human beings, is completely developed. When man comes into the world he is completely sealed (just like a nut), and now each one has to be opened gradually. That is what one calls his life. Life opens each one slowly, and by that means, then, only slowly does man emerge from his shell, . . . and many experience the opening of their shell and the emergence of the human being, and then there is a cry as if it were a miracle: the beautiful human being, the good human being. (*OM,* 192)

Most of the problems in the world result, according to the *Nussmensch,* because "human beings do not yet know how beautiful they are. I don't know why they have forgotten that" (*OM,* 285). The *Nussmensch* sees no need for a new man but only for the understanding and realization of man as he exists. This idea also recurs in Bahr's essays and in the drama *Das Prinzip* (1912), which closely resembles *O Mensch* thematically. On the basis of the view of universal brotherly love and of his attempt in these two works to present the essence of his characters stripped of surface superficiality Bahr must be recognized as one of the earliest pioneers of expressionism.

In addition to the religious dimension of the novel Bahr continues his discussion of the social situation in Austria. Surprisingly, considering his previous animosity toward the institution of *Hofrat,* he uses Hofrat Stelzer as the spokesman for the theme of isolation, which he extends to outright hostility of Austrians for each other, especially for anyone attempting to accomplish anything. Stelzer was clearly speaking for Bahr, who in *Wien* and other essays had frequently attacked the manner in which Austrians treated even their greatest artists from Grillparzer to Mahler. After his nearly twenty years in Vienna in the service of art Bahr too suffered the "Austrian fate" and was left disillusioned at the ingratitude his efforts had aroused. Bahr's lingering bitterness is revealed in Stelzer's remark: "Austria will never change; he is a fool who imagines that he can still improve the situation. I have given up. I would only like to sit somewhere peacefully for my few remaining years and rejoice about the fall and spring" (*OM*, 247). Two years later in 1912 Bahr fulfilled this prophesy by moving to Salzburg.

Six years passed before Bahr resumed his chronicle of Austria with the autobiographical novel *Himmelfahrt* (1916), which again treats the theme of religion, specifically the intellectual's way to Catholicism. The novel was widely reviewed at the time and was either praised or attacked, depending upon the critic's attitude toward Bahr. Most attention was focused on the novel as the product of Bahr's latest transformation rather than on the work itself. *Himmelfahrt* represents Bahr's attempt once again to come to grips with what he considered to be the major problem of his time: its lack of religiosity. He had already dealt with this problem intensively in *Inventur* (1912) and now attempted to fictionalize his personal conflict and its resolution. The theme of the novel is the need for twentieth-century man to end his frantic pursuit of all the trendy "isms" of the age and instead to find a solid anchor within himself through religion. Significantly, in *Himmelfahrt* it is not simply religion but organized religion that has become important. Despite the universal natural religion espoused in *O Mensch*, man is now enjoined not to seek God directly but to use the mediation of the church. Count Flayn decides to seek peace of mind in Catholicism, for as a born Catholic he has a choice between believing or not believing, but if he believes it must be as a Catholic. True to his usual practice Bahr makes no attempt to insist that this is the right road for everyone. Domherr Zingerl, Bahr's principal spokesman throughout the Austrian novels, comments that for him Catholicism is the only way, but it is immaterial whether one becomes a Turk or a Jew as long as one believes genuinely.

Bahr's protagonist is Count Franz Flayn, thirty-seven years old, a man of reason who has lost the ability to follow his emotions, a painter who has never managed to become a real artist, an amateur scientist, and a "dilettante of life" in all respects. He returns home after years of traveling throughout the world without having found the peace of mind that he is seeking. Psychologically Count Flayn already contains the seeds of religious transformation within him at the time he arrives home. His passage from the family brewery to the estate via the path called *Himmelfahrt* represents a symbolic foreshadowing. Typically there is no suspense in the novel, for it is evident from the very beginning that Flayn will find the way to faith. The only uncertainty is how the path will be negotiated.

As we have come to expect in Bahr's novels, there is virtually no plot but many dialogues and inner monologues that convey in detail the psychological processes leading Flayn inexorably toward his final conversion. Although Flayn hears on all sides that there is no path for the intellectual to find religion through reason, Bahr himself seems to be presenting a rational case for faith in this novel, logically eliminating one avenue of escape after another until Flayn has no further choice except to believe. The stimulus for the final conversion, however, does not result from the discussions about religion but from the outbreak of World War I. Flayn, who was a sincere admirer of Archduke Franz Ferdinand, as Bahr was also, feels that he must join the war effort after the assassination. In accepting this goal for his life he performed an act that enables grace to enter his soul. On his way home from the last of many lengthy discussions with the Domherr, Flayn is suddenly moved to enter a small neighborhood church and confess. He discovers that the faith which he has long sought has entered his soul silently and mysteriously.

One noticeable quality of Bahr's Austrian novels is their seriousness, for there is no irony, no skepticism, no attempt to shock readers through outrageous statements. Bahr is deeply concerned about the diseased soul of his generation and would like his views to be taken seriously. *Himmelfahrt* continues not only the religious ideas of *Inventur* but also the diagnosis of the malady of twentieth-century man: the frenetic business activity ("Der Betrieb"), to which Bahr's generation has fallen victim. Bahr had also experienced the curative powers of nature in Salzburg, just as Flayn does, and was convinced of the virtues of provincial life. In the words of the Domherr: "The experience that was decisive for me was the discovery of real human beings, the discovery of the people [Volk]. In the country I found what no longer exists anywhere else today: people who stick together, whole people, people with a center."[7] The same local populace that had caused such misery for Baron Furnian and Drut are now shown in a positive light.

Like the other novels, *Himmelfahrt* is linear in construction. It is an intelligent, thoughtful analysis of the conflict between rationality and faith that Bahr took extremely seriously, as evidenced by his 1917 essay entitled "Vernunft und Wissenschaft," which he retitled "Vernunft und Glaube" when it was reprinted in 1921. Except for Count Flayn, Bahr devotes little time to characterization, possibly because many of the characters have been introduced in previous novels. Moreover, the characters are important only as spokesmen for Bahr's ideas. Bahr excels at the descriptions of the landscapes and people of Upper Austria, and at capturing the anguish of the aesthete-intellectual who exists without higher purpose.

Flayn wants to believe, but as a rationalist he would like proof before he will accept the Catholic faith. He wants the church to convince him, to persuade him logically, but he learns that this is not the role of the church. The church is there to be available to men who have made an inner decision to accept faith. He is informed that he cannot be cured of his problem through reason, because his rationality is the problem (*H*, 116). Flayn needs only to ask for grace and it will be granted: "Ask for that which you require and you will have it, you will receive what you need, even if it may not be precisely what seems necessary to you, for you must leave that decision to the giver, he knows better!" (*H*, 240).

Flayn's transformation to faith is also influenced by his love for Klara, the symbol of pure womanhood. Bahr had developed a new respect for women through his love for Anna Mildenburg and through his intensive study of Goethe. In his earlier works women were presented most often as sex objects, consistent with the attitude of his youth. Now in *Himmelfahrt,* as previously in *Die Rahl,* woman is depicted as the inspiration that leads man to his higher self. Since Klara is a deeply religious person, Flayn's love and respect for her become an integral part of his overall religious transformation.

Another influence on Flayn is the lowly servant, Blasl, an idealized eccentric figure analogous to the *Nussmensch* in *O Mensch.* Blasl is the author of a series of writings that argue the case for religion. When the war breaks out Blasl reveals himself to be Don Tadeo, the Spanish Infant, who disappeared years before to lead an authentic Christian life of poverty. He had wearied of his role as heir apparent and sought refuge among the common people to learn their needs and to share their way of life. Now the war situation awakens his sense of duty, and he prepares to return home to fulfill his responsibility to his country. This unconvincing masquerade of Don Tadeo contributes little to the novel beyond adding another dimension to the discussion of religiosity. Yet he symbolizes the strength of Bahr's religiosity and embodies the ideal of the simple Christian life that Bahr (like Tolstoi) envisioned. Blasl is the precise opposite of the "fictitious" twentieth-century man, inwardly bankrupt and committed to soulless materialism, whom Bahr had decried since *Inventur*. He repeats here also the idea found in *Kriegssegen* and *Das österreichische Wunder* that perhaps the war was inflicted on Europe as a horrible test to determine whether mankind could change its destructive course before the situation became irreversible (*H*, 358).

Other characters in the novel such as Hofelind, Radauner, and Vickerl also reinforce the religious theme from different perspectives. The painter Höfelind reflects upon the role of God in art. Just as Bahr had planned to characterize Austrian society in twelve novels, Höfelind projected twelve pictures to capture the "personnel of humanity" (*H*, 100) or the "twelve ideas." Unlike Bahr, Höfelind agonizes between doubt and belief but without finding any resolution to the dilemma. However, he resembles the mature Bahr in believing that art like every human action is dictated from above: "my contribution to my pictures . . . is no greater and also of no other quality than the contribution of the canvas, the brush, and the paints. For all his deeds man is only the tool. They happen through him, to be sure. . . . He is the apparatus, the channel, the pipeline, the conduit, the telegraph wire, but he himself need not be active at all, his voice only disturbs the process" (*H*, 110).

In stark contrast to Höfelind stands the painter Radauner, who has devoted his life to painting the same field of clover in an attempt to discover the secrets of nature. He retains his negative view of God and religion and ends in lunacy. Another perspective is provided by Vickerl, the wild illegitimate girl from *Drut*, who finds solace in becoming a nun. These contrived fates, rewarding those who find religion and punishing those who do not, diminish rather than enhance the novel, for in their patness they trivialize the dilemma of the protagonist.

In 1919 Bahr completed *Die Rotte Korahs,* his longest and most ambitious, complex, and profound novel. This work shows him at the peak of his narrative powers and totally involved in his attempt to analyze not only the temper of the time, but also the nature of Austrian character that he felt would guarantee the continued existence of the country. In *Drut, O Mensch,* and *Himmelfahrt* Bahr had concentrated on analyzing provincial life in Upper Austria. Now he expanded his view to encompass Vienna and Austrian conditions in general at the critical period near the end of World War I. The novel contains the sum total of Bahr's thought on major questions of the day and is filled with insightful observations on fundamental human and social problems. Like the preceding works, *Die Rotte Korahs* consists primarily of essays presented either in the form of dialogues or monologues. Still, it is the most engrossing of his novels. Despite its length of more than six hundred pages, it maintains its intensity, and even the lengthy dialogues sustain a high emotional level. While the work is directed toward his own day, like all of Bahr's works it transcends its age by dealing with such issues as anti-Semitism, the nature of race, the essence of Austrian character, and the future mission of Austria.

The plot concerns a prominent, wealthy Jewish entrepreneur named Jason, who is brought to trial for fraud. He dies while testifying in court, and leaves his entire estate to Count Ferdinand Drzic, whom he claims as his natural son. The count, a wounded war hero, had been raised without knowledge of his true parentage, although his mother and his legal father, Baron Drzic, were both aware of it. Ferdinand was raised as the son of an old Austrian family and now must come to grips with his new identity as a Jew, with the problem of managing his inherited wealth, and with the task of building a new life for himself.

Ferdinand's first reaction is to reject the money, because he does not want the Jewish identity that accompanies it. However, everyone, including his father, grandfather, and even Domherr Zingerl, advises him against such a foolish step, for whether he accepts the money or not, the fact of his Jewish identity will remain. Realistically, he can protect himself against prejudice better with wealth than he can without it. He can also make better use of the money by supporting good causes rather than turning it over to the state. Like Count Flayn in *Himmelfahrt,* Ferdinand has many conversations with a variety of people and engages in much soul searching before he emerges transformed to accept the inheritance. He also resolves to marry Paula, who is pregnant with his child, and to move with his family to an estate in the provinces. There he intends to establish roots and realize as best he can the fullness of life attainable only to one with the inner peace that comes from having ties to the soil.

Family and homeland become the conservative values that Bahr advocates throughout his remaining works.

The novel contains two major interrelated themes: racial identity and the twentieth-century blight of business activity. The two topics are interconnected because, according to Bahr, the concept of driving productivity that he deplores was created by the Jews. Jason represents the epitome of this constant urge to make money for its own sake. He is not liked even by other Jews, but is useful for what he could accomplish. According to Beer (from *Die Rahl*), now a military surgeon who saved Ferdinand's life, the entire history of Europe since the Renaissance is a continuing process of non-Jews imitating Jews like Jason in the chase for money. But Europeans must accept the responsibility for the trend, for only Jews like Jason were liberated and cultivated to perform the tasks that non-Jews wanted done but did not care to do themselves. Beer calls such a Jew *Epikores,* meaning a youth who has decided not to be cheated any longer but instead to become the cheater: "Epikores is the ancestor of all Jasons . . . who procures everything. Manly pride? Independence? Free opinion? You can have them! . . . Epikores does everything and deals with everyone; he turns everything into money. . . . The whole contemporary world of culture is carried on by the Epikores."[8] In this context, Jewishness is measured by one's attitude toward the manipulation of money and is not restricted to individuals with Jewish blood. Bahr, who had been responsible during his radical political years for aiding Schönerer in his efforts to segregate Jews by blood and to make anti-Semitism a racial rather than a cultural phenomenon, had now adopted a diametrically opposed position. The determining factor is not race but whether one is an *Epikores* or not. *Die Rotte Korahs* is Bahr's strongest, most compelling statement against racial anti-Semitism.

The antithesis of the *Epikores* is represented by Beer, an ardent Zionist. He despises Jews like Jason and tells Ferdinand (echoing Viktor Adler) "One has to be a Jew, Sir, in order . . . to be an anti-Semite" (*RK,* 120). He has no sympathy for the type of Jews so prominent in Viennese society, the monied Jews who operate businesses. His sympathies are with the other type of Jews, those without money who represent the old traditions of the Jewish nation. He fervently believes that the Jews have the sacred mission of producing the perfect human being. It is his hope that the Jews will regain their identity through the reestablishment of their own homeland. He insists that, like most people, Ferdinand does not know what Jews are really like, because he has only met the one type belonging to *Die Rotte Korahs,* "with which finally Jehovah himself did not know how to cope except by opening a crack in the earth and swallowing them up with all the houses of Korah and with all their property . . ." (*RK,* 367–68). Domherr Zingerl reinforces Beer's viewpoint that the quarrel is not between Aryans and Jews but between decent people with humanistic values and those who put the triumph of money over human beings: "For money brings spirit into a far more frightening danger than the curse of the dullest blood" (*RK,* 534). Beer is a bitter and fanatical Zionist, but Ferdinand wins him over at the end of the novel to a slightly broader perspective and understanding by showing him that the real Austria lies buried and unknown beneath the surface, just as the true Jews go unrecognized.

The novel also depicts a third type of converted Jew like the attorney, Dr. Raibl, who is thoroughly assimilated, considers himself an Austrian, and has no desire to emigrate to Palestine. Like the Zionists, Dr. Raibl recognizes that the Jews will remain nomads until they have a homeland, but he draws a different conclusion from this premise. He believes that Palestine will be a great disappointment to the Zionists, that they will feel as foreign there as they do in Austria. He agrees that the Jews need their own land, need the connection with the soil that alone constitutes and sustains a nation. In his view there no longer is any Jewish nation but only nomads, gypsies, wanderers, fugitives, in any case not an organic entity but uprooted, despised outcasts. He agrees with Beer that the Jews need land to have a fatherland but argues that it need not be in Palestine. He believes that Aryans have made a major mistake in following the bad example of the uprooted Jews who lost contact with the soil: "it is not a question of race any longer. Our current widespread anti-Semitism is addressed falsely, it is the defense of all nations against the European trend toward nomadism. All of Western culture is based on the soil. A culture bears only a very limited number of uprooted people. Being uprooted is . . . the problem, and not only for the Jews but for all the nations of Europe" (*RK,* 422–23). Ferdinand is so moved by the advice of the attorney that he resolves to move to an estate in Upper Austria, which will provide a solid basis for his life.

Bahr repudiates race and blood as the determining factors in the behavior of man and places the emphasis on the human spirit as the dominant force (*RK*, 393, 504). Thus even though Ferdinand has a Jewish father, his upbringing by an old Austrian aristocratic family has determined his race rather than his parentage: "Look around you in the world! Everywhere you see the most intellectually different races side by side in the same nation, even in the same family. Two brothers have the same father and the same mother, but the one is a born master . . . and the next to him plods the other, a born slave. . . . Do you not think that a member of the Chinese master class feels more related to his Tyrolean or British counterpart than to the servants in his own nation?" (*RK*, 394). To Ferdinand's father, reflecting Bahr's belief in astrology, the star one is born under is more important for one's intellectual race than the nation.

The antithesis of Ferdinand is Franz Heitlinger. Despite the promise that he had shown at the end of *Die Rahl*, he has developed into a shallow opportunistic individual, an anti-Semite, an Aryan *Epikores*, and a member of *Die Rotte Korahs*. Beer despises his former friend, and Ferdinand, while recognizing the contemptibility of Heitlinger, is at the same time attracted by his ingratiating charm that will enable him to succeed in life despite the pettiness and meanness of his soul. Heitlinger's character is completely flexible. He makes no effort to conceal his anti-Semitism yet has no scruples about asking Ferdinand for a loan to start an anti-Semitic newspaper. Ferdinand, who underestimates Heitlinger and sees no harm or threat in this precursor of Nazism, agrees to lend him the money.

Die Rotte Korahs is written in a religious spirit and reflects Bahr's revitalized Catholicism. As was true of Bahr's own life, Ferdinand notes that the right thing has always met him at the right moment in his life as if by chance. Yet even though chance has been beneficial, the thought of being merely a pawn of fate causes him to rebel inwardly. However, he becomes reconciled to the situation by accepting (as did Bahr) chance or fate as divine guidance, which leads men to the good, true, and beautiful; "No, it is not chance! Everything is guidance! I am led! Only first I must learn to understand properly what the leader intends. I must first learn to obey properly. I must learn to surrender myself" (*RK*, 464).

As in *Himmelfahrt*, Domherr Zingerl resolves the novel by putting Ferdinand's life into perspective and also by presenting a thoughtful view of European conditions past and future. He shifts the discussion from anti-Semitism to the future of Austria, which henceforth became the major theme of Bahr's writings. The Domherr feels that Austria's strength resides in its ordinary people and that through such people, who radiate the spirit of Stifter,[9] and Grillparzer, Austria will fulfill its mission of serving as a cultural and political mediator within the framework of the European community: "We do not need a new Austria, we only need to renew the virtues of Austria in the people. The West needs Austria because it needs our type of human being, for we have a talent for virtue which is rare in other nations" (*RK*, 550). This speech, in fact, this novel, is written out of Bahr's heart of hearts and reflects his sincere belief as well as his fervent hope for the future of Austria. *Die Rotte Korahs* represents his attempt after the war to unite his countrymen, to reawaken their national pride, and to energize them to face the future with optimism. He used this novel to accomplish what he had hoped to do as Burgtheater director but lacked the time to complete.

After a lapse of eight years Bahr continued the series with *Der inwendige Garten* (1927). His world had changed significantly with the reduction of Austria to a small nation and the shift from monarchy to republic, changes that he accepted grudgingly. Although Bahr retained his usual optimism for the future, he retreated even further into the Upper Austrian world of Stifter to create a portrait of society as he believed it should be: tranquil, in harmony with nature, and populated by humans who know how to create a meaningful life anchored in Catholicism. To convey the symbolic intent of his novel, Bahr created a fictitious village governed by Count Ahamb, a conservative defender of the values of Old Austria. The tranquillity of the count's home is threatened when his wife falls in love with his friend Raderer. Through reason and faith the problem is happily resolved, and the count restores order both to the family and to the populace, which had threatened to stage a political revolt.

The purpose of this tendentious novel is to deliver a homily on the importance of maintaining agreements, particularly the marriage contract. Bahr preaches that marriage is sacrosanct and that divorce is not permissible, because the "sacredness of marriage rests on its indissolubility."[10] Only death can dissolve marriage. The happiness of individuals is of no consequence; the marriage contract is all that matters. The count warns his wife that he will never grant her a divorce, but he is not averse to her having an affair with Raderer, if they behave discreetly. The law is more important than the individual, and the meaning of every person's life is to serve the law. Everything else is inconsequential. In the count's view, if two people recognize that there is no escape from their marriage, they will work out their problems. As proof of his theory the novel concludes with the countess, having restored the "alphabet of her inner life," having reorganized her "inner garden," by severing her still Platonic relationship with Raderer and announcing that she is expecting a child by the count. The final word is spoken by the count rather than by the countess, so the reader has only his opinion that she has happily adjusted to circumstances. It would have been more convincing if the countess had spoken for herself, but it is typical of Bahr's view of women that their lives are controlled by men.

This weakness of the ending is representative of the novel as a whole, possibly the thinnest and least artistic work of the series. *Der inwendige Garten* is the most tendentious of Bahr's novels and leads to the speculation that Bahr may have been asked by his friends in the church to write a defense of marriage. The novel lacks vitality because of its sermonizing and because of its sketchy abstract nature. Usually Bahr's ability to create believable characters is the strongest feature of his novels, but these figures are never more than one-dimensional spokesmen for his ideas. Even the love affair between the countess and Raderer lacks feeling, for it is only reported. They never meet alone and hence can never display or even discuss the great love that they are supposed to feel. In essence, *Der inwendige Garten* is less a novel than a detailed outline for one. Since it is an idealization, perhaps Bahr felt less obliged to create convincing characters and design a believable plot. As it stands, the work serves no better than a hypothetical discussion would have done to give the count an occasion to present his views on marriage.

Bahr's inflexible viewpoint reflects how far his thinking had changed from 1909 when he had obtained a divorce from Rosa Jokl after having tolerated an unsatisfactory marriage for more than a decade. Some eighteen years later Bahr seems to have forgotten the unpleasantness that he was spared by divorce and the happiness he found with Anna Mildenburg. By 1927 he was so thoroughly imbued with Catholic doctrine and the need for absolute standards in all aspects of life that he became intolerant and dogmatic. This shift in attitude can be seen in his stress now on the indispensable role of the church. In complete contrast to the natural religion of the

Nussmensch in *O Mensch* Bahr now maintains that God wants the fulfillment of the formal rituals in church as a sign of obedience. Only illness or extraordinary circumstances permit dispensation from this duty, which cannot be replaced by private meditation outside the church. Man exists to serve God, according to the count, and his happiness lies solely in God's will: "That is the secret of the art of life" (*IG,* 174).

The value of the novel lies in its examination of the importance of form: form in "inner life" by arranging one's "inner alphabet" or inner garden, form in outer life through tact and discretion, form in society through agreements, and form in religion through church attendance. Bahr extends the discussion of form to art and allows Raderer to digress on the nature of the novel as a genre. A proper novel is not simply a mirror of reality but "ein schaffender Spiegel" ("a creative mirror"). Literature should reflect a better future, but not through falsification of reality. Rather it should emulate music, which banishes reality and transports its listeners to a higher plane of feeling. The author must rise above reality and extract the essential meaning from his material: "We need a mirror that does not simply reflect, but also conveys the meaning of life" (*IG,* 123). As early as 1889 Bahr had attempted to overthrow naturalism and replace it with symbolism, by which he meant an art of nerves. His mature view of art, which he derived from Goethe and from classical Greek authors, is idealistic, symbolic, and intended for moral uplift. Bahr tried to demonstrate his theory by means of his own novel. Unfortunately, *Der inwendige Garten* is too weak a work to illustrate Bahr's elevated concept of the novel except theoretically.

Bahr's final novel, *Österreich in Ewigkeit* (1929), continues his attempt to hold a creative mirror up to his time. The motto taken from Stendhal's *Le Rouge et le Noir* conveys the intent: "Ah, Monsieur, a novel is a mirror that walks with us on the high road."[11] Regrettably the mirror of the novel is more reflective than creative, and while the work deals with topical issues and circumstances— anti-Semitism, Hitler's Brown Shirt Movement, pacifism, the annexation of Austria, and the future of Austria—it does so only in a sketchy, superficial way. Like its predecessor, this novel seems more like a detailed outline for a novel than the completed work.

The setting is again Upper Austria, where the Princess Uldus, the symbol of old Austria, is arranging a festival to celebrate her ninetieth birthday. She is a typical Upper Austrian with a rebellious nature, a tender heart, and a tendency to do the opposite of what people suggest. As the descendant of one of the oldest families in Austria the princess is proud of her Austrian heritage and has unlimited faith in the future of her homeland. She is adamantly opposed to the annexation of Austria and believes that Austria can and will maintain itself independently in the future.

The remaining characters around the princess represent a cross section of social and political views. The state attorney, the father of the Hitler enthusiast Höd Hiedel, is an old liberal and Austrian patriot. Although he does not share his son's view that Austria's future lies in annexation by Germany, he has grown disenchanted with liberalism and sympathizes with the search of youth for a strong leader to save the West from its predicaments (*OE,* 146). Bahr had always been an advocate of strong leaders like Bismarck or Napoleon, but he never endorsed Hitler. However, in Hiedel he shows how Hitler, like Schönerer before him, captivated the imagination of young men who became his fanatical followers. Hiedel is thoroughly enchanted with the promise represented by Hitler and is also infected with rabid Hitlerian anti-Semitism. He is a typical product of his era, devoting his time to sport, participating in duels to prove his courage, and failing his examinations, as Bahr adds to undercut Hiedel's seriousness. In Hiedel and his father Bahr foreshadows the conflict that would divide families as the year 1938 approached. However, as he is portrayed Hiedel appears more ludicrous than menacing. His father, who lightly dismisses his son's excesses as signs of immaturity, illustrates why the older generation did not feel threatened by the frightening ideas of the young Nazi.

The antithesis of Höd Hiedel is the Jew Guido Grün, a decorated war hero who is now a pacifist. Hiedel tries to persecute him because he is the only Jew in the area, but Grün challenges him to a duel and wounds him. They become friends, and Grün, the symbol of peace, tries to educate Hiedel, the symbol of hate. Given the cheerful optimistic tone of the novel and Hiedel's good nature, the indications are that he will be successful, another sign that at the time the novel was written Hitler and the possibility of annexation were not considered serious threats. Bahr may have modeled Hiedel on his own past as a student radical. The princess ridicules Hiedel's anti-Semitism by asserting that race is not important. It is not a question of what one brings into the world at birth but what one can accomplish with one's inheritance that matters. Everyone is his own creation and his own fate. Hiedel, on the other hand, contends that all great men like Napoleon believed in a higher fate. It is the will that makes the difference: "That is the meaning of the whole game that fate plays with us" (*OE,* 133). Bahr does not resolve the problem but leaves it open. He had touched upon the key issue in the rise of the Nazi movement, the matter of will, without realizing its significance.

Several characters reappear from the preceding novels including Princess Uldus, Prelate Zingerl, and Höfelind. Zingerl is now the prime minister of Austria, and in his characteristics and views he seems clearly modeled on Bahr's personal friend, Prelate and Minister Ignaz Seipel. Höfelind, who now calls himself Mister Nobody, has returned to painting after his period of introversion and soul searching. His painting parallels Bahr's mature view of art as a creative mirror that does not reproduce what already exists in nature but extracts its essence: "Art wants more, it wants to reach the secret mysteries of the pine tree, it wants to get to the very basis of the pine tree—do you understand now how art makes us so happy" (*OE,* 58–59).

The novel concludes on a note of reconciliation in a conversation between the state attorney, who is seeking a substitute for the old liberalism, and the liberal notary (possibly modeled on Bahr's father), who is an Austrian patriot resisting any talk of change. Despite their disagreement they both share the hope that Austria will continue to exist forever: "The Austrian is always modest. . . . We do not luxuriate in great plans, we are thankful if we are allowed to live at all, we worry ourselves ahead a little bit farther each day, and if we progress slowly with patience and caution, we cannot fail, then ultimately there will remain an Austria in eternity! In this hope I will blissfully die!" (*OE,* 163–64).

In artistic terms, Bahr's novels demonstrate what he recognized about himself, namely, that his ability to shape his material was not as strong as his gift for conceiving ideas. Although his novels treat universal problems, he lacked the creative talent to give them the necessary polished and rounded expression to enable them to endure. Another limitation is Bahr's highly subjective approach. This inability ever to escape from himself, to be able to portray a problem in objective terms more or less as an anonymous author, restricted the literary significance of his novels. Bahr wanted to speak to his age directly, and his novels reflect this intention. They gain much of their force from the personality of Bahr that suffuses these works. His novels provide finely drawn characterizations, sensitive and provocative analyses of major problems as well as an accurately depicted cross section of Austrian institutions. Despite their artistic limitations they have sacrificed none of their readability. However, their primary significance lies in their value as literary and cultural documents of their time.

Chapter Seven
The World as Theater

Given his great native ability as a conversationalist, his love of dialectically clashing ideas, and his gift for dialogue and mimicry, the dramatic form was an ideal medium for Bahr. His extensive background as a theater critic and his considerable experience as *Regisseur* and *Intendant* gave him a working knowledge of the craft of playwriting shared by few dramatists. Yet with all his expertise Bahr never wrote a play of sufficient substance to endure. His thirty-four dramas are all commentaries on issues of his day (*zeitgebunden*) and involve the same social criticism found in his essays and novels. His light comedies, including his most popular and appealing play, *Das Konzert* (1909), never aspired to the higher levels of comedy. Bahr himself relegated his dramatic works to the level of Eduard von Bauernfeld, who in the preface of his comedy *Leichtsinn aus Liebe* had written: "This comedy opens the series of those lightly cast dramatic productions that make it their task to mirror on the stage the relatively harmless society of earlier days. By means of pleasing dialogue, a cheerful atmosphere, and good characterization, a play of real life came into being on the boards that offered the actors rewarding roles—thus one pardoned or overlooked the lack of a truly significant plot and the loose conception."[1] Bahr remarked that this same statement could be applied to his own dramas beginning with *Das Tschaperl* (1898). However, in contrast to Bauernfeld Bahr always dealt with the circumstances of his own time even if his plays were set in the past.

Throughout his career as a dramatist Bahr used the criterion of theatrical effectiveness to determine whether a play was good or bad. His standard for a good drama was simple: a play that could produce in the audience the mood desired by the dramatist was a success; otherwise it was a failure.[2] The audience had to be swept into the action immediately and then had to be sustained by it. The primary aim of his plays was to entertain. If they also achieved the status of literature, that must come in addition to their theatrical merits, not in their place. Secondarily they were to educate, to uplift, and ultimately to help unify the public. In view of this conception of the theater it is understandable that in most of Bahr's plays the first act is the longest and often the best. However, it would be unfair to call him a dramatist of the first act. His plots often reveal clever twists and amuse by turning accepted notions inside out. At times he had to resort to such stock devices as the *deus ex machina* or the services of a *raisonneur* to resolve the action. As in his novels Bahr's creative ability frequently failed to equal the level of his conceptions. Yet because he was so thoroughly at home in the theater, knew the capabilities of performers, and possessed a gift for witty dialogue and realistic characterization, he managed to conceal the weaknesses of plot, at least during performances. He utilized every theatrical device, including the interjection of songs and dances in the manner of the Viennese folk-play tradition, and he often tailored roles to specific performers.

Bahr began his career as a dramatist with the tendentious political plays *Die neuen Menschen* (1887) and *Die grosse Sünde* (1888), which illustrate his attraction to topical subjects. They also reflect Bahr's tendency to "direct" the production by means of lengthy stage directions. Following the conversational farce *La Marquesa d'Amaeguie* (1888), which displays his fondness for antithesis, and *Die Mutter* (1891), his one experiment in using decadent themes in drama, Bahr wrote *Die häusliche Frau* (1893), a comedy in four acts that offers all the features of technique, style, and dialogue that characterize his subsequent comedies. The plot, which is set in Berlin, concerns an averted seduction: a wife who is taken for granted by her philistine husband becomes vulnerable to the advances of a sculptor friend, a typical aesthete. The danger is avoided after numerous complications, and the action is happily resolved. Bahr revised this play in 1898 under the title *Veilchen,* shifting the locale to Vienna, but the new version was never published.

In 1893 Bahr also collaborated with Carl Karlweis on a folk play in three acts entitled *Aus der Vorstadt,* which was a failure, as was their second collaboration, the "Wiener Revue" *Wenn es euch gefällt* (1899). The two intervening plays, *Die Nixe* (1896) and *Juana* (1896), which were unsuccessful in performance and published only as stage manuscripts, reflect Bahr's attempt to put into practice his theories of the actor's preeminence in the theater. The texts were loosely written to allow the actors the latitude to improvise: "My idea was to share the theme with the performer: He has the violin,

I merely want to accompany him on the piano."[3] Bahr felt that he might not yet have found the right division or possibly that he was attributing more to the actor than he was capable of achieving, but the experiment had to be made. All four plays are minor experimental works.

Bahr felt that his series of comedies began with *Das Tschaperl* (1898), which he considered an experiment in producing a theatrically effective drama. The play is called neither comedy nor tragedy but simply "ein Wiener Stück." The plot, which deals with the topical themes of women's emancipation and the elimination of the double standard, concerns the jealousy of an unsuccessful music critic, who is celebrating a triumph as the composer of an acclaimed operetta. He has always considered his wife a *Tschaperl* (Viennese dialect for an awkward person not quite capable of coping with life), for he is a chauvinist who believes in male superiority. He frantically tries to maintain his dominance over his wife, whose career now overshadows his, but every new laurel she wins widens the gap between them. She leaves him after he abuses her physically, and he discovers that it was he who was the *Tschaperl* all along.

This bourgeois melodrama, with its overtones of Ibsen's *The Doll's House*, may serve as a representative example of Bahr's formula for producing successful theater: a blend of comic and tragic elements, a mixture of wit and irony, a surprising twist of plot, spritely dialogue, theatrical effects, a dash of pathos, the use of Viennese dialect, and well-drawn main characters. Bahr vainly tries to present basic problems in such a way that the audience is forced to confront them from a new perspective.

More successful in combining theatrical and literary values is the comedy *Josephine* (1899), which retains its comic vitality with its good-naturedly humorous demythologizing of Napoleon.[4] Not only are the roles of Napoleon and Josephine rewarding parts for performers, but Bahr also incorporated into the text his view of the actor's importance as a model for life. Napoleon is a hero but needs instruction from the actor, Talma, to learn how to act like one. It is Talma who suggests the famous Napoleonic pose.

Josephine is an important work reflecting Bahr's belief in the power of fate as the controlling force in life, a theme that recurs in the dramas *Der Athlet* (1899) and *Der Meister* (1904), as well as in the novels *Das Theater, Die Rahl, Drut,* and *O Mensch*. Man as a pawn of fate was a popular theme among all of the *Jung-Wien* writers. For

Bahr fate became a substitute for the God he was trying to avoid until he finally regained his religiosity in 1914. He employs the metaphor of the world as a theater with fate as the director, who ensures that people play their allotted role in life whether they like it or not. Originally he had intended to write a trilogy portraying the three basic stages of existence: "How man presumes to live for himself but then is ordained by fate to carry out his destiny until he has done his duty, performed his task, played his role to the end, and can be released again by fate."[5]

Whether it was because of the difficulties he experienced with *Josephine* (adverse audience reaction to the irreverent treatment of Napoleon and accusations of plagiarism by Karl Bleibtreu) or whether it was simply that his interests shifted, Bahr completed only the first part of the trilogy. An unambitious Napoleon, who wishes to remain near his beloved wife Josephine, is forced to carry out his destiny against his own will. Josephine forces him to accept command of the army in Italy, where his jealousy over reports of her conduct in Paris drives him to daring military maneuvers to shorten the campaign so that he can return home. Thus the brilliant career of the intrepid world conqueror is actually launched by Josephine's infidelity. It was Bahr's genial notion to stress the erotic element as the catalyst of the action. However, the theme of sexuality is only incidental to his main idea of fate as the driving force of life.

The idea of fate controlling life is demonstrated again in *Der Star* (1899), another "Wiener Stück" that presents essentially a less successful version of the novel *Das Theater,* and *Der Athlet* (1900). It features Baron Gustav von Handel, an egotistical domineering man of action who believes only in power: "The only thing that gives life meaning is to have power—power over nature, power over other people, power over oneself."[6] Handel's psychological need to prove his superiority is reflected in his attempts to reform the incorrigible criminal Loisl, who also possesses a strong personality. The philanthropic purpose is only a screen to mask Handel's true motivation of satisfying his own ego. In the manner of a French thesis play Handel learns that there are forces in the world stronger than his will.

The catalyst for the action is the confession of Handel's wife Marie that for reasons she cannot explain rationally she has had an affair with a young army officer. Handel is less concerned about Marie than about his own ego, and demands the satisfaction of a duel to avoid being consumed by frustration. Through a psychological twist he undergoes a change of heart and is brought to greater insight about life. His antipathy for his pedestrian bureaucratic brother and the bourgeois conventions that he represents serves to deflect Handel's anger, enabling him to approach Marie with a maturity that was absent previously. Bahr eschews a light happy ending in favor of a more realistic conclusion that is cautiously optimistic about Handel's future life with Marie: "Forgive—no, Marie! That I cannot do. Something between us has been destroyed, it is over! But we have our work, our duties, our concern for other people around the whole region here. We shall cling to this—it will sustain us! Without it we could no longer live."[7] This confrontation with his own vulnerability has made Handel a sadder but wiser man. In Hofmannsthal's terms, one could say that the baron, who had been living in a state of preexistence, has now been forced by his wife's infidelity to enter painfully into real life with the suffering as well as the rewards that this transition will bring.

Der Athlet contains features of the *Volksstück* in the interludes of singing and dancing as well as in the use of dialect. It also provides many good observations about life in Upper Austria, which Bahr knew intimately and enjoyed portraying. The structure is unsophisticated with the strong contrasts Bahr favored, such as the diametrically opposed characters of the two brothers, who represent intellect and nature respectively. Even though the central theme, that there are higher powers in life stronger than any individual, is timeless and universal, *Der Athlet* with its stock figures, including a *Raisonneur,* appears dated.

Bahr's choice of setting and form in *Der Athlet* reflected his recently discovered interest in the provinces and his reaction against Vienna. This newest programmatic tendency becomes even more pronounced in *Die Wienerinnen* (1900), one of his more successful and enduring comedies. In the vacuous rich young Viennese socialites, Daisy and Marie, Bahr portrays his current negative view of Vienna: devoid of substance and giddily pursuing every superficial craze in order to be considered fashionably modern.

Die Wienerinnen treats the conflict between genuineness and artificiality in life as well as in art. The world of integrity and wholesomeness is represented by Josef Ulrich (modeled on Joseph Olbrich), an architect and strong-willed individualist from the provinces who marries Daisy. They quarrel over her foolish ideas of modernity but reconcile after he convinces her of the soundness of his point of view. Bahr shows how serious ideas such as modernity, the equality of women, and the Secession were perverted into ridiculous fads. He also airs several of his pet grievances: the difficulty of accomplishing anything in Vienna because of bureaucratic obstacles, the hostility of the Viennese toward those who strive for progress, and the sorry treatment of artists. The play represents Bahr's defense of Olbrich, who left Vienna to work in Darmstadt, where he felt more appreciated.

In several lengthy speeches that parallel the ideas found in the essays of *Secession* Bahr stresses the importance of work and displays his enthusiasm for the craftsmanship of applied art: "I have respect for whoever has learned to make or create something, even if it is only a chair or a boot! I esteem every shoemaker and mason because he is useful and that is finally the only thing that gives our life meaning and value."[8] Despite the serious and polemical nature of Bahr's various theses, *Die Wienerinnen* avoids becoming tedious or heavy because of the sparkling repartee, the humorous situations, and the excellent characterizations of the two leading characters. It is one of Bahr's comedies that is still revived occasionally with success.

Bahr's glorification of the provinces at the expense of Vienna finds its epitome in the dialect play *Der Franzl* (1900), a warmly sentimental tribute to his compatriot, the Upper Austrian dialect poet Franz Stelzhamer. The play, which is subtitled "Five scenes from the life of a good man," is an early form of expressionist "Stationendrama" or of epic theater. The overview of Stelzhamer's life is given unity only by the central figure and is lacking in dramatic conflict. The play is dedicated to Austrian youth, which is to bring about the new humanity of the future on the model of independent-minded men, "wirkliche Menschen" like Stelzhamer. Bahr's affectionate esteem for Stelzhamer, which is well documented in his essays and diaries, enabled him to produce in *Der Franzl* one of his most heartfelt and genuine works. Despite its dramatic deficiencies the play was well received by the critics, who appreciated Bahr's sincerity as well as his choice of subject matter.

The five scenes cover fifty years of Stelzhamer's life from his carefree youth as a wandering minstrel who enjoyed gambling and drinking to his death on 14 July 1874, concluding with tributes showing that he was universally loved and respected: "This was the greatest man we ever had in our land. He was such a good man."[9] Each act depicts one or more characteristics that Bahr felt made up his unique significance: his openness toward life and his indifference to money, his deep affection for his family and for his homeland, his refusal to compromise his independence by bowing to any man regardless of the favors he could bestow, his sense of honor and responsibility, and his infectious optimism and general joy in life. Bahr's essays in the period after 1900 concern themselves almost entirely with these values, particularly *Buch der Jugend* (1908), which contains an essay on "Stelzhamer."

Bahr's hostility toward politicians and bureaucracy gave him in *Der Apostel* (1901) the idea of re-creating the entire parliament (some three hundred people) on stage in realistic fashion, in order to give the public an opportunity to view their representatives in action both officially and behind the scenes. It was Bahr's bold attempt to introduce the kind of verisimilitude that is achieved today by documentary theater. The play uses the theater as a tribune to expose the corruption and incompetence of politicians, who are incapable of regenerating society because they spend most of their time working for their own advantage rather than for the benefit of the people and the country. Bahr's execution fell far short of the ambitious task he had set for himself. The characterizations are weak and one-dimensional except for the prime minister, who is known as the Apostle. Even he is not consistently drawn, for Bahr became so captivated by his own protagonist that he changed him from a satiric to a saintly figure, causing a serious discrepancy in the overall conception of the drama.

The plot involves party politics, bribery scandals, and the personal ambition of some politicians who will stop at nothing to achieve political power. Finally, the resolution of the problems leads the Apostle and Andri, the leader of the opposition party, to discover that they share many ideas about society and politics. They resolve to forswear party affiliations in the future in order to appeal to the people directly.

Bahr's favorite ideas of this period are all represented in the play, whose major weakness results from Bahr's enchantment with the saintliness of his protagonist to the point that he ignored his own plot. All the complications are left unresolved as the play concludes with the euphoric sermon of the Apostle. Again Bahr sacrificed dramatic unity for a theatrical ending, a utopian alternative to party politics. The intended satire of politicians dissolves into a euphoria of love and benevolence. Had Bahr written this play a decade later it would have fitted into the context of expressionist drama with its antirational stance and its fervent plea for the universal brotherhood of man. As it was, *Der Apostel* left most of Bahr's contemporaries bewildered and dissatisfied. Even his close friend Max Burckhard dismissed the play with the categorical statement that the Apostle was an idiot!

The politics of Austria also serve as the theme of *Der Krampus* (1902), one of Bahr's most popular comedies that is still revived today. The title refers to a Viennese devil with a long red or black tongue, a lizard's tail, and either a whip or a trident to chastize bad children. He also has a sack or basket to carry off those who misbehave. This mythical figure accompanies St. Nicholas on his rounds on 6 December in Austria. In the play the retired Hofrat Negrelli is called *Der Krampus* because of his caustic nature and sharp tongue. He is a crotchety old man who is impossible to please. The play is intended to illustrate Bahr's view that the Hofrat was a malicious force not only within his own family, but also within the nation. In this instance the senile protagonist will not permit the marriage of his niece to the young man she loves, partly because he has already arranged for her marriage to a man of his choosing and partly because her choice is the nephew of the woman who spurned the *Hofrat* thirty years before. Because the niece and her mother are financially dependent upon him, the *Hofrat* can control their lives to suit his whims. The play could easily have turned tragic, but instead Bahr resolves the conflict with the grace, charm, and delicacy of the rococo period in which it is set. In keeping with the conventions of comedy the gruffness of the *Krampus* turns out to be superficial, and after numerous complications and the intervention of his former beloved to soften his heart, the young lovers are happily united.

One of Bahr's aims in *Der Krampus* was to test whether it was still possible to write historical plays. To insure the accuracy of historical detail, Bahr read a number of works from the late eighteenth century, which he cites in an appendix to the drama. He also indicates the play's indebtedness to Goldoni, probably the play *Burbero benefico*. *Der Krampus* is also related to the *Volksstück* tradition through its interludes of music and dance. Another feature of the play is the reliance on gestures, for the writing of *Der Krampus* coincided with Bahr's experiments in pantomime.

In *Der Meister* (1904), which was awarded the Bauernfeld Prize, Bahr again presented a domineering title figure surrounded by subordinate characters who represent viewpoints rather than being fully realized individuals. The play resembles *Der Athlet* in its technique of antithesis, in its attack on rationality as the guiding force in life, and in its focus on the double standard, the rights of women, and the subservience of all men to the laws of nature. The influence of Ibsen and Dumas is seen in the tendentiousness of the play and that of Nietzsche in the Master's philosophy of supremacy. The Master feels sovereign in the world because of his powerful will which has led to his success as a self-made man. Like *Der Athlet,* he must learn that he does not control life but plays only a subordinate role.

The Master, a renowned surgeon, is married to an independent-minded American woman, the daughter of a millionaire, who works as his associate. Their relationship is based on practicality rather than love, and for erotic diversion the Master engages in affairs which he makes little attempt to conceal. He is known for his liberal philosophy and his advocacy of equality for women. The events of the play test his principles when he discovers that his wife is having an affair with a count. True to his views, the Master refuses to duel after convincing the count of his prowess as a marksman, for he is willing to grant his wife her freedom as he has taken his. However, his wife confounds his logic by refusing to accept his magnanimous offer of forgiveness. She declines to return to him for, although they have shared a satisfying intellectual comradeship, he has never satisfied her emotionally and he has never needed her. Like *Der Athlet* the Master is temporarily shaken by this blow to his ego and loss of control over his environment. There is a chance that he may undergo a transformation of his character as a result of this experience. For the present he allows his wife to leave him without making any attempt to hold her.

The play is resolved by a *raisonneur,* the Master's Japanese assistant Kokoro, who dispassionately analyzes his behavior and outlook. The introduction of an exotic character reflects the Japanese craze of the time, but it also enables Kokoro to be objective. He explains that the Master's "icy reason" repels people. Human beings are all pawns in the hands of a higher power. People should feel emotions. Instead of being a master, man is only a clown. Human happiness lies solely

The World as Theater 123

in the feeling that a higher power propels us in any direction it wishes and that we have to obey: "We are innocent; it is stronger. How stupid of us now to become so emboldened as to be cleverer than fate, which exerts its control through our passions—if we cut them off with the scissors of reason, then dear Master—oh!"[10]

Following the lightweight satirical skit *Unter sich* (1904), Bahr wrote *Sanna* (1905), one of the works he set his hope on for posterity. While most critics reacted negatively to the premiere directed by Max Reinhardt in the Kleines Theater in Berlin in March 1905, others like Bahr's disciple Willi Handl hailed the work as Bahr's masterpiece: "This intellectual approach to classic fate tragedy and the purity of evenly proportioned form give the play a classic dignity and beauty. It belongs technically and poetically to Bahr's most perfect works. It is a masterpiece in which the central idea and the formative creative power have combined into a wonderful unity of the sensual and the rational."[11]

Sanna is essentially a variation on *Der Krampus* in a tragic key. It treats the same conflict between individual feeling and social convention set two generations later in 1847, the Biedermeier or *Vormärz* period when resignation was the prevailing spirit. The play illustrates Bahr's belief that the principal goal of life was personal fulfillment. He was opposed to the suppression of instincts and inclinations, which he saw as the aim of both school and family in his own day. When one of his daughters reproves her father for having taught them wrongly, he replies: "And the law? And duty? And the state? Eh, the state? That is the main point!" Her response is emphatic. "No, old man. The point is that one lives, lives, lives!"[12] The importance to Bahr of self-fulfillment, independence of spirit, and following one's instincts in life can be seen in their treatment in *Die Rahl*, *Wien*, and *Buch der Jugend* in successive years. For Bahr the individual was more important than the state or any other institution, and he lashed out violently at the system that robbed its citizens of their individuality, initiative, and personal happiness. To expose the roots of this Austrian system historically and to show its detrimental effects on the Austrian character was the purpose of *Wien*.

The villain in *Sanna* is an eighty-year-old senile *Hofrat*, who perversely enjoys dominating his family, which caters to his whims in order to inherit his money. Sanna's father, Trost, whose name symbolizes his conciliatory nature, recognizes early that the *Hofrat* is a tyrant, but because of his inner weakness, feelings of inferiority, and greed he is incapable of protesting. Sanna's mother is also a pitiable individual, who feels she has been cheated out of life. She is also too weak to defy the *Hofrat,* because she is blinded by the misery of her own life and the desire to inherit the money. She has become hardened over the years and finds refuge in the thought that no one dies from suffering. She is proven wrong, for when Sanna's fiancé withdraws after learning of the *Hofrat*'s refusal to provide a dowry, Sanna commits suicide. She had witnessed the shadowy, broken existence of her older sister, who had also been refused permission to marry, and prefers death to a pseudolife. Shocked by the tragedy, Trost finally finds the courage to declare his independence from the *Hofrat*'s control, suggesting the possibility of hope for a better life for the youngest daughter. Beyond this vague glimpse of optimism Bahr does nothing to lighten the gloomy oppressive atmosphere of the drama.

Although *Sanna* is set in 1847, Bahr was addressing his own age, presenting the demonic side of the same world of Upper Austria he had glorified in *Der Franzl.* In a letter to Hofmannsthal, in which he summarized the critical opinions on *Sanna,* Bahr explained his purpose: "I consider it my best play next to *Der Franzl,* and the necessary correction of *Franzl.* Or, more precisely, the two plays together express for me the Austrian Catholic world precisely as I see it, as one in which ordinary people talented in resignation, like Stifter, or those who ironize it perceptively, like Stelzhamer, can become something quite wonderful; they are all healthy people, but they all cannot avoid being destroyed."[13] The powerful emotion in *Sanna* was fueled by Bahr's hostile feelings toward his countrymen because of their timidity and false liberalism, which led to hypocrisy, repression, and resignation.

In *Sanna* all of the characters have been twisted in some manner by repressed emotions until they become a caricature of a family. The influence of the psychological ideas of Breuer and Freud is strong in this drama, not only in the embittered, frustrated mother and the disturbed older sister, but also in the teacher Zingerl, who makes his first appearance here and becomes a continuing character in the novels. Although he later becomes a positive character, Bahr portrays him here as a dissembling lecher, reflecting his antipathy toward school and church officials.

From the standpoint of technique *Sanna* is more tightly constructed than any of the earlier plays. Bahr utilized a starkly realistic manner, and the language is concise and taut, with frequent use of fragmentary sentences to convey emotional tension and heightened feelings. There is emphasis on gesture and pantomime to reflect inner states. The detailed stage directions leave nothing to chance despite Bahr's belief in the actor's preeminence in the theater. This technique shows Bahr's confidence as a director, as well as the seriousness with which he approached this particular work. The harmful psychological effect of repression, the negative impact of the school system on young people, the conspiracy of home and school against youth, the tyranny of the *Hofrat,* and the cruelty of family life when it is perverted by greed, opportunism, and misguided principles were all themes then close to his heart.

Bahr's interest in the psychology of repression and in the idea of the fluid ego acquired from Ribot's *Maladies de la personalité* and Mach's *Die Analyse der Empfindungen* became the basis of *Die Andere* (1906), Bahr's most complex psychological drama. In 1904 he had written two essays on Mach: "Der Philosoph des Impressionismus," in which he described Mach's ideas as the basis of the impressionist's view of life, and "Das unrettbare Ich," in which he explained Mach's theory of the nonfixed ego. Because of this fluid condition of the ego the human being is capable of unlimited transformation of character, an idea that became a basic theme for Bahr as well as for Hofmannsthal.

In addition to the psychological basis of *Die Andere,* Bahr also deals with the conflict between civilization and nature *(Geist* and *Natur),* defining *Geist* as the sum of social pressures. In the *Dialog vom Marsyas* (1905) Bahr had affirmed the ascendancy of life over art, and the play reflects this orientation toward a natural existence based on instinct as opposed to one dominated by cultural, social, or political forces.

Bahr, who had fervently evangelized for the new humanity from his first drama *Die neuen Menschen,* now expressed his disappointment over the lack of progress by lashing out at the institutions that he felt made change impossible. He had come to the conclusion that it was impossible for individuals to surmount their environment and that therefore the institutions must be changed so that man can develop. Throughout his writings, he had repeatedly shown that individuals who tried to bring about social change were defeated by their own deep-seated training and atavistic feelings, which could not be overcome. His belief in the necessity of reforming society explains his eagerness for revolution during his political phase. His shift to a cultural approach to the problem raised the hope that the desired change could be accomplished rationally by the aesthetic education of man, who would be led by beauty to a higher, better self. When he now recognized that this hope, which he had derived from Marx, was illusory, he became pessimistic. Nevertheless, *Die Andere* ends on a note of cautious optimism. The outbreak of revolution in Russia symbolizes not only the rebirth that society needs, but also represents in Bahr's view the only way to accomplish social change.[14]

Die Andere, written in five acts instead of the four Bahr usually used, is his most ambitious and complex drama. On one level, the author explores the compulsion of an individual to follow his destiny when he is impelled by subconscious drives. Leta Lent, an accomplished violinist, is having an affair with Professor Heinrich Hess, who is slavishly devoted to her even though he is a calculating rationalist who has never surrendered to his feelings before. He was never able to love Frau von Jello, his mistress for five years, who is passionately attached to him. Similarly, Leta does not love Hess but is hopelessly and, as it turns out, fatally attracted to her agent Amschel, who uses her shamelessly. He holds a hypnotic power over her, and in his presence she becomes a puppet without a will of her own. Frau von Jello behaves the same way toward Heinrich, and the normally officious, even imperious Heinrich loses his will when Leta is involved. Through this analogous behavior Bahr shows how the power of love causes individuals to undergo behavior modification.

The relationship between Leta and Amschel borders on the perverse and masochistic. No matter how badly he mistreats her, she remains attracted to him. Hess finds himself in the same situation with Leta. No matter how many times she leaves him to return to Amschel, he cannot break free of her. Bahr was always fascinated by the power of eroticism because he felt that this elemental force could not be feigned and hence revealed the real person. Hess explains to Frau von Jello that this necessity to obey a call that emanates from the subconscious and is beyond reason is the happiness of love.[15]

Die Andere also treats a political theme which Bahr introduces in two ways. Heidern, a student whose life has been strongly influenced by Hess's lectures, invites him to join his uncle's government in order to put his policies into practice. Heidern tells Hess that he was "the first real person" who taught the students what life can be. Although a government post had been his fondest wish in the preceding year, Hess now declines, for he is a changed person. He no longer believes that it is possible to help people through politics, law, and culture: "That is the thousand-year delusion. That is what is suffocating us. . . . The law has choked us. Away with it, back to ourselves, clear away the lies and—freedom, freedom. . . . We do not need to rescue our culture, we need to be rescued from our culture, from morality, from the law . . . perhaps then we can get back to ourselves."[16]

The antithesis of the conservative Heidern is the young radical August, who believes that society cannot be changed except by destroying it to allow a new system to arise. Individuals cannot alter the system because everyone is contaminated. Therefore everything must be destroyed to permit a new beginning. Nature does not intend people to suffer. If they do, it is because social institutions are not functioning properly and need to be eliminated so the new man can arise. The news of the revolution in Russia represents Heinrich and August's hope for the future.

A more conservative alternative to the problem of culture is offered by Besenius, an eccentric who has withdrawn from society and lives in nature. Formerly he was, like Hess, a man guided by his reason and a believer in culture and education. Besenius does not miss other human beings, because he is convinced that words are lies and that at the moment one says anything it is already distorted. He feels that the inner man cannot survive present social conditions which make any moral improvement impossible: "With the same words in his mouth, the same distress in his heart, always chasing the same hopes, caught up in the same business deals, tormented by the same vanities, always in the same place—and they call that sanity. God, I am happy that I am crazy."[17] Besenius cites Angelus Silesius to support his view that in order to survive society must reduce its level of culture *(entbilden)*.

Die Andere, which is dedicated to Anna Mildenburg, has the densest thematic texture of any of Bahr's dramas, as the author attempts to interweave psychological, cultural, and political levels of action. The play tries to capture dramatically the idea of the changed personality by portraying a human being, Hess, who becomes so estranged from the person he was previously that he can no longer assume responsibility for the actions of the former without completely denying the new person he has become. Bahr felt that he had failed: "The problem is beyond the reach of my creative powers. Ultimately it can be represented only in a mythical figure."[18] Schnitzler pointed out some of the play's flaws in a letter of 30 July 1905, stating that the themes did not blend into a unified whole, and that only after reading the fifth act could one understand the threads running through the earlier acts. But the first four acts had not prepared him for the fifth: "If one says, *therefore* two times two equals four, this *therefore* is the result of a prior calculation. Naturally you feel this *therefore* very well—but you have not made me feel it dramatically."[19] Schnitzler also criticized Besenius, whom he compares to a pianist playing a prelude and having no further part in the performance. He feels that the play would have been more convincing if Amschel had been made more sympathetic. Finally, he disliked the melodramatic last act, which contains no explanation of how Leta came to find her death in such disreputable surroundings. Schnitzler's perceptive critique illuminates not only the basic faults in the construction of *Die Andere,* but also Bahr's general weaknesses in dramatic craftsmanship.

One of Bahr's best and most accomplished works is the one-act drama *Der arme Narr* (1906), which had its premiere in the Burgtheater on 29 November 1906 with Kainz in the title role. The play once again reflects his preoccupation with the conflict between intellect and nature. Bahr repeats his injunction to follow the dictates of feeling and live life to the fullest. As he frequently does, Bahr employs the antithesis of two brothers, Vincenz, who has lived his entire life in anxiety and resignation, and Hugo (possibly modeled on Hugo Wolf), who has dared to venture to the extremes of life even at the risk of his own sanity. The play turns on the central paradox that the sickly protagonist, who has nearly lived himself to death, emerges as the stronger force and is shown to have made the wiser choice.

The most surprising feature of the play is its strict economy of means in contrast to the excessively detailed stage directions and verbose speeches usually employed by Bahr. Possibly because the drama was written for Kainz, Bahr suppressed his directorial tendencies in order to allow latitude for the actors. This same austerity is found in the language, which is almost expressionistic in its unadorned simplicity and in the use of color imagery. The play is intended to make a strong emotional impact; and since there is no action, the forcefulness must be rendered through language and gestures. The influence of Nietzschean vitalism is strongly in evidence, as is the Goethean idea of "stirb und werde" ("dying and becoming") and Mach's fluid ego. Hugo tells Sophie, the daughter of Vincenz: "Die daily, live eternally. This is my legacy to you: live yourself to death. In so doing you praise God, the Lord!"[20]

Vincenz represents Bahr's view of the Viennese at this time, as he characterized them also in *Wien,* where he maliciously commented that the major problem of the day was "to make human beings out of Austrians."[21] Hugo provides a lesson in life by telling Vincenz that his barren, joyless existence is a sign that such a fearful, introverted life is not regarded with favor by God. Hugo lived to the fullest, undergoing constant transformations in the crucible of an active existence: "With both feet into life. Into the fire. And [he] burned. And [he] became smoke. And out of the smoke emerged a new person. And into life again and burned again. Burning without end. And from that I am now yellow with blessings. Burning is life. . . . Everywhere I am so richly filled with ripe blissful blue hours, fully laden, with every sense alert. Everything is open, everything is granted to the sinner."[22] Vincenz, who had brought Hugo home from the sanitarium to triumph over him, instead must learn that he, and not Hugo, is the poor fool who will be denied a good death because he has failed to give his life meaning. There is no illuminating transformation of character, for Vincenz remains uncomprehending to the end.

No matter how serious his message might be or how straightforwardly he presented it, Bahr had great difficulty in being properly understood. As Duke Oriole states in *Der Klub der Erlöser,* the first of the three one-act plays comprising *Grotesken* (1907): "I suffer the misfortune that when I try to be very serious one only considers me witty."[23] Bahr therefore employed the form of the grotesque to mask his serious purpose in these additional variations on the conflict of intellect and nature that were written out of deep conviction. While neither the first play nor the third, *Die tiefe Natur,* a light comedy dedicated "to the memory of *Anatol"* because of its resemblance to Schnitzler's drama, is particularly significant, the second play, *Der Faun,* raises an important issue concerning the conflict between the sexes and the double standard. Two husbands vacationing in the mountains with their wives provide alibis for each other in order to have affairs. Neither of them has the slightest suspicion that the women involved are their own wives, who have informed each other of the flirtation and have exchanged rooms, so that each man visits his own wife without knowing it. When the truth is revealed the following day the husbands feel deceived.

The Faun of the title is a natural individual, who makes no pretenses or excuses about his openly erotic nature and life-style. He is the only honest character in the play, while the married couples dissemble and conceal their true feelings from one another. Bahr's attempt to make a serious statement about the psychological and erotic relationship of married couples resembles the fifth scene in Schnitzler's *Reigen,* where the young husband explains to his wife the difference between her and the women who become mistresses. In *Der Faun,* Helmine tries to understand the masculine viewpoint when her husband justifies his conduct by explaining that it stems from man's nature. She cannot fathom why it is not also the nature of woman. She fails to see why a husband makes love to his wife in a very reserved manner and saves his most passionate, honest lovemaking for his mistress. By using the woman's perspective in the play, Bahr complements Schnitzler's scene, in which the wife makes no response to her husband's views. Helmine is one of the most articulate and fully realized of Bahr's female characters, and this scene, which is left open-ended, is one of his most thoughtful contributions to the subject of marriage and the relationship of the sexes.

Ringelspiel (1907) continues the same preoccupation with the problem of fidelity combined with the idea of the flexible ego and the round dance of life around man's sexual drives. The point of departure seems to be Schnitzler's *Reigen,* as Bahr attempts to show in comic fashion that man is a pawn of his sexuality. Although it appears to mock all values, the play has a serious purpose. The problem is one treated frequently by Hofmannsthal: how can one remain faithful to oneself and one's personal growth and also fulfill one's commitments to others. In contrast to *Reigen* the round dance here is caused not simply by man's erotic drives but by a fundamental personality change in terms of Mach's philosophy.[24]

The reaction to the play, which Bahr directed in Berlin, was negative because critics dismissed it as a persiflage based on events in Bahr's own life.[25] The deeper meaning was completely overlooked.

Yet, even though it failed, Bahr refused to revise it. His seriousness is seen in the care with which he delineated each of his principal figures. There is no possibility of judging these characters because, as in *Die Andere,* Bahr is attempting to show that they are all subject to changes of personality that are beyond their control. The play is related to the *Grotesken* in its bold approach to the question of the relationship between the sexes and its complete disregard for moral considerations. However, the attractive setting on the Lido in summer, the charming nature of the characters, and the lightness of the dialogue keep it from being offensive.

The congenial Julius Eggers, who has lived apart from his wife Franzl for several years, is preparing to divorce her to marry Rune, a more serious-minded woman better suited to his present personality. Although he has outgrown Franzl, Julius has always kept in touch with her as a link to his previous self. She appears on the Lido with her latest suitor, Harold, a thoroughly pedestrian individual about whom Franzl herself jokes. Franzl explains to Rune that Julius will seek another mistress after he marries her, and she proposes that, since Rune is replacing Franzl as his wife, she, Franzl, assume the role of mistress. The situation is not resolved, for Franzl goes sailing with a new conquest while the others wait for her to join them for dinner on the beach. The scene is filled with erotic tension and suspense: Harold waits for his fate at the hands of the mercurial Franzl, Rune is alarmed over the reawakened attraction of Julius for his former wife, and Julius finds himself in an ambivalent state of excitement. There is no resolution to the play, as there is no solution to the problem. The comedy concludes with a theatrical flourish as the children of all nationalities join in a bacchantic dance to symbolize the universal and timeless centrality of eros in the lives of human beings.

In *Die gelbe Nachtigall* (1907) Bahr returned to the world of the theater, basing the play loosely on his experiences while working for Reinhardt without, however, intending a "drama à clef." As in the novel *Das Theater,* he defends the artificiality of the theater, arguing that it is not deceptive because audiences expect it to be a world of make-believe. He portrays the theater as a symbol of life and as a desirable influence on society. Whereas in *Das Theater* and *Der Star* Bahr had tried to demonstrate the thesis that the world of the theater cannot be united with the real world, here he shows that it is possible to do so. In *Wien,* Bahr had shown how his countrymen leave their true self at home when they venture outside. They face reality with dissembling and role-playing until they no longer know how to be honest. In this sense performers can serve as a model, for they know when they are pretending: "At least we only deceive from seven until ten, then we take off our makeup! After ten we are free. This advantage, dear friend, we have over the rest of mankind: we are able to take off our makeup."[26]

Das Konzert (1909), with its additional variations on the themes of marriage, role-playing, and the erotic round dance of life, is a continuation of the freethinking ideas about marriage in *Ringelspiel*, although it is more conservative in its approach and conclusions. Bahr did not regard this comedy as superior to his other plays and never understood its success, although he attempted to account for it by observing: "It was a world success, however, not of mine but of Vienna. People throughout the world have never tired of speaking or hearing about our Austrian manner."[27] This explanation fails to explain the appeal of the play adequately; for when the director Leo Dietrichstein changed the setting from Vienna to New York for the American stage it was the hit of the New York season.[28] The popularity of *Das Konzert* can more properly be attributed to its ageless plot and sympathetic characters.

A husband and wife who genuinely love and understand each other find they can hold their marriage intact by being tolerant of each other's basic nature. For the concert pianist Gustav Heink this involves the idea that man is impelled by his deepest nature to indulge in extramarital escapades. As a piano teacher he is constantly surrounded by young women who lead him into temptation. On these occasions Heink announces that he is going to give a concert, a euphemism which his wife Marie understands clearly. However, she has always ignored his escapades to preserve their harmonious home life. She knows that the lothario role is losing its appeal for Heink. However, he is trapped by his personality and his vanity into continuing his liaisons in order to protect his youthful image and his reputation, which attracts the wealthy piano pupils. Marie, one of the most intelligent, positive women in Bahr's works, controls the action of the play as she does her marriage and her husband. She knows that he is driven by forces that he is incapable of understanding. She also recognizes that these escapades are emotionally meaningless and serve merely as ego gratification. If she is patient, they will eventually cease.

A crisis arises after Heink has embarked upon a concert with Delphine, the seventeen-year-old wife of Dr. Jura, a realist and emancipated male, who loves his wife and is prepared to allow her full freedom. He will even release her if it will bring her happiness. He and Marie have been alerted about the rendezvous by Eva, a vamp in the Klimt fashion, who is jealous that Heink preferred another to her. Because of Jura's sincerity Marie decides to disrupt the "concert." She and Jura follow their mates to the mountains and pretend to have an affair. Heink seems not unhappy to have his plans interrupted. He tried to explain to Marie how he becomes involved without even trying: "One is bored. A real conversation is not possible with our women. You cannot be impolite. Just to have something to say you look at them and remark that spring will soon be coming again. Then you are lost. Or you say Goethe and Frau von Stein and then you are completely lost."[29] Thus Heink shows how he is trapped by circumstances into playing a role that is becoming increasingly difficult to maintain, but which he is powerless to break away from. Despite the happy reunion of the two couples, Heink at the end of the play is shown mechanically embracing Eva as he resignedly comments: "I must, I must."

This humorous conclusion contains tragic implications, for Heink is really a victim of his own nature. Despite his immature views of women and his belief in a double standard, he is not malicious and makes no effort to take advantage of anyone. If anything, he gives the impression that he is the one being exploited. As in *Ringelspiel,* Bahr seems to suggest that there is no end to this game until old age or death intervene, for Heink is a type who will never mature. Yet he possesses qualities that make it possible for a woman of Marie's intelligence to love and find happiness with him. This serious dimension invests *Das Konzert* with its deeper significance and elevates it from the level of farce to true comedy.

Das Konzert bears somewhat the same relationship to Schnitzler's *Intermezzo* (1905) as *Die tiefe Natur* does to the same author's *Abschiedssouper*—it is a variation on a theme. Whereas Schnitzler showed that two people who have an open marriage cannot survive the freedom because the situation is never equal, Bahr portrays a marriage that survives only because the wife does not demand the same freedom. Originally Bahr had conceived *Das Konzert* as a libretto for Richard Strauss, to whom the play is dedicated and on whom Heink may be loosely modeled. The original text was to be called

"Intermezzo," but Bahr proved unequal to the task. He finally conceded defeat, leaving Strauss to write his own libretto for the opera by that name.[30]

In his next two plays Bahr returned to the dichotomy of reality and appearance which he had treated so frequently in earlier works. In *Das Tänzchen* (1911) he satirizes politicians who live two lives. As in *Der Apostel*, the plot, which this time is set in Berlin, involves election politics, sexual entrapment, and a blackmail scandal. Audiences in Berlin rejected the play, possibly believing that the Viennese author was satirizing German politics; and it lasted for only two performances. By contrast, the comedy *Die Kinder,* which concerns double adultery, premiered at the Leipzig Schauspielhaus on 23 December 1910 and simultaneously on twenty-seven other stages. Bahr was attempting to develop more fully an idea that he had touched upon in *Das Tänzchen,* where the daughter of Baron von Biest married into the family of the Jewish entrepreneur Lawin: the blood of the aristocracy needed renewal from the outside. Bahr, who from his early years had dismissed the aristocracy as a vital force, emphasizes the strength of the bourgeoisie as compared to the nobility and rejoices that nature can override moral considerations to insure the world's renewal.

The following dramas all continue to offer variations on established themes. The comedy *Das Prinzip* (1912) returns to the moral world of *Der Apostel* and depicts in a humorous manner the idea of the innate goodness of human beings found in the novel *O Mensch* and in the essays of *Inventur*.

The conflict of intellect and nature reappears as the theme of *Das Phantom* (1913), which is built upon the clever paradox that a Platonic affair may be as serious in its effects as an actual one. The play illustrates well what by now had become Bahr's formula for successful popular comedy: "Love, marriage, and adultery . . . a little cultural apostolic posing and a proper dose of farce, many witty paradoxes and some skepticism, a little 'new psychology' and a dash of ethics, amazing leaps of thought, and here and there a few malicious comments against the philistines—out of such elements Bahr creates a piquant mixture which when served gracefully is certain of success."[31]

In late 1912 Bahr moved to Salzburg, and his play *Der Querulant* (1914) shifts away from his standard theme of eroticism to the problems of guilt, punishment, and justice in a rural setting. An old poverty-stricken peasant nicknamed Hias (Job), who was a decorated hero in the war of 1870, now lives alone, despised by most men, suspected of being insane by others, and neglected by everyone. His only friend is his mongrel dog, which is shot one day by the forester. When Hias attempts to obtain justice by having the forester punished for murder, his case is dismissed and the forester suffers no penalty. Consequently Hias determines to gain retribution by killing the forester's daughter Marie. However, when he attempts to strangle her one dark night, his conscience will not allow him to kill her. The compassionate Marie refuses to testify against Hias, but his integrity compels him to confess. At the end the judge assures Marie that nothing will happen to Hias because the jurors will see that he is suffering from diminished capacity.

As is frequently the case in Bahr's dramas, the first act of the play, in which Hias dominates the action, is the best. He is a type that Bahr loved to portray, somewhat on the order of *Der Franzl*, speaking dialect, flinty, independent, an integral part of nature which he loved. The play belongs to Hias; the other characters are all stock figures filling their function in the play merely as necessary adjuncts to the plot.

Although Bahr calls *Der Querulant* a comedy, he was serious about his basic theme of the inadequacy of justice. True justice on earth will be possible only when all men live in the spirit of true Christianity. The judge agrees that the law is not infallible, but at present there is no better alternative. In his view the order of the state would collapse without the courts, and people would be worse off than they are. Meanwhile the pastor has tried to persuade Hias to accept a higher form of justice based on a system of divine compensation in life. If one suffers a wrong, it will be balanced out in some other way: "We are all subject to the mercy of God. Let us not be so anxious about justice."[32]

Bahr reacted to the outbreak of World War I with the propagandistic essays *Kriegssegen* (1914) and *Das österreichische Wunder* (1915), in which he viewed the war as a means of unifying the Germans and Austrians and also as a way for people to relinquish role-playing and reveal their real character. These patriotic themes were incorporated in *Der muntere Seifensieder* (1915), a trivial topical play subtitled "Ein Schwank aus der deutschen Mobilmachung." This farcical work gave Bahr an opportunity to satirize the ridiculous excesses at the beginning of the war: arresting people as spies, shooting at stars thinking they are enemy planes, hasty marriages, people trying to hide their physical defects to enlist, and other foolish responses. While his plea for unity and an end to role-playing was sincere, the vehicle was too shallow for the play to make any impact.

Die Stimme (1917), the reworking of the theme of *Himmelfahrt*—an intellectual's way to religious faith—was Bahr's last attempt at a major play. It is a literary rather than a theatrical work and is one of three plays (the others being *Der Franzl* and *Sanna*) on which he set his hopes for posterity. The seriousness of Bahr's purpose can be seen in his efforts to rise above superficial stage effects and to portray the inner growth of his protagonist during the course of the play. *Die Stimme* is a purely psychological drama portraying the intellectual fencing of the protagonist and his introspective soul-searching. One can only empathize with his spiritual transformation and in a sense accept it as he does on faith, since it cannot be proved or demonstrated factually.

As in *Himmelfahrt* the protagonist of *Die Stimme,* Hans von Ule, is an intellectual and dilettante whose characterization would fit Bahr very well: "A man of high intellect, broad education, honest will, an unusual, perhaps, according to his gifts, even a significant man. Yet, it is uncertain whether his qualities qualify him as the 'praeceptor Germaniae' he would like to be."[33] Hans, a religious free thinker, marries a young girl who is a fervent Catholic. The one source of disharmony between them results from her constant unsuccessful attempts to lead him to religious belief. Suddenly she dies. Hans takes a trip to relieve his distressed state of mind and is visited by what he thinks is his wife's voice imploring him to leave the train at the next stop. He does so and later learns that a wreck left no survivors in his compartment. At this point the drama proper begins.

Only now does Hans learn from his mother-in-law that his wife had willed herself to death, hoping that the shock might jar him into religious faith. Hans would like to consider his wife's voice as a sign sent by God to persuade him to believe, but he cannot find any authority or logical reason to support this view. In fact, as in the novel, Domherr Zingerl flatly opposes any such interpretation: "You would like to be gripped by grace and dragged with force. You would like to be seduced by God."[34] However, the church cannot provide that service for Hans. Only he can accept faith, and in this situation his reason is useless. There is no path to religious belief through the intellect.

Since Hans can neither persuade himself nor be convinced by anyone else to accept faith, his wife's death and his rescue from the train wreck have ostensibly been to no avail. However, at the end of the play, while still protesting that he is unable to believe, Hans is suddenly gripped once more by what he thinks is his wife's voice. He is brought to his knees and suddenly feels that he has been visited by faith. The introduction of the voice at the end was the most criticized feature of the drama, for critics considered it a *deus ex machina*. However, it is not intended as a supernatural phenomenon but as the expression of Hans' own inner conscience. Bahr used this externalization of internal psychological processes to show how belief grips and takes possession of the spirit when the proper inner attitude has been achieved. The process occurs of itself totally beyond the control of the will.

Bahr's subsequent plays show a marked decline in substance and quality and add nothing to his reputation as a dramatist. In *Der Augenblick* (1917), written the same year as the volume of essays entitled *Um Goethe,* Bahr reworked the plot of Goethe's *Der Mann von fünfzig Jahren* into a psychological comedy of fidelity with the message that virtue cannot be imposed from the outside but must come from inner conviction.

In *Der Unmensch* (1919), which is set in the immediate post–World War I period in Vienna, Bahr was possibly following Lessing's injunction to write comedies after a war. The central theme is reminiscent of Schnitzler's *Das weite Land:* a man encourages his wife to be unfaithful because in this way she can perhaps save the life of another man. At the same time Bahr was satirizing postwar conditions to show that nothing essential had really changed in the transition of Austria from monarchy to republic. As he repeatedly stated, the strength of Austria lay in its ordinary citizens, and the form of government was of little consquence.

Ehelei (1920), which presents Bahr's views on the function of adultery as a means of preserving an indissoluble Catholic marriage, was the last comedy published in book form. The final plays were published only in the form of stage manuscripts, an indication that even Bahr took them lightly. They are all repetitious in theme and in the use of characters from previous works. For example, the three one-act comedies comprising *Spielerei* (1919) are all related thematically to *Der Unmensch* and poke gentle fun at the postwar situation in Austria. *Altweibersommer* (1924) involves an aging Anatol-type who is still driven to new conquests to satisfy his ego. This farce is so thin and weak that Bahr attempts to forestall disaster by warning the audience that it has an obligation to contribute to the play's effectiveness. He concludes by appealing to the audience directly for applause.

Bahr's final play, *Die Tante* (1928), repeats the themes of love, marriage, and adultery. The play ends with no change in either the characters or the situation. This comedy is redeemed only by the good nature of the characters who are so charming and ingratiating in their shallow amiability that it is impossible to dislike them. Bahr, who had begun his career as a dramatist with high aspirations, ended on a trivial note, turning out hack works much like the artist in *Die gute Schule.*

The importance of the plays today is their reflection of Bahr's world, for they supplement his novels and essays as an important aspect of his literary and cultural contribution. They provide a survey of the theater in Austria over a forty-year period, reflecting changing dramatic styles and attitudes and serving as an historical reflection of the era in which they were written. They are highly personal documents, as Bahr noted: "Concerning my plays. Moments in which I sense with enormous pleasure the mysteries of existence and the riddle of my own being—sometimes it is in the smile of a woman, the breeze from the incoming tide, or the touch of a loving hand that gives me these moments. And I suffer great fear that they will fade away and never return. But at the same time I have the feeling that I can hold on to them, make them part of myself, can keep the fleeting moment for myself. My works are beakers that catch the outpouring of the moment. I am surprised that others can have any relationship to them at all."[35]

Bahr's dramatic oeuvre contains several plays of genuine merit—*Josephine, Der Franzl, Sanna, Der Meister, Der arme Narr, Der Faun, Das Konzert,* and *Die Andere*—and many of theatrical effectiveness. *Das Konzert* has proved to be his most durable play rather than *Der Franzl, Sanna,* or *Die Stimme,* on which he had predicted his future reputation would rest. And yet overall, if one excludes the plays of Hofmannsthal and Schnitzler, one can agree with Castle's final assessment: "If one looks back over the total production of the last thirty years of German comedy, one will have to say that Bahr did not raise himself above his time, but he also did not sink below it."[36]

Chapter Eight
Conclusion and Assessment

It is impossible to investigate all of the many facets of Bahr's career within the limitations of an introductory study. However, this examination of the main aspects of his life and works is intended to provide sufficient evidence to document the central importance of Bahr within his generation and the major significance of his contributions as a theorist, critic, essayist, novelist, and dramatist. Bahr was not a literary genius on the order of Hofmannsthal, attempting to answer timeless questions, or a painstaking diagnostician of a small segment of Viennese society like Schnitzler, or a meticulous craftsman like Beer-Hofmann. He was willing to sacrifice depth for breadth, durability for immediate effect, and detailed logical argument for sweeping generalizations. His ambition to stay in tune with his generation and to serve as its spokesman often led him to changes of direction and excesses that distracted attention from the importance of his ideas. Yet, his involvement in every important activity in the realm of the arts during his lifetime, his position in the avant-garde, particularly during the 1890s, and his constant visibility through his many publications and public appearances made him a force equaled in impact by few other Austrian writers of his day.

Bahr's major achievement was his promotion of the idea of modernity, which contributed to a complete transformation of values in Austria at the turn of the century. The success of the *Jung-Wien* writers, of the Secessionist painters, the awakening of a general enthusiasm for culture, the development of an awareness of European trends, and the wish to give Austrian literature its own identity are all accomplishments that can be directly attributed, in varying degree, to Bahr's efforts as a mediator and publicist. How much he actually helped individual writers, artists, musicians, and actors is difficult to document, but the instances of his readiness to use his considerable influence to promote and support his colleagues provide tangible evidence of his instrumental role in guiding the course of the arts in Austria. Despite the efforts of Karl Kraus to destroy his credibility, Bahr remained a powerful force in the society of his day. Indeed, if he had not been such a prestigious and influential spokesman of his generation, Kraus would not have devoted forty years to the attempt to discredit him.

Bahr's life proceeded in a circle beginning with belief in the absolute values that he learned from Joseph Steger in Salzburg and returning to these same ideals later in life. He was a Catholic by birth and died a Catholic by conviction. He was raised on the values of nineteenth-century liberalism and in his last years embraced the liberal view of social progress through evolution and enlightenment. In art he proceeded through all of the fashionable trends of the day before returning to the idea that artists are born and that art should be judged according to strict aesthetic criteria. His generation initially rejected the heritage of its literary tradition, but Bahr concluded his career as an advocate of tradition and particularly of the values of Goethe, Stifter, and Grillparzer. Born into a family of patriots, he repudiated Austria and urged a merger with Germany only to become the most dedicated spokesman for the continued independence of Austria. By the time of his death, he had completed the circle of his life to an exceptional degree.

Bahr's greatest enthusiasm was reserved for fostering the virtues of "Old Austria." Through his concept of the unifying capability of the baroque, which he expanded to contain a political and social as well as an artistic meaning, he envisioned Austria as a center of supranational Europe because of its unique citizenry and central geographical position. Today with its new United Nations office center, the second largest after that in New York, Austria is fulfilling the role as a mediator among the nations of the world that Bahr foresaw for it.

Bahr was given to sweeping visions, and yet the evolution of his thinking reveals many practical ideas intended to help create a nation of happy, free-spirited people and to make the world a pleasanter, more comfortable place in which to live. It is not desirable for people to stay modern, that is, to remain in tune with their changing environment? Do not institutions need to be updated constantly? Would it not be helpful if the state assumed more responsibility through the schools for educating young people to an appreciation of the arts and to become what Bahr called "wirkliche Menschen"? Would it not enhance the quality of life if art and craftsmanship were more often united, and if, as Bahr desired, people lived in better homes and books were bound in a better way? In short, would not society benefit by fulfilling Bahr's vision of a world in which art played a significant role as a meaningful part of culture instead of remaining separate from life?

Most of Bahr's commentaries on society and politics were neither new nor novel; for example, his belief in the basic goodness of man or in the need for honest politicians. Indeed, he claimed that all of the ideas necessary for the betterment of mankind had long been known. All that was necessary was to put them into practice. Most of his writings were motivated by his desire to encourage the moral improvement of society: his attacks on soulless materialism, on constant business activity, on a society uprooted from the soil, on the lack of national unity, and on a bureaucracy that had its own rather than the nation's interests at heart.

Bahr's novels and dramas are all reflections, from a highly personal viewpoint, of the age in which they were written. He once referred to his writings as *Lebensspuren* ("the tracks of his life") to indicate their subjective nature. As a writer he never succeeded in creating a character that has remained alive in literature in the manner of Schnitzler's Anatol or Hofmannsthal's Claudio, nor did he ever create a work that contains even a hint of his true nature. This is why *Das Konzert,* the one work with which he is immediately identified today, fails to convey an accurate idea of Bahr's significance. Most of his novels can be read with pleasure and profit today, particularly *Die Rotte Korahs;* and several dramas, first and foremost *Das Konzert,* can still delight audiences. If one applies Bahr's own critical standards to his writings, one arrives at the conclusion that he was not a poet in the German sense of *Dichter* but a highly gifted journalist and cultivated man of letters, who was also a visionary, an educator, and the conscience of his age. He had a gift for reading the "demands of his time" and the willingness to respond to them. It was this sensitivity to nuances of change and shifts of attitude that enabled him to remain in the forefront of developments. Because of the diffuse nature of Bahr's role as a cultural mediator, his contribution must be viewed as in the total aggregation of all his activities rather than from the standpoint of any single accomplishment.

Since Bahr has been shown to hold a central position in his generation, and since turn-of-the-century Vienna has become one of the most fashionable and enthusiastically researched topics of the last decade, one may properly ask why such a highly productive figure has not attracted greater attention. How was it possible, for example, for the eminent critic of this period, Carl Schorske, to write his Pulitzer Prize winning book, *Fin-de-siècle Vienna,* without a single mention of Bahr's contribution or significance? This is not to fault Schorske but merely to illustrate how completely Bahr has been overlooked and neglected. He has been ignored while the other *Jung-Wien* writers have become fashionable and the subject of intensive research. The collected works of all of the other *Jung-Wien* writers have been reprinted in their entirety, while Bahr's writings have never been published in either a collected or selected edition, and few have been reprinted. The only work that has remained in print is *Das Konzert* thanks to the efforts of the publisher Reclam. The unavailability of Bahr's works has acted as a deterrent to research. Moreover, at the time of his death Bahr was generally dismissed by literary critics as irrelevant and unimportant. Except for the evaluation by Eduard Castle in 1937 nothing of consequence was written about Bahr until Heinz Kindermann's book in 1954. Bahr is not generally included in literature courses, partly for lack of available books and partly because most academics have taken their view of Bahr from Kraus's prejudiced judgment without ever having read the original works. It is certain that Kraus's forty-year polemic influenced critical and scholarly opinion of Bahr. Another problem stems from Bahr's frequent transformations, which make it difficult to generalize about him. There is a wide variety of Hermann Bahrs, and one must always know precisely what period of his life is being considered in order to discuss him intelligently. Finally, Bahr was given to verbosity and repetition. It is necessary to read through considerable chaff in his one hundred and twenty volumes in order to find the wheat.

For all of these reasons Bahr's reputation has faded, and he is forgotten at a time when the period of which he was the center is enjoying a renaissance. The discrepancy cannot continue to exist, and it is certain that Bahr's importance will soon begin to be recognized. To assist in this task of properly understanding and restoring his significance is the principal aim of the present study.

Notes and References

Chapter One

1. *Selbstbildnis* (Berlin, 1923), 1–2. All translations are by the author.
2. *Glossen zum Wiener Theater (1903–1906)* (Berlin, 1907), 408.
3. *Selbstbildnis,* 13.
4. Ibid., 15.
5. Ibid., 49.
6. Ibid., 51.
7. In 1931 Bahr donated his extensive library (about 10,000 volumes) to the University of Salzburg, and he also intended to leave his literary estate to the library after his death. However, after a series of complications the literary estate was permanently housed in the Theater Collection of the National Library in Vienna. See Donald G. Daviau, "Hermann Bahr's Nachlass," *Journal of the International Arthur Schnitzler Research Association* 2 (Autumn 1963):4–27.
8. See motto.
9. *Selbstbildnis,* 100.
10. Cf. Donald G. Daviau, "Hermann Bahr and the Radical Politics of Austria in the 1880s," *German Studies Review* 5, no. 2 (May 1982):163–85.
11. *Selbstbildnis,* 170.
12. *1917* (Innsbruck, 1918), 210.
13. *Hermann Bahr: Briefwechsel mit seinem Vater,* ed. A. Schmidt (Vienna, 1971), 192.
14. *Adalbert Stifter* (Vienna, 1918), 12.
15. *Selbstbildnis,* 223.
16. Cf. Donald G. Daviau, "The Misconception of Hermann Bahr as a 'Verwandlungskünstler,' " *German Life and Letters* 11 (April 1958):182–92.
17. Cf. "Holz," in *Bilderbuch* (Vienna, 1921), 78–87.
18. "Bonaparte," in *Moderner Musen-Almanach* 2 (1894):251–65. This play later became the first act of *Josephine* (1898).
19. *Josef Kainz* (Vienna, 1906); see also *Die Briefe von Josef Kainz,* ed. Hermann Bahr (Vienna, 1921).
20. "Eleonora Duse," in *Der Thespikarren* (Vienna: W. Andermann 1943), 315–21; this is a reprint of an article from the *Frankfurter Allgemeine Zeitung.* See also "Die Duse," in *Studien zur Kritik der Moderne* (Frankfurt, 1894), 251–57; hereafter cited as *Studien.*

21. Many essays from *Die Zeit* not published in book form by Bahr were included by Gotthart Wunberg in *Das junge Wien: Österreichische Literatur und Kunstkritik, 1887–1902,* 2 vols. (Tübingen: Max Niemeyer, 1926). Of the 513 essays in the two volumes 143 are by Bahr.

22. Peter de Mendelssohn, *S. Fischer und sein Verlag* (Frankfurt am Main: S. Fischer, 1970), 191–192.

23. *Renaissance* (Berlin, 1897), ii.

24. "Die Menschen," in *Wirkung in die Ferne* (Vienna, 1902), 244–54.

25. Quoted in Erich Widder, *Hermann Bahr: Sein Weg zum Glauben* (Linz, 1963), 103.

26. These diaries and letters are contained in a file marked "Anna" in the Theater Collection of the National Library in Vienna. Anna Mildenburg edited this material and expunged explicit passages. What, if any, documents she may have destroyed is unknown.

27. Widder, *Hermann Bahr,* 92.

28. *Selbstbildnis,* 289.

29. *Kriegssegen* (Munich, 1914), preface.

30. *1918* (Innsbruck, 1919), 252.

31. He never traveled to the United States, about which he knew very little beyond his reading of a few authors such as Whitman, Poe, Emerson, and Sinclair Lewis. Bahr was not widely translated into English, but *Josephine, The Master, The Poor Fool, The Concert,* and *The Mongrel (Der Querulant)* were performed in both England and America. See Donald G. Daviau, "Hermann Bahr's Cultural Relations with America," in *Österreich und die Angelsächsische Welt,* ed. Otto Hietsch (Vienna, 1968), 482–522.

Chapter Two

1. *Selbstbildnis,* 221.

2. For a more detailed treatment of this topic see Donald G. Daviau, "Hermann Bahr and Decadence," *Modern Austrian Literature* 10, no. 2 (1977):53–100.

3. *Studien,* 94–95.

4. Cf. Donald G. Daviau, *"Dialog vom Marsyas:* Hermann Bahr's Affirmation of Life over Art," *Modern Language Quarterly* 20, no. 4 (December 1959):360–70. In his *Selstbildnis* Bahr states that he was "born to affirm" (235).

5. *Russische Reise* (Dresden, 1893), 66, 104, 172, 194.

6. "Des Esseintes is absolutely the richest and clearest example of Decadence" (*Studien,* 23). Erwin Koppen, who has written an excellent book on the reception of decadence in Germany, concurs with Bahr's view (*Dekadenter Wagnerismus* [Berlin: Walter de Gruyter, 1973], 36–37).

7. *Selbstbildnis,* 237.

8. Fritz Martini first established Bahr's importance for carrying decadence to Germany and Austria: "The Austrian critic Hermann Bahr had imported the concepts of Decadence and fin de siècle as literary formulas (modeled on the comedy *Fin de siècle* by Michard and Jouvenot in 1884)," in *Reallexikon der deutschen Literaturgeschichte,* vol. 1, ed. Paul Merker and Wolfgang Stammler, 2d ed. (Berlin: Walter de Gruyter, 1958), 227. See also *Dekadenter Wagnerismus* by Erwin Koppen, who acknowledges Bahr's major role in the spread of decadence in Germany.

9. "Yet I may console myself, because it is still a nice thought and flattering that between the Volga and the Loire, from the Thames to the Guadalquivir, nothing is perceived today that I could not understand, analyze, and put into artistic form, and that the European soul has no secrets from me" ("Das junge Österreich," in *Studien,* 95).

10. "Villiers de l'Isle-Adam," in *Zur Kritik der Moderne* (Zurich, 1890), 1:196.

11. "Salon 1889," in ibid., 1:204–15.

12. In an essay "Zur Kritik der Kritik" Bahr calls for a new criticism to accompany the new trends in literature, and Lemaître is cited as a model of the desired modern style (ibid., 1:251–52).

13. "Salon 1889," in ibid., 1:214.

14. "Der Buddhismus," in *Die Überwindung des Naturalismus* (Dresden, 1891), 100.

15. "Die Überwindung des Naturalismus," in ibid., 152–60. This formulation earned Bahr the name "Der grosse Überwinder" among his contemporaries. Karl Kraus began his forty-year polemic against Bahr with an essay entitled "Die Überwindung des Hermann Bahr," *Die Gesellschaft* 9 (May 1893):627–36.

16. "Die Überwindung des Naturalismus," in *Die Überwindung des Naturalismus,* 157.

17. "Der Naturalismus im Frack," in ibid., 63.

18. See, for example, "Die Krisis im Naturalismus," in ibid., 72.

19. "Die Überwindung des Naturalismus," in ibid., 155.

20. "Salon 1889," in *Zur Kritik der Moderne* 1:214–15.

21. "Zur Kritik der Kritik," in ibid., 1:253.

22. Cf. "Puvis de Chavanne," in ibid., 1:241–47.

23. "Maurice Maeterlinck," in *Die Überwindung des Naturalismus,* 193.

24. Ibid., 196.

25. "Die Decadence," in *Studien,* 19–26; "Symbolisten," in ibid., 26–32; and "Satanismus," in ibid., 33–42.

26. "Die Decadence," in ibid., 19–20.

27. Ibid., 21–22.

28. "Maurice Barrès," in ibid., 162–77.

29. "Even closer to me than Huysmans was Maurice Barrès. No poet of my generation exerted such a profound influence on me, and again and again for twenty years. . . . I felt the inner connection so strongly, Barrès was so instantly familiar to me, even before I met him in person, that it seemed really almost as if he were my twin" (*Selbstbildnis,* 237–38). *Studien* is dedicated to Barrès.

30. "Decadence," in *Renaissance,* 11.

31. "Sacher-Masoch," in ibid., 107.

32. "Notiz 119" (1895), quoted in Josef Gregor, *Meister und Meisterbriefe um Hermann Bahr* (Vienna, 1947), 184.

33. *Selbstbildnis,* 239.

34. Otto Brahm, "Die gute Schule," *Freie Bühne für Modernes Leben* 1:616.

35. *Die gute Schule* (Berlin, 1890), 10.

36. Ibid., 11.

37. Ibid., 163.

38. Cf. Brahm, "Die gute Schule," 616–17.

39. *Die gute Schule,* 2d ed., ii–iii.

40. This story is based on Bahr's meeting with Viktor Adler in Paris, where he told the Marxist leader he was giving up politics. In his *Selbstbildnis* Bahr reported that Adler immediately noticed the profound change in him. "The Marxist had turned into an impassioned spiritualiste; since then he [Adler] no longer trusted any intellectual or artist in the party" (230).

41. The second printing was approved for sale in France but not in Germany.

42. This sentence played a vital role in Bahr's original reaction against naturalism and in his attraction to decadence: "We could not get beyond the incantation of Macbeth's witches with our new aesthetics. But why then did I sit for days and nights crossing out what I had written. Now I understood for the first time. Now it was confirmed to me through that sentence: 'Une phrase bien faite est une bonne action.' And now I recognized also that we in Berlin had completely misunderstood French naturalism. We interpreted it materialistically, we took it literally, we did not perceive that it was intended by the French only as a reaction against romanticism, as a means of returning to their classical tradition, even if by a marvelous detour" (*Selbstbildnis,* 223–24).

43. Erwin Koppen, *Dekadenter Wagnerismus* (Berlin: De Gruyter, 1973), 253.

44. *Studien,* 157.

45. *Selbstbildnis,* 257.

46. Bahr felt that the relationship between the mother and the clown was not properly understood: "That part about the third sex, about sexless

desire, about the substitution of common sexual organs by the more refined nerves, has been my idea for a long time. In *Die Mutter,* which nobody understood, there is a relationship between the mother and the clown that no one grasped. They have never desired each other; thus they can get along well with one another. Their souls can merge in pure and fervent impulses, because their bodies are held apart by different vices. But I hoped for such seraphic virtue at that time only from the ultimate degree of sin. It can probably happen that at the conclusion of long carnal pleasures and depravities a fresh and joyful race will be born" (*Russische Reise,* 132).

47. *Selbstbildnis,* 257.
48. *Studien,* 92.
49. *Russische Reise,* 1.
50. Ibid., 112–13.
51. Ibid., 172.
52. *Dora: Drei Novellen* (Berlin, 1893), 90.
53. *Selbstbildnis,* 236.
54. In his *Selbstbildnis* Bahr elaborated on his intentions: "I went so far in my indifference to form that the worst content seemed desirable, because precisely through this means form would have the best opportunity to show the miracle of its power. To one collection of novellas I gave the name *Caph.* Every content of an earthly existence appeared to me to be filth out of which the purest gold gleams when the artist touches it with the divine ray of form" (230).

Chapter Three

1. *Expressionismus* (Munich, 1916), 82.
2. *Selbstbildnis,* 280.
3. "Zehn Jahre," in *Bildung* (Berlin, 1900), 176.
4. *Liebe der Lebenden* 3 vols. (Hildesheim, 1921–23), 1:15.
5. *Selbstbildnis,* 277.
6. *Studien,* 77–78.
7. Felix Salten, "Aus den Anfängen," *Jahrbuch deutscher Bibliophilen und Literaturfreunde* 18–19 (1932–33):37.
8. *Selbstbildnis,* 282. For a detailed discussion of the relationship of Bahr and Schnitzler, see Donald G. Daviau, *The Letters of Arthur Schnitzler to Hermann Bahr* (Chapel Hill, 1978).
9. Willi Handl, *Hermann Bahr* (Berlin: S. Fischer, 1913), 37.
10. *Studien,* 95.
11. Eugen Wolff, "Zehn Charakteristiken," *Deutsche Universitäts-Zeitung* 1, no. 1 (1888).
12. "Die Herkunft der Weltanschauungen," in *Zur Kritik der Moderne,* 1:16.
13. Ibid., 1:17.

14. "Henrik Ibsen," in ibid., 1:65.
15. Ibid., 1:79.
16. "Die Krisis des Burgtheaters," in ibid., 1:141. See also "Zur Kritik der Kritik," in ibid., 1:250.
17. "Die Moderne," in *Die Überwindung des Naturalismus*, 2.
18. Ibid., 3.
19. Ibid., 6.
20. "Die Zukunft der Literatur," in *Studien*, 18–19.
21. "Bildende Kunst in Österreich," in ibid., 214.
22. "Die Duse," in ibid., 255.
23. "Das junge Österreich," in ibid., 87.
24. "Edouard Rod," in ibid., 155.
25. "Ferdinand von Saar," in ibid., 107.
26. Ibid., 108–9.
27. *Selbstbildnis*, 240.
28. Ibid., 284.
29. "Peter Altenberg," in *Renaissance*, 46–47.
30. "Schweine," in ibid., 186.
31. "Der Garten der Erkenntnis," in ibid., 44.
32. Ibid., 45. This same idea of seeking the harmonious unity of life recurred in "Ein Sonderling" (in *Renaissance*, 27).
33. "Johanna Ambrosius," in ibid., 90.
34. Ibid., 93.
35. "Orpheus," in ibid., 16.
36. "Entdeckung der Provinz," in *Bildung*, 191.
37. Preface to ibid., ix.
38. "Cultur," in ibid., 5.
39. Ibid., 6.
40. "Bei Goethe," in ibid., 16.
41. "Volksbildung," in ibid., 29.
42. Ibid., 34.
43. "Die plastische Kraft," in ibid., 97.
44. "'s Katherl," in *Wiener Theater* (Berlin, 1899), 492.
45. "Die Hauptstadt von Europa," in *Bildung*, 116–22.
46. *Selbstbildnis*, 277.
47. "Zehn Jahre," in *Bildung*, 176–77.
48. "'s Katherl," in *Wiener Theater*, 493.

Chapter Four

1. A representative view is that of Kristian Sotriffer: "Within the hundred years from 1860 to the present day, the Secession forms a peak of international importance in the arts" (*Modern Austrian Art* [New York: Praeger, 1965], 8).

2. "Malerisch," in *Studien*, 195.
3. For a concise view of historicism in Vienna see Sotriffer, *Modern Austrian Art*, 10–11.
4. *Hermann Bahr: Briefwechsel mit seinem Vater*, 417.
5. Ibid., 418.
6. Ludwig Hevesi, "Villa Bahr," in *Acht Jahre Secession* (Vienna: Carl Konegen, 1906), 515.
7. Christian M. Nebehay, *Ver Sacrum (1898–1903)* (Vienna: Edition Tusch, 1975, 25. See also Hans Ulrich Simon, *Secession* (Stuttgart: Metzler, 1976), 98–99.
8. Nebehay, *Ver Sacrum*, 35.
9. "Ver Sacrum," in *Secession*, 14; originally published under the title "Secession" in *Ver Sacrum*, January 1898, 8–13.
10. *Hermann Bahr: Briefwechsel mit seinem Vater*, 417.
11. Cf. "Theodor von Hörmann," in *Renaissance*, 230–37, and "Der erste Secessionist," in *Secession*, 101–8.
12. "Erste Ausstellung der Vereinigung bildender Künstler Österreichs," in *Secession*, 32.
13. "Malerei 1894," in *Renaissance*, 175.
14. "Schweine," and "Rothe Bäume," in *Renaissance*, 185–90 and 197–202, respectively.
15. "Malerei 1894," in *Renaissance*, 178–79.
16. These views are contained in the series of articles comprising "Bildende Kunst in Österreich," in *Studien*, 200–223.
17. "Künstlerhaus," in *Renaissance*, 223.
18. Ibid., 226–27.
19. Quoted in Christian M. Nebehay, *Gustav Klimt* (Munich: DTV, 1976), 29.
20. For more details on the history as well as the founding of the Secession see Robert Waissenberger, *Die Wiener Secession* (Munich: Jugend und Volk, 1971), especially 33–38; and Peter Vergo, *Art in Vienna 1898–1918* (New York: Phaidon Press, 1975), 18–44.
21. "Unsere Secession," in *Secession*, 8.
22. Nebehay, *Gustav Klimt*, 102. Reinhard Heller cites different figures: 56,802 visitors and half of the 410 exhibited works sold: "Recent Scholarship on Vienna's 'Golden Age,' Gustav Klimt, and Egon Schiele," *Art Bulletin*, March 1971, 112.
23. Franz Endler, *Das k. u. k. Wien* (Vienna: Überreuter, 1977), 76.
24. "Erste Kunstausstellung der Vereinigung bildender Künstler Österreichs," in *Secession*, 21.
25. "Im eigenen Hause," in ibid., 69.
26. "Vorwort," in ibid., vii.

27. Nicolas Powell, *The Sacred Spring: The Arts in Vienna 1898–1918* (London: Studio Vista, 1974), 63.
28. "Meister Olbrich," in *Secession*, 61.
29. Endler, *Das k. u. k. Wien*, 36.
30. "Im eigenen Haus," in *Secession*, 66–67.
31. Bahr met with Olbrich in Mainz in May 1900 to discuss the design of the theater: "the form of the building, the lighting, decoration, costumes, acting, acoustics . . ." (*Glossen*, 468). Bahr then wrote a programmatic essay to disseminate their plans. See "Ein Dokument," in ibid., 467–77.
32. "Ein Brief an die Secession," *Ver Sacrum* 4 (1901):238.
33. "Josef Olbrich," in *Buch der Jugend* (Vienna, 1908), 74.
34. "Im eigenen Haus," in *Secession*, 84–85.
35. Ibid., 86–87.
36. Ibid., 116.
37. "Malerei," in ibid., 121.
38. Ibid., 120.
39. "Die vierte Ausstellung," in ibid., 123–24.
40. Hans Weigel, *Karl Kraus oder die Macht der Ohnmacht* (Vienna: Fritz Molden, 1968), 264.
41. *Rede über Klimt* (Vienna, 1901), 12–13.
42. *Gegen Klimt*, Foreword by Hermann Bahr (Vienna: Eisenstein, 1903), 9. It is noteworthy that Bahr refused to include in this volume any of the critical remarks against Klimt by Kraus. Bahr never acknowledged Kraus's existence in any of his writings.
43. Ibid., 4.
44. "Architektur," in *Secession*, 40.
45. "Kunstgewerbe," in ibid., 33–34.
46. Ibid., 36.
47. *Tagebuch* (Berlin, 1909), 237–38.
48. "Das Landhaus," in *Secession*, 48–53. For an additional description of Bahr's villa, which no longer exists, see Ludwig Hevesi, "Villa Bahr," in *Acht Jahre Secession* (Vienna: Konegen, 1906), 512–16.
49. "Der englische Stil," in *Secession*, 187.

Chapter Five

1. *Wiener Theater* ii.
2. *Selbstbildnis*, 285.
3. *Zur Kritik der Moderne*, 250.
4. *Rezensionen* (Berlin, 1903), title page.
5. "Entsagung," *Wiener Theater*, 259.
6. In *Erinnerung an Burckhard* (Berlin, 1914), a warm testimonial to his friend, Bahr gave major credit to his production of Schiller's *Don*

Carlos, in which he applied the new style of acting developed for productions of Ibsen, Holz, and Hauptmann to a classical work. In opera, Burckhard's experiment was duplicated by Mahler, who applied the staging technique developed for Wagner to Mozart, and both influenced Reinhardt, who carried their ideas to fruition (101–3).

7. "Burgtheater," in *Wiener Theater*, 168–75.
8. "Die rothe Fahne," in *Wiener Theater*, 94; see also "Zwei glückliche Tage," in ibid., 206–7.
9. "Verismo," in ibid., 478.
10. "Niobe," in ibid., 17.
11. Ibid., 22.
12. "Adele Sandrock," in ibid., 65.
13. Ibid., 65–66.
14. Cf. Donald G. Daviau, "Experiments in Pantomine by the Major Writers of *Jung-Wien*," in *Österreich in amerikanischer Sicht* (New York: Austrian Institute, 1981), 19–26.
15. "Pantomime," in *Die Überwindung des Naturalismus*, 44–49.
16. "Sada Yacco," in *Rezensionen*, 207.
17. "Ein Dokument," in *Glossen*, 474.
18. "Der Philosoph des Impressionismus," in *Dialog vom Tragischen* (Berlin, 1904), 102–14. For a discussion of Mach's ideas see also "Das unrettbare Ich," in ibid., 79–101.
19. "Jugend von heute," in *Premièren* (Munich, 1902), 18.
20. "Zwei Eisen im Feuer," in ibid., 29–30.
21. Karl Kraus, *Die Fackel* 2, no. 69 (February 1901):7–8.
22. Herbert Nedomovsky compared the newspaper and book versions of Bahr's Volkstheater reviews and reported that he was unable to find any essential variation ("Der Theaterkritiker Hermann Bahr" [Ph.D. diss., University of Vienna, 1949]).
23. For a detailed analysis of these productions see Heinz Kindermann, *Hermann Bahr: Ein Leben für das europäische Theater* (Graz, 1954), 230–41.
24. Gregor, ed., *Meister und Meisterbriefe um Hermann Bahr*, Notiz 178, 20 December 1906, 197.
25. Ibid., Notiz 173, 9 December 1906, 196.
26. Ibid., 188.
27. Ibid., 155.
28. Leopold von Andrian, "Meine Tätigkeit als Generalintendant," *Neue Freie Presse*, 28 October 1928, 1.
29. Heinz Kindermann, *Das Burgtheater* (Leipzig: Adolph Luser, 1939), 12.
30. *Kritik der Gegenwart* (Augsburg, 1922), 5.
31. Daviau, ed., *The Letters of Arthur Schnitzler to Hermann Bahr*, 117.

32. "*Die natürliche Tochter,*" in *Glossen,* 463.
33. *Kriegssegen,* 47.
34. "Burgtheater," in *Neue Freie Presse,* 17 November 1918.
35. Cf. his comments in *Österreich in Ewigkeit* (Hildesheim, 1929), 107.
36. *Liebe der Lebenden,* 2:130.
37. "Goethebild," in *Sendung des Künstlers* (Leipzig, 1923), 40.
38. Ibid., 39.
39. *1919* (Leipzig, 1920), 307-8.
40. Ibid., 319.
41. *Burgtheater* (Vienna, 1920), 15.
42. Ibid., 14.
43. Ibid., 15. Bahr repeated in *Schauspielkunst* (Leipzig, 1923) the idea that a public that had learned to participate in the theater would become more closely knit as a nation. For the theater to accomplish this unifying function the spectator "must not simply attend the play, he must also participate in the play" (32).
44. "Goethebild," in *Sedung des Künstlers,* 41.
45. Gregor, ed., *Meister und Meisterbriefe um Hermann Bahr,* letter of 26 July 1918 (180).
46. *Liebe der Lebenden,* 1:195.
47. Ibid., 182.

Chapter Six

1. *Selbstbildnis,* 292.
2. *Theater* (Berlin, 1897), 222; hereafter cited in the text as *T.*
3. Cf. the essays "Maximen" and "Ekstase," in *Dialog vom Tragischen,* 115-19, 131-39.
4. *Die Rahl* (Berlin, 1908), 61; hereafter cited in the text as *R.*
5. *Drut* (Berlin, 1909), 530; hereafter cited in the text as *D.*
6. *O Mensch* (Berlin, 1910), 241-42; hereafter cited in the text as *OM.*
7. *Himmelfahrt* (Berlin, 1916), 353; hereafter cited in the text as *H.*
8. *Die Rotte Korahs* (Berlin, 1919), 139-40; hereafter cited as *RK.*
9. Bahr had devoted the year 1918 to the study of Stifter. The year 1919 was dedicated to Walt Whitman, "a Stifter on a grand scale, with broader horizons . . . supranational . . . and timeless. Whitman has everything we need, precisely we, precisely now" (*1919,* 27-28).
10. *Der inwendige Garten* (Hildesheim, 1927), 160; hereafter cited in the text as *IG.*
11. *Osterreich in Ewigkeit,* motto on title page; hereafter cited in the text as *OE.*

Chapter Seven

1. *Selbstbildnis,* 287.
2. "Ein unbeschriebenes Blatt," in *Wiener Theater,* 336.
3. "Verismo," in *Wiener Theater,* 481–82.
4. For a detailed treatment see Donald G. Daviau, "Hermann Bahr's *Josephine:* A Revisionist View of Napoleon," *Modern Austrian Literature* 12, no. 2 (1979):93–111.
5. *Josephine* (Berlin, 1898), vii–viii.
6. *Der Athlet* (Bonn, 1899), 48.
7. Ibid., 147.
8. *Die Wienerinnen* (Bonn, 1900), 130.
9. *Der Franzl* (Vienna, 1900), 375.
10. *Der Meister* (Berlin, 1904), 107–8.
11. Willi Handl, *Hermann Bahr* (Berlin: S. Fischer, 1913), 146.
12. *Sanna* (Berlin, 1905), 121–22.
13. Gregor, ed., *Meister und Meisterbriefe um Hermann Bahr,* 166.
14. The ending alludes to the revolution on "Bloody Sunday," 22 January 1905, when imperial troops fired on strikers assembled before the palace of Nicholas II, an example of how Bahr incorporated current events into his works.
15. *Die Andere* (Berlin, 1906), 94.
16. Ibid., 101–2.
17. Ibid., 15.
18. *Inventur* (Berlin, 1912), 47.
19. Daviau, ed., *The Letters of Arthur Schnitzler to Hermann Bahr,* 89.
20. *Der arme Narr* (Vienna, 1906), 89.
21. *Glossen,* 129.
22. *Der arme Narr,* 88–89.
23. *Der Klub der Erlöser,* in *Grotesken* (Vienna, 1907), 42.
24. *Tagebuch,* 26–27.
25. Cf. Friedrich Düsel, *Berliner Theater* 20, no. 1 (1906–7):470–71.
26. *Die gelbe Nachtigall* (Berlin, 1907), 193.
27. *Selbstbildnis,* 288.
28. For a more detailed discussion of this and other plays by Bahr on the American stage see Daviau, "Hermann Bahr's Cultural Relations with America," 487–522.
29. *Das Konzert* (Berlin, 1909), 131.
30. Cf. Gregor, ed., *Meister und Meisterbriefe um Hermann Bahr,* 49–144.
31. Karl Berger, "Das Phantom," *Bühne und Welt* 16, no. 1 (1913–14):327.
32. *Der Querulant* (Munich, 1914), 54.

33. *Die Stimme* (Berlin, 1916), 104.
34. Ibid., 122.
35. Gregor, ed., *Meister und Meisterbriefe um Hermann Bahr,* Notiz 180, 7 January 1907, 198.
36. Edward Castle, "Die neue Generation um Hermann Bahr," in *Deutsch-österreichische Literaturgeschichte,* ed. J. Nagl, J. Zeidler, and E. Castle, vol. 4 (Vienna: Carl Fromm, 1937), 1697–98.

Selected Bibliography

PRIMARY SOURCES

1. Bibliographies

Nimmervoll, Hermann. "Materialien zu einer Bibliographie der Zeitschriftenartikel von Hermann Bahr (1883–1910)." *Modern Austrian Literature* 13, no. 2 (1980):27–110.
Thomasberger, Kurt. "Bibliographie der Werke von Hermann Bahr." In *Ein Leben für das europäische Theater,* edited by Heinz Kindermann, 347–68. Graz-Cologne: Böhlau, 1954.

2. Works

Die Einsichtslosigkeit des Herrn Schäffle: Drei Briefe an einen Volksmann. Zürich: Schäbelitz, 1886.
Die neuen Menschen: Ein Schauspiel. Zürich: Schäbelitz, 1887.
La Marquesa d'Amaëgui: Eine Plauderei. Zürich: Schäbelitz, 1888.
Die grosse Sünde: Ein bürgerliches Trauerspiel. Zürich: Schäbelitz, 1889.
Zur Kritik der Moderne. Zürich: Schäbelitz, 1890.
Die gute Schule: Roman. Berlin: S. Fischer, 1890.
Fin de Siècle. Berlin: Ad. Zoberbier, 1891.
Die Mutter: Drama. Berlin: Sallisscher Verlag, 1891.
Die Überwindung des Naturalismus: Zweite Folge von "Zur Kritik der Moderne." Dresden: Pierson, 1891.
Russische Reise. Dresden: Pierson, 1893.
Die häusliche Frau: Lustspiel. Berlin: S. Fischer, 1893.
Dora: Drei Novellen. Berlin: S. Fischer, 1893.
Neben der Liebe: Roman. Berlin: S. Fischer, 1893.
Der Antisemitismus. Berlin: S. Fischer, 1893.
Aus der Vorstadt: Volksstück. Vienna: Konegen, 1893. W. H. C. Karlweis.
Caph: Skizzen. Berlin: S. Fischer, 1894.
Studien zur Kritik der Moderne. Frankfurt: Rütten & Loening, 1894.
Die Nixe: Drama. Munich: Rubinverlag, 1896.
Juana: Drama. Munich: Rubinverlag, 1896.
Renaissance: Neue Studien zur Kritik der Moderne. Berlin: S. Fischer, 1897.
Tschaperl: Ein Wiener Stück. Berlin: S. Fischer, 1897.
Theater: Roman. Berlin: S. Fischer, 1897.
Josephine: Ein Spiel. Berlin: S. Fischer, 1898.

Der Star: Ein Wiener Stück. Berlin: S. Fischer, 1898.
Wiener Theater (1892—1898). Berlin: S. Fischer, 1899.
Die schöne Frau: Novellen. Berlin: S. Fischer, 1899.
Der Athlet: Schauspiel. Bonn: Albert Ahn, 1899.
Wienerinnen: Lustspiel. Bonn: Albert Ahn, 1900.
Secession: Essays. Vienna: Wiener, 1900.
Der Franzl: Fünf Bilder eines guten Mannes. Vienna: Wiener, 1900.
Bildung: Essays. Berlin: Schuster & Loeffler, 1900.
Der Apostel: Schauspiel. Munich: Albert Langen, 1901.
Rede über Klimt. Vienna: Wiener, 1901.
Der Krampus: Lustspiel. Munich: Albert Langen, 1902.
Wirkung in die Ferne: Novellen. Vienna: Wiener, 1902.
Premièren. Munich: Albert Langen, 1902.
Rezensionen (Wiener Theater 1901—1903). Berlin: S. Fischer, 1903.
Dialog vom Tragischen. Berlin: S. Fischer, 1904.
Der Meister: Komödie. Berlin: S. Fischer, 1904.
Unter sich: Ein Arme-Leut'-Stück. Vienna: Wiener, 1904.
Sanna: Schauspiel. Berlin: S. Fischer, 1905.
Dialog vom Marsyas. Berlin: Bard, Marquardt & Co., 1905.
Die Andere: Schauspiel. Berlin: S. Fischer, 1906.
Der arme Narr: Schauspiel. Vienna: Konegan, 1906.
Josef Kainz: Monographie. Vienna: Wiener, 1906.
Glossen zum Wiener Theater (1903—1906). Berlin: S. Fischer, 1907.
Ringelspiel: Komödie. Berlin: S. Fischer, 1907.
Grotesken (Der Klub der Erlöser; Der Faun; Der arme Narr). Vienna: Konegen, 1907.
Wien (In der Sammlung "Städte und Landschaften"). Stuttgart: Carl Krabbe, 1907.
Die gelbe Nachtigall: Lustspiel. Berlin: S. Fischer, 1907.
Die Rahl: Roman. Berlin: S. Fischer, 1908.
Stimmen des Bluts: Novellen. Berlin: S. Fischer, 1908.
Tagebuch. Berlin: Paul Cassirer, 1909.
Buch der Jugend: Essays. Vienna: Heller, 1908.
Drut: Roman. Berlin: S. Fischer, 1909.
Dalmatinische Reise. Berlin: S. Fischer, 1909.
Das Konzert: Lustspiel. Berlin: Reiss, 1909.
O Mensch: Roman. Berlin: S. Fischer, 1910.
Die Kinder: Komödie. Berlin: S. Fischer, 1911.
Das Tänzchen: Lustspiel. Berlin: S. Fischer, 1911.
Austriaca: Essays. Berlin: S. Fischer, 1911.
Das Prinzip: Lustspiel. Berlin: S. Fischer, 1912.
Inventur: Essays. Berlin: S. Fischer, 1912.
Essays. Leipzig: Insel, 1912.

Selected Bibliography 159

Parsifalschütz ohne Ausnahmegesetz. Berlin: Schuster & Loeffler, 1912.
Bayreuth (von Anna Mildenburg and Hermann Bahr). Leipzig: Rowohlt, 1912.
Das Phantom: Komödie. Berlin: S. Fischer, 1913.
Das Hermann Bahr-Buch. Berlin: S. Fischer, 1913.
Dostojewski: Essays. Munich: Piper, 1914.
Der Querulant: Komödie. Munich: Delphin, 1914.
Erinnerung an Burckhard. Berlin: S. Fischer, 1914.
Kriegssegen. Munich: Delphin, 1914.
Salzburg. Berlin: Bard, 1914.
Das Osterreichische Wunder. Stuttgart: "Die Lese," 1915.
Rudigier. Kempten: Kösel, 1915.
Der lustige Seifensieder. Berlin: S. Fischer, 1915.
Expressionismus. Munich: Delphin, 1916.
Himmelfahrt: Roman. Berlin: S. Fischer, 1916.
Die Stimme. Berlin: S. Fischer, 1916.
Um Goethe: Essays. Vienna: Urania, 1917.
Schwarz-Gelb. Berlin: S. Fischer, 1917.
Vernunft und Wissenschaft. Innsbruck: Tyrolia, 1917.
Der Augenblick (nach Goethe). Berlin: Ahn & Simrock, 1917.
1917: Tagebuch. Innsbruck: Verlagsanstalt Tyrolia, 1918.
Adalbert Stifter: Eine Entdeckung. Vienna: Amalthea, 1918.
1918: Tagebuch. Innsbruck: Verlagsanstalt Tyrolia, 1919.
Die rotte Korahs: Roman. Berlin: S. Fischer, 1919.
1919: Tagebuch. Leipzig: Tal, 1920.
Ehelei. Berlin: Ahn & Simrock, 1920.
Der Unmensch. Berlin: Erich Reiss, 1920.
Spielerei. Berlin: Ahn & Simrock, 1920.
Burgtheater (In der Sammlung "Theater und Kultur"). Vienna: Wiener literarische Anstalt, 1920.
Summula. Leipzig: Insel, 1921.
Bilderbuch. Vienna: Wiener literarische Anstalt, 1921.
Liebe der Lebenden. 3 vols. Hildesheim: Borgmeyer, 1921–23.
Kritik der Gegenwart. Augsburg: Haas & Grabherr, 1922.
Sendung des Künstlers. Leipzig: Insel, 1923.
Selbstbildnis. Berlin: S. Fischer, 1923.
Schauspielkunst. Leipzig: Zellenbücherei, Dürr, & Weber, 1923.
Notizen zur neueren spanischen Literatur. Berlin: Stilke, 1926.
Der Zauberstab: Tagebucher von 1924 bis 1926. Hildesheim: Borgmeyer, 1926.
Der inwendige Garten. Hildesheim: Borgmeyer, 1927.
Himmel auf Erden. Munich: Verlag ars Sacra, Josef Müller, 1928.
Das Labyrinth der Gegenwart. Hildesheim: Borgmeyer, 1929.

Österreich in Ewigkeit. Hildesheim: Borgmeyer, 1929.
Die Hexe Drut. New ed. Munich: Siebenstäbeverlag, 1929.

3. Collections

Mensch, werde wesentlich. Edited by Anna Bahr-Mildenburg. Graz: Styria, 1934.
Essays. Edited by Heinz Kindermann. Vienna: H. Bauer, 1962.
Kritiken. Edited by Heinz Kindermann. Vienna: H. Bauer, 1963.
Sinn hinter der Komödie. Edited by Rudolf Holzer. Graz: Stiasny, 1965.
Zur Uberwindung des Naturalismus. Edited by Gotthart Wunberg. Stuttgart: Kohlhammer, 1968.
Das junge Wien: Österreichische Literatur- und Kunstkritik. Edited by Gotthart Wunberg. 2 vols. Tübingen: Niemeyer, 1976. Includes 134 essays of Bahr, 1887–1902.

4. Correspondence

Daviau, Donald G., ed. *The Letters of Arthur Schitzler to Hermann Bahr.* Chapel Hill: University of North Carolina Press, 1978.
Fellner, Fritz, ed. *Dichter und Gelehrter: Hermann Bahr und Josef Redlich in ihren Briefen, 1896–1934.* Salzburg: Neugebauer, 1980.
Gregor, Joseph, Ed. *Meister und Meisterbriefe um Hermann Bahr.* Vienna: Bauer, 1947.
Hirsch, Rudolf, ed. "Hugo von Hofmannsthal und Hermann Bahr: Zwei Briefe." *Phaidros* 1 (1947):85–88.
Schmidt, Adalbert, ed. *Hermann Bahr: Briefwechsel mit seinem Vater.* Vienna: Bauer, 1971.

SECONDARY SOURCES

Andrian, Leopold Freiherr von. "Meine Tätigkeit als Generalintendant der Wiener Hoftheater." *Neue Freie Presse,* 28 October, 4, 8 November 1928.
Brecker, Egon W. "Hermann Bahr and the Quest for Culture: A Critique of his Essays." Ph.D. dissertation, University of Wisconsin, Madison, 1978.
Burdach, Konrad. "Wissenschaft und Journalismus (Betrachtungen über und für Hermann Bahr)." *Preussische Jahrbücher* 193 (1923):17–31.
Chandler, Frank W. "The Austrian Contribution: Schnitzler, Bahr, Schönherr, von Hofmannsthal." In *Modern Continental Playwrights,* 345–65. New York: Harper & Row, 1931.
Chastel, Emile. "Hermann Bahr, son oeuvre et son temps." 2 vols. Ph.D. dissertation, University of Paris, 1974.

Selected Bibliography 161

Cysarz, Herbert. "Alt-Österreichs letzte Dichtung, 1890–1914." *Preussische Jahrbücher* 211 (1928):32–51.

Daviau, Donald G. "*Dialog vom Marsyas:* Hermann Bahr's Affirmation of Life over Art." *Modern Language Quarterly* 20 (December 1959):360–70.

———. "Experiments in Pantomime by the Major Writers of *Jung-Wien*." In *Österreich in amerikanischer Sicht,* 19–26. New York: Austrian Institute, 1981.

———. "The Friendship of Hermann Bahr and Arthur Schnitzler." *Journal of the International Arthur Schnitzler Research Association* 5 (Spring, 1966):4–37.

———. "Hermann Bahr and Decadence." *Modern Austrian Literature* 10, no. 2 (June 1977):53–100.

———. "Hermann Bahr and Gustav Klimt." *German Studies Review* 3, no. 1 (February 1980):27–49.

———. "Hermann Bahr and the Radical Politics of Austria in the 1880s." *German Studies Review* 5, no. 2 (May 1982):163–85.

———. "Hermann Bahr and the Secessionist Art Movement in Vienna." In *The Turn of the Century German Literature and Art, 1890–1915,* edited by Gerald Chapple and Hans H. Schulte, 433–62. Bonn: Bouvier, 1981.

———. "Hermann Bahr as Director of the Burgtheater." *The German Quarterly* 32 (January 1959):11–21.

———. "Hermann Bahr's Cultural Relations with America." In *Österreich und die angelsächsische Welt II,* edited by O. Hietsch, 482–522. Vienna: Braumüller, 1968.

———. "Hermann Bahr's *Josephine:* A Revisionist View of Napoleon." *Modern Austrian Literature* 12, no. 2 (June 1979):93–111.

———. "Hermann Bahr's Nachlass." *Journal of the International Arthur Schnitzler Research Association* 2 (Autumn 1963):4–27.

———. "The Misconception of Hermann Bahr as a Verwandlungskünstler." *German Life and Letters* 11 (April 1958):182–92.

———. "The Significance of Hermann Bahr to Austria." Ph.D. dissertation, University of California, Berkeley, 1955.

Diersch, Manfred. "Hermann Bahr: Der Empiriokritizismus als Philosophie des Impressionismus." In *Empiriokritizismus und Impressionismus,* 46–82. Berlin: Rütten & Loening, 1973.

Drake, William A. "Hermann Bahr." In *Contemporary European Writers,* 184–91. New York: John Day, 1928.

Ende, Amelia V. "Literary Vienna." *Bookman* 38 (September 1913–February 1914):141–55.

Hirsch, Otto Michel. "Hermann Bahr, der Novellist und Dramatiker." *Xenien* 2, no. 11 (1909):279–89.

Hofmannsthal, Hugo von. "Die Mutter." In *Prosa I*, 16–23. Frankfurt am Main: S. Fischer, 1950.

———. "Zum Direktionswechsel im Burgtheater." *Neue Freie Presse*, 5 July 1918, 1–2.

Jahnichen, Manfred. "Hermann Bahr und die Tschechen." In *Slawische-Deutsche Wechselbeziehungen in Sprache, Literatur und Kultur*, edited by W. Kraus, J. Belic, and V. I. Borkovskij, 363–77. Berlin: Akademie Verlag, 1969.

Kindermann, Heinz. *Hermann Bahr: Ein Leben für das europäische Theater*. Graz: Böhlau, 1954.

Kronegger, M. E. "L'écrivain dans une Société en mutation. Le cas de Hermann Bahr (1863–1933)." *Literaturwissenschaftliches Jahrbuch* 20 (1979):173–82.

Lehner, Friedrich. "Hermann Bahr." *Monatshefte* 39, no. 1 (1947):54–62.

Macken, Mary M. "Chronicle: Hermann Bahr, 1863–1934." *Studies: An Irish Quarterly Review* 23 (March 1934):144–46.

———. "Hermann Bahr: His Personality and his Works." *Studies: An Irish Quarterly Review* 15, no. 57 (March 1926):34–46.

Meridies, Wilhelm. *Hermann Bahr als epischer Gestalter und Kritiker der Gegenwart*. Hildesheim: Borgmeyer, 1927.

———. "Hermann Bahrs religiöser Entwicklungsgang." *Das heilige Feuer* 15 (March 1928):270–78.

Nadler, Josef. "Vom alten zum neuen Europa." *Preussische Jahrbücher* 193 (1923):32–51.

———. "Hermann Bahr und das katholische Österreich." *Die neue Rundschau* 34 (1923):490–502.

———. *Literaturgeschichte Österreichs*, 397–406, 414–16. Salzburg: Müller, 1951.

Nagl, J., Zeidler, J., and Castle, E. *Deutsch-Österreichische Literaturgeschichte*, 1649–1702. Vienna: Fromm, 1937.

Nirschl, Karl. *In seinen Menschen ist Österreich: Hermann Bahrs innerer Weg*. Linz: Oberösterreichischer Landesverlag, 1964.

Oswald, Victor, A. "The Old Age of Young Vienna." *Germanic Review* 27, no. 3 (October 1952):188–99.

Pollard, Percival. "Bahr and Finis." In *Masks and Minstrels of New Germany*, 290–99. Boston: John W. Luce, 1911.

Romero, Christine Zehl. "Die konservative Revolution: Hermann Bahr und Adalbert Stifter." *Germanische-Romanische Monatsschrift* 56 (1975):439–54.

Salten, Felix. "Aus den Anfängen, Erinnerungskizzen." *Jahrbuch deutscher Bibliophilen* 18–19 (1932–33):31–46.

Simmons, Robert Edward. "Hermann Bahr as a Literary Critic: An Analysis and Exposition of his Thought." Ph.D. dissertation, Stanford University, 1956.
Sprengler, Joseph. "Hermann Bahr—der Weg in seinen Dramen." *Hochland* 2 (1928):352–66.
———. "Hermann Bahr Tagebücher." *Das literarischer Echo* 22 (1919–20):262–65.
Wagner, Peter. *Der junge Hermann Bahr.* Giessen: Druck der Limburger Vereinsdruckerei, 1937.
Widder, Erich. *Hermann Bahr: Sein Weg zum Glauben.* Linz: Oberösterreichischer Landesverlag, 1963.

Index

Adler, Viktor, 5, 148n40; *Die Gleichheit*, 5
Alt, Rudolf von, 62
Altenberg, Peter, 53, 68
Ambrosius, Johanna, 49
Andrian, Leopold von, 11, 18, 48, 49, 82, 83; *Der Garten der Erkenntnis*, 49
Arendt, Wilhelm, 40; *Moderne Dichtercharaktere*, 40
Auernheimer, Raoul, 20, 79; *Das Wirthaus zur verlorenen Zeit*, 20
Auspitzer, Emil, 10

Bach, Johann Sebastian, 86
Bahr, Alois, 1
Bahr, Engelbert, 1
Bahr, Hermann:

WORKS—DIARIES:
Tagebuch (1909), 16, 96

WORKS—DRAMAS:
Altweibersommer, 138
Die Andere, 125, 126–28, 131, 138
Der Apostel, 12, 120–21, 134
Der arme Narr, 128, 138
Der Athlet, 13, 116, 117, 118, 122
Der Augenblick, 137
Aus der Vorstadt, 115
Ehelei, 137
Der Franzl, 11, 12, 119, 124, 136, 138
Die gelbe Nachtigall, 78, 81, 131
Die grosse Sünde, 7, 8, 115
Grotesken (Der Klub der Erlöser, Der Faun, Der arme Narr), 93, 98, 129, 130, 131, 133, 138
Die häusliche Frau, 115
Josephine, 13, 116, 117
Juana, 115
Die Kinder, 134
Das Konzert, 114, 132–33, 138, 143
Der Krampus, 12, 96, 121–22, 123
Der liebe Augustin, 77
La Marquesa d'Amaëgui, 115
Der Meister, 12, 13, 115, 122–23, 138
Der Minister, 77
Der muntere Seifensieder, 135

Die Mutter, 8, 9, 10, 23, 31, 32, 115, 148–49n46
Die neuen Menschen, 5, 7, 115, 125
Die Nixe, 115
Pantomime vom braven Manne, 77
Das Phantom, 134
Das Prinzip, 99, 134
Der Querulant, 134–35
Ringelspiel, 81, 130–31, 132, 133
Sanna, 12, 95, 96, 123–25, 136, 138
Spielerei (Spielerei, Der Selige, Der Umsturz), 137
Der Star, 78, 117–18, 131–38
Die Stimme, 19, 136, 138
Die Tante, 138
Das Tänzchen, 134
Tschaperl, 114, 116
Der Unmensch, 14, 137, 138
Unter sich, 12, 123
Wienerinnen, 11, 118–19

WORKS—ESSAYS:
Austriaca, 96
Bayreuth (von Anna Mildenburg and Hermann Bahr), 14
Bildung, 11, 12, 48, 51, 52, 53, 54
Buch der Jugend, 92, 95, 96, 99, 120, 123
Burgtheater, 19, 86, 88
Dalmatinische Reise, 16, 96
Dialog vom Marsyas, 12, 13, 76, 125
Dialog vom Tragischen, 12, 13, 80
Die Einsichtslosigkeit des Herrn Schäffle, 5
Expressionismus, 19
Inventur, 14, 46, 54, 100, 101, 103, 134
Kriegssegen, 17, 84, 103, 135
Notizen zur neueren spanischen Literatur, 8, 79
Das österreichische Wunder, 18, 103, 135
Renaissance, 11, 32, 48, 49, 50, 76
Rudigier, 18
Russische Reise, 9, 23, 32, 33
Schwarzgelb, 18
Secession, 11, 48, 63, 119
Selbstbildnis, 1, 20
Sendung des Künstlers, 19
Schauspielkunst, 19, 78, 88

Index

Studien zur Kritik der Moderne, 11, 39, 40, 45, 46, 53
Die Überwindung des Naturalismus, 7, 25, 40, 43, 44
Um Goethe, 75, 137
Vernunft und Wissenschaft, 19, 102
Wien, 14, 96, 99, 123, 129, 131
Zur Kritik der Moderne, 8, 42, 43, 44

WORKS—INDIVIDUAL ESSAYS:
"Adalbert von Goldschmidt," 45
"An das Publikum," 74
"Bildende Kunst in Österreich," 46
"Der Buddhismus," 24
"Cultur," 51
"Decadence," 26, 48
"Die Dekadenz," 45
"Ein Amt der Entdeckung," 54
"Entdeckung der Provinz," 11
"Erleben," 54
"Die falsche Secession," 65
"Ferdinand von Saar," 45
"Geschichte der modernen Malerei," 42
"Die Hauptstadt Europa," 53
"Henrik Ibsen," 42
"Die Herkunft der Weltanschauungen," 42
"Das junge Österreich," 39, 45
"Das jüngste Deutschland," 45
"Die Krisis im Burgtheater," 43
"Kritik," 45
"Das Landhaus," 68
"Loris," 45
"Die Moderne," 36, 43
"Der neue Stil," 46
"Der Naturalismus im Frack," 25
"Das österreichische Wunder," 103
"Der Philosoph des Impressionismus," 125
"Die plastische Kraft," 52
"Salon 1889," 24
"Satanismus," 45
"Stelzhamer," 120
"Die Symbolisten," 45
"Über Rodbertus," 5
"Die Überwindung des Naturalismus," 24
"Das unrettbare Ich," 125
"Ver Sacrum," 58
"Vernunft und Glaube," 19, 102
"Venunft und Wissenschaft," 102
"Vom jüngsten Frankreich," 45
"Die Weltanschauung des Individualismus," 42
"Zehn Jahre," 53

WORKS—NOVELS AND NARRATIVE PROSE:
Caph, 24, 33, 46, 149n54
Dora (Dora, Jeanette, Die Schneiderin), 24, 32, 33
Drut, 90, 95–98, 99, 103, 104, 116
Fin de siècle (Niklaus der Verräter, Der verständige Herr), 8, 9, 30, 31, 34
Die gute Schule, 8, 23, 27, 29, 30, 33, 56, 90, 138
Himmelfahrt, 19, 90, 100–103, 104, 107, 136
Der inwendige Garten, 90, 108–10
Neben der Liebe, 23, 29, 30, 32, 90
O Mensch, 90, 98–100, 102, 104, 110, 116, 134
Österreich in Ewigkeit, 90, 110–12
Die Rahl, 78, 90, 92, 94–95, 98, 102, 105, 107, 116, 123
Die Rotte Korahs, 90, 103–108, 142
Theater, 13, 78, 90, 91–92, 94, 116, 117, 131
Wirkung in die Ferne (Der Garten, Die Menschen), 12, 13

WORKS—THEATER REVIEWS:
Glossen zum Wiener Theater (1903–1906), 48, 71
Premièren, 12, 48, 71
Rezensionen (Wiener Theater, 1901–1903), 12, 48, 71
Wiener Theater (1892–1898), 11, 48, 70, 71, 72

Bahr, Wilhelmine, 2
Bahr-Mildenburg, Anna, 14, 15, 20, 21, 81, 102, 109, 127, 146n26
Balzac, Honoré, 90; *Comédie Humaine,* 90
Barrès, Maurice, 7, 8, 26, 27, 33, 36, 50, 75; *Les Déracinés,* 50
Bauernfeld, Eduard, 114, 122; *Leichtsinn aus Liebe,* 114
Beer-Hofmann, Richard, 18, 36, 38, 53, 76, 83, 140; *Der Tod Georgs,* 76; *Jaákobs Traum,* 83, 84
Bernhardt, Sarah, 78
Bettelheim, Anton, 73
Bing, Samuel, 67
Blake, William, 49
Blei, Franz, 68
Bleibtreu, Karl, 117
Blumenthal, Oskar, 74; *Niobe,* 74
Böcklin, Arnold, 59

Bourget, Paul, 25
Brahm, Otto, 9, 27, 70, 72
Breuer, Josef, 124
Bukowics von Kiss-Alacska, Emmerich, 79, 80
Burckhard, Max, 11, 35, 57, 72, 73, 83, 85, 88, 121, 152–53n6

Calderon de la Barca, Pedro, 78, 79; *Hombre pobre todo es trazas*, 78
Carrès, Michel, 76; *L'enfant prodigue*, 76
Castle, Eduard, 138, 143, 153
Chamberlain, Houston Stewart, 36; *Foundations of the 19th Century*, 36
Conrad, Michael Georg, 6
Conradi, Hermann, 46
Crane, Walter, 59, 67

Dante Alighieri, 75
Degas, Edgar, 25
Devrient, Max, 82
Dietrichstein, Leo, 132
Dörmann, Felix, 37
Dumas, Alexandre, 122
Duse, Eleonora, 9, 46, 70, 74, 78

Ebner-Eschenbach, Marie von, 35
Egidy, Moriz von, 52
Endler, Franz, 62
Engelhart, Josef, 65
Ernst, Otto, 78; *Jugend von heute*, 78
Ernst-Ludwig, Großherzog von Hessen, 51, 59, 64
Ewers, Hanns Heinz, 68

Felix, Eugen, 61
Feuchtersleben, Ernst Freiherr von, 53
Fontane, Theodor, 35
Franz Ferdinand, Erzherzog, 101
Freie Bühne, 8, 9, 25, 27, 38
Freie Bühne (Wien), 38
Freud, Sigmund, 124

Ganghofer, Ludwig, 10
Gervex, Henri, 25
Ghil, René, 26
Girardi, Alexander, 74
Goethe, Johann Wolfgang, 7, 8, 12, 19, 47, 49, 52, 75, 78, 83, 84, 85, 86, 95, 102, 110, 129, 137, 141; *Faust II*, 86; *Der Mann von fünfzig Jahren*, 137; *Die natürliche Tochter*, 83, 84, 85
Goldoni, Carlo, 121; *Burbero benefico*, 121

Goldschmidt, Adalbert von, 38
Gregor, Joseph, 81
Greinz, Rudolf, 50
Grillparzer, Franz, 53, 78, 93, 99, 108, 141; *Sappho*, 93

Halm, Friedrich, 78
Handl, Willi, 38
Hartleben, Otto Erich, 75
Hauptmann, Gerhart, 25, 72, 75; *Vor Sonnenaufgang*, 25
Heine, Albert, 83, 84, 88
Hevesi, Ludwig, 58, 59, 79
Heyden, Hubert von, 49, 60
Heyse, Paul, 40
Hirth, Georg, 62
Hitler, Adolf, 21, 110, 111
Hoffmann, E. T. A., 78
Hoffmann, Josef, 35, 61, 66, 68
Hoffmann, Ludwig von, 60
Hofmannsthal, Hugo von, 10, 11, 12, 17, 18, 19, 21, 35, 36, 37, 38, 39, 46, 48, 49, 57, 60, 75, 76, 82, 87, 88, 118, 123, 124, 125, 130, 138, 140, 142; *Everyman*, 82; *Gestern*, 39; *Jedermann*, 87; *Österreichische Bibliothek*, 17
Holz, Arno, 5, 8, 9, 40; *Buch der Zeit*, 40; "Modern," 40
Hörmann, Theodor von, 59, 60
Huysmans, Joris-Karl, 7, 23; *A Rebours*, 7, 23, 27

Ibsen, Henrik, 5, 37, 42, 43, 65, 72, 81, 116, 122; *Doll's House*, 116; *Hedda Gabler*, 81; *Komödie der Liebe*, 81; *The Pretenders*, 37

Jenny, Urs, 50
Joachim, Jacques, 37, 38
Jokl (Joël), Rosa, 14, 15
Jones, Edward Byrne, 67
Jugendstil, 62, 63
Jung-Wien, 6, 12, 36, 37, 53, 57, 59, 69, 116, 140, 143

Kafka, Eduard Michael, 10, 36, 37, 38; *Moderne Dichtung*, 10, 36, 37
Kahane, Arthur, 38
Kainz, Josef, 9, 35, 74, 128
Kanner, Heinrich, 10, 11
Kant, Immanuel, 19
Karlweis, Carl, 115
Kessler, Harry, 81

Index

Khnopff, Ferdinand, 59
Kienzl, Hermann, 79
Kindermann, Heinz, 143
Klimt, Gustav, 11, 35, 58, 61, 62, 65, 66, 67, 69
Klinger, Friedrich Maximilian, 59
Koppen, Wolfgang, 31
Korff, Arnold, 37
Kornfeld, Paul, 83; *Himmel und Hölle*, 83
Kralik, Richard, 35
Kraus, Karl, 11, 16, 17, 21, 37, 66, 79, 80, 140, 141, 143, 147n15, 152n42; *Die demolirte Literatur*, 37; *Die Fackel*, 16, 79
Kulka, Julius, 37
Künstlerhaus Genossenschaft, 57, 58, 59, 61
Kürnberger, Ferdinand von, 44

Lagarde, Paul de, 52
Langbehn, Julius, 40; *Rembrandt als Erzieher*, 40
Laube, Heinrich, 83, 87
Lemaître, Jules, 24, 45, 75
Lessing, Gotthold Ephraim, 137
Lienhard, Friedrich, 50
Liliencron, Detlev von, 46
Loos, Adolf, 35, 57, 68; *Ornament und Verbrechen*, 57; *Die potemkinsche Stadt*, 57
Loris. *See* Hofmannsthal, Hugo von

Mach, Ernst, 7, 13, 35, 78, 125, 129, 130; *Die Analyse der Empfindungen*, 125
Maeterlinck, Maurice, 25, 38, 39, 59; *Les Aveugles*, 38; *L'Intruse*, 38
Mahler, Gustav, 35, 86, 99, 153n6
Mann, Heinrich, 94; *Professor Unrat*, 94
Marx, Karl, 5, 42, 126
Mendelssohn, Peter de, 10
Mendès, Catulle, 24
Michel, Robert, 82
Mildenburg, Anna. *See* Bahr-Mildenburg, Anna
Millenkovich, Max von, 82
Millet, Jean-François, 60
Mitterwurzer, Friedrich, 74
Moll, Carl, 65, 66
Montesquiou, Robert Graf, 26
Morris, William, 67
Moser, Koloman, 35, 59, 66
Müller-Guttenbrunn, Adam, 11
Munch, Edvard, 59
Murray, J. Middleton, 44
Muther, Richard, 57

Nadler, Josef, 3, 82, 88
Napoleon Bonaparte, 112, 116, 117
Nebehay, Christian M., 58
Nietzsche, Friedrich, 7, 28, 46, 52, 85, 122, 129; *Menschliches allzu Menschliches*, 85
Novelli, Ferdinand, 74

O'Henry (pseudonym for William Sydney Porter), 31
Olbrich, Joseph, 35, 51, 59, 62, 63, 64, 68, 69
Orlik, Emil, 66

Popper, Joseph, 35; *Phantasies of a Realist*, 36
Powell, Nicolas, 63
Puvis de Chavannes, Pierre, 25, 59

Racine, Jean, 83; *Phèdre*, 83, 85
Redlich, Joseph, 16, 17, 20, 21
Reicher, Emanuel, 9, 14
Reinhardt, Edmund, 80
Reinhardt, Max, 19, 35, 68, 70, 72, 77, 80, 81, 82, 85, 87, 123, 131, 153n6
Reinhold, Babette, 73
Ribot, Theodule, 78, 125; *Les Maladies de la Personnalité*, 78, 125
Rod, Edouard, 47; *Les Idées Morales du Temps Present*, 47
Roller, Alfred, 35, 66
Rops, Felicien, 59
Rosegger, Peter, 35, 50
Rossetti, Dante Gabriel, 67
Rudigier, Franz Josef, Bischof von Salzburg, 18
Rysselberghe, Theo van, 59

Saar, Ferdinand von, 35, 47, 53, 54; *Herr Fridolin und sein Gluck*, 47
Sacher-Masoch, Leopold, 26
Salten, Felix, 38
Sandrock, Adele, 74, 75
Schäffle, Albert, 5; *Die Aussichtslosigkeit der Sozialdemokratie*, 5
Schiller, Friedrich, 65, 74, 75, 83; *Maria Stuart*, 74
Schlenther, Paul, 73
Schmoller, Gustav, 5
Schnitzler, Arthur, 12, 13, 14, 18, 20, 21, 35, 36, 37, 38, 72, 73, 76, 84, 88, 128, 129, 130, 133, 138, 140, 142; *Abschiedssouper*, 133; *Anatol*, 129; *Casanova in Spa*,

84; *Der einsame Weg*, 76; *Der grüne Kakadu*, 73; *Intermezzo*, 133; *Ein Leben in Wien*, 20; *Reigen*, 130; *Der Ruf des Lebens*, 13; *Der Schleier der Beatrice*, 73
Schnitzler, Julius, 12
Schönberg, Arnold, 35
Schönerer, Georg Ritter von, 5, 111
Schopenhauer, Arthur, 52
Schorske, Carl, 143; *Fin de siècle*, 143
Schreyvogel, Joseph, 78
Schullern, Heinrich von, 50
Segantini, Giovanni, 59
Seipel, Ignaz, 20, 84, 112
Shaw, George Bernard, 20
Singer, Isidor, 10, 11, 14
Sophokles, 83
Sorma, Agnes, 81
Specht, Richard, 37
Speidel, Ludwig, 43, 53, 70, 79
Steed, Wickham, 20
Steger, Josef, 4, 5, 141
Stelzhamer, Franz, 49, 119, 124
Stendhal, Henri Beyle, 110; *Le rouge et le noir*, 110
Stifter, Adalbert, 53, 108, 124, 141
Stoclet, Adolphe, 68; Palais Stoclet, 68
Strauss, Richard, 15, 19, 133, 134; *Intermezzo*, 134
Stuck, Franz von, 56
Sudermann, Hermann, 72

Talma, François Joseph, 116
Tolstoi, Leo, 103
Torresani, Baron Karl, 37

Tressler, Otto, 74

Ver Sacrum, 11, 57, 58, 68
Verlaine, Paul, 24
Villiers de l'isle-Adam, Jean Marie, 24, 27
Voltaire, François, 13; *Candide*, 13

Wagner, Adolf, 5, 6, 14
Wagner, Otto, 35, 63, 64, 65, 67, 68, 79; *Architektur*, 64
Wagner, Richard, 5, 15, 153n6
Wärndorfer, Fritz, 66
Waser, Maria, 81
Wedekind, Frank, 72
Weidlich, Wilhelmine. *See* Bahr, Wilhelmine
Weigel, Hans, 66
Weininger, Otto, 35
Whistler, James A., 59
Wiener Werkstätte, 56, 58, 63, 66, 67, 68, 69
Wilde, Oscar, 26
Wildgans, Anton, 83, 88; *Die Irae*, 83, 84
Witt, Lotte, 9, 32, 74
Wittmann, Hugo, 73, 79
Wolf, Hugo, 35, 128
Wolff, Eugen, 40; "Zehn Charakteristiken," 40

Yacco, Sada, 76

Zola, Emile, 6, 7, 30, 46
Zweig, Stefan, 16, 20, 21, 35; *Die Welt von gestern*, 20